Political Pluralism, Disagreement and Justice is a powerful and original defense of a polycentric political order. And it is an important contribution to a fresh approach to political philosophy, "New Diversity Theory," according to which moral diversity is not moral reasoning gone awry, or a feature of free societies to be managed, but a fundamental moral phenomenon that can be a resource to discover better ways of living together. This book shows Julian Müller to be one of the young, innovative, thinkers who may well change the face of political philosophy.

Gerald Gaus, *University of Arizona, USA*

Julian Müller's book is not only one of the best introductions and accounts of the increasingly influential literature on polycentric governance systems but also it is an important contribution to it, advancing in significant ways the frontier of our understanding of polycentric democracy in both the analytical-explanatory and the normative-applied directions.

Paul Dragos Aligica, *George Mason University, USA*

This essay brings together problems from political theory with tools from epistemology and economics to provide a very astute tour de horizon of a great deal of scholarship whose individual elements often remain out of touch with one another. One of the themes of the work is that diversity of judgment is a tool and not merely a problem. Müller shows how bringing together a diversity of ideas and approaches can help us understand problems about diversity itself.

Fred D'Agostino, *The University of Queensland, Australia*

Routledge Frontiers of Political Economy

Commodity
The Global Commodity System in the 21st Century
Photis Lysandrou

Uncertainty and Economics
A Paradigmatic Perspective
Christian Müller-Kademann

Discourse Analysis and Austerity
Critical Studies from Economics and Linguistics
Edited by Kate Power, Tanweer Ali and Eva Lebdušková

A Macroeconomic Analysis of Profit
Andrea Carrera

The Dark Places of Business Enterprise
Reinstating Social Costs in Institutional Economics
Pietro Frigato and Francisco J. Santos Arteaga

Economic Woman
Gendering Economic Inequality in the Age of Capital
Frances Raday

The Economics of Military Spending
A Marxist Perspective
Adem Yavuz Elveren

Political Pluralism, Disagreement and Justice
The Case for Polycentric Democracy
Julian F. Müller

For more information about this series, please visit: www.routledge.com/books/series/SE0345

Political Pluralism, Disagreement and Justice

This book poses the question: How can we organize society in such a way that our disagreement about facts and norms works to the benefit of everyone? In response, it makes the argument for polycentric democracy, a political arrangement consisting of various political units that enjoy different degrees of independence.

It is argued that to progress towards justice, we first need to change our attitude towards reasonable disagreement. Theorists have always viewed reasonable disagreement as nuisance, if not as a threat. However, this work puts forward that the diversity of perspectives that underlie reasonable disagreement should be viewed as a resource to be harvested rather than a threat to be tamed. Resting on two key arguments, the author proposes the idea of polycentric democracy as the most capable method of making pluralism productive. The essay explores what such a political order might look like and concludes that only an institutional system that is capable of profiting from diversity, such as polycentric democracy, might reasonably be expected to generate an overlapping consensus.

Continuing in the tradition of Karl Popper and Friedrich August von Hayek, this essay lies at the intersection of philosophy, political economy and political theory. It will be of great interest to academics and scholars working in philosophy, politics and economics.

Julian F. Müller is a Research Associate at the University of Hamburg, Germany. He works at the intersection between political philosophy, social epistemology and political economy. His research into political disagreement has won several research awards.

Political Pluralism, Disagreement and Justice

The Case for Polycentric Democracy

Julian F. Müller

Routledge
Taylor & Francis Group
LONDON AND NEW YORK

First published 2019
by Routledge
2 Park Square, Milton Park, Abingdon, Oxon OX14 4RN

and by Routledge
605 Third Avenue, New York, NY 10017

First issued in paperback 2020

Routledge is an imprint of the Taylor & Francis Group, an informa business

British Library Cataloguing-in-Publication Data
A catalogue record for this book is available from the British Library

Library of Congress Cataloging-in-Publication Data
A catalog record for this book has been requested

ISBN 13: 978-0-367-72889-2 (pbk)
ISBN 13: 978-1-138-22896-2 (hbk)

Typeset in Bembo
by Apex CoVantage, LLC

To Inger

Contents

Illustrations

Tables

Figure

Acknowledgments

Sometimes, I wish that the essay, as a medium, would be more fluid and not that set in stone. The reason for that is perhaps that my thought process on the issue of polycentric democracy is still evolving. Nevertheless, I decided to publish my current thoughts on this topic because I hope that others might take up the baton and carry the project to new places.

My thinking on polycentric democracy has greatly benefited from a range of friends, colleagues and advisors. I am particularly grateful to Jerry Gaus, who hosted me at the University of Arizona back in early 2014. Even though my thoughts on polycentricity were a hot mess at the time, he helped me to organize my ideas and encouraged me to pursue the project.

I also want to give special thanks to John Tomasi and Dan D'Amico for taking me on as a postdoctoral research associate at Brown University's Political Theory Project (PTP). Spending time at the PTP provided me with valuable time to refine the present essay and learn the ropes of professional philosophy. Spending time at Brown between 2016 and 2018 allowed me to butt heads with a number of great minds, among them of course David Estlund and Charles Larmore – an experience that I will forever cherish.

Over the years, I have received a lot of kindness. I am especially grateful to Fred D'Agostino, who supported my work even though we never met in person. My thanks also go to my advisors, Christoph Lütge and Thomas Schramme, for taking me on as a research assistant and granting me ample space to explore new ideas and to travel widely. I also want to thank the Friedrich Naumann Foundation, which sponsored this project over many years as well as various research visits. Moreover, I want to give a shout-out to the Edmund Siemers Foundation and the Roman Herzog Institute for honoring my research with their respective research awards.

Last but not least, I want to acknowledge the importance of a number of friends and colleagues that were crucial in a variety of ways in the development and the publication of the present essay: Matthew Braham, Benjamin Buchthal, Rosoline Candella, Dan D'Amico, Brennan Davis, Gianna Englert, Jan Gogoll, Anton Howes, Chad van Schoelandt, David and Emily Skarbek, John Thrasher and Fabian Wendt.

Introduction

Modern democracies are marked by pervasive disagreement. Reasonable people disagree about the content of the core values of the political realm, such as justice, legitimacy, liberty, equality, authority and autonomy. Since we cannot agree on the meaning, trade-off rate, or correct application of these values, we also disagree on the legitimate scope of government. We can neither agree on the constitutional essentials for a modern democracy, nor about specific political issues. There is no agreement on issues of social security, health care, drug and educational policies, or basic issues of paternalism. Should the state tell us what to drink, what to eat or – more generally – what to put in our bodies? If so, should the state act in a heavy-handed manner or gently nudge us in the 'right' direction? We can also find no agreement when it comes to questions of domestic security. Some people present good arguments in favor of government surveillance of the internet; others find good arguments against it. There is not even agreement about whether the state should have a monopoly over the use of physical force. In short, when it comes to politics, we face broad evaluative diversity between reasonable people. Moreover, not only do we disagree about ends, but also about means – especially with regard to the political realm. There is no agreement between reasonable people on how to efficiently produce a desirable level of security, education, social security, or public health. Furthermore, there is disagreement about how to best manage the economy, how to prevent financial meltdowns, or how to recover from them. Therefore, disagreement between reasonable people is fueled not only by evaluative, but also by instrumental diversity.

Disagreement leads to friction and conflict

In the political realm, disagreement leads to friction and friction leads to conflict. We might imagine a world in which disagreement between reasonable people would motivate the involved parties to abstain from all political action until they reach a general consensus through joint deliberation. We could also imagine a world in which deliberators accept, say, the standard of "blameless liberty" as a default decision rule.[1] In such a world, to simplify a bit, deliberators would push only for those laws that are a (moral) improvement over the current situation from the point of view of all parties concerned. In modern democracies, reasonable people – for better or for worse – do not restrain themselves in such a fashion. Instead, reasonable people both push for and vote for laws that they deem justified.[2] Seen from this angle, the institutions of our current democracy – the constitution, democratic elections and decisions, the judiciary and so forth – can be best understood as *modus vivendi arrangements*. Modus vivendi arrangements, as John Gray points out, are not set up "to still the conflict of values," but rather for purposes of reconciliation and peaceful cooperation.[3] Since political factions, activists, social scientists, intellectuals, philosophers and interest groups forever 'discover' new social problems and opportunities for enhancing efficiency, and imagine new ways and modes of organizing society, our modus vivendi arrangements produce a constant stream of new *modus vivendi bargains*.

From the point of view of the parties to our modus vivendi arrangements, the continuous stream of modus vivendi bargains has its blessings and its misfortunes – and they are not necessarily evenly distributed. New modus vivendi bargains might impinge on Mia's freedom to practice her religion, or put such a burden on her company that she will have to file for bankruptcy. Other pieces of legislation might force her to pay for the whims of special interest groups or to finance the losses of reckless investors, and even outlaw her favorite midnight snack. A new winning coalition might require her to pay an additional tax to finance a war or threaten to draft her son by reintroducing conscription. At the same time, if the party that represents Mia is part of a winning coalition, she, in turn, might be able to impose on others the laws she deems legitimate.

Escaping modus vivendi

The question that then arises, is whether we – as a society – cannot do better than settling for a "mere modus vivendi."[4] Shouldn't we be able to do better than to bargain and push each other around within modus vivendi arrangements? Some philosophers call for caution: "The very phrase 'a mere modus vivendi' suggests a certain distance from the political," writes Bernard Williams. He continues: "Experience (including at the present time) suggests that those who enjoy such a thing are already lucky."[5] Williams is certainly right. During the last fifty years, modern democracies have overcome some of the gravest social ills, such as extreme poverty, illiteracy, segregation and legal discrimination against women. Although this is true, all modus vivendi arrangements are undeniably and inherently strained, as I outlined earlier.

The question that this essay sets out to answer is then, simply put, *whether modern societies can do better than to settle for modus vivendi arrangements*. This question, of course, is not new in political philosophy. Indeed, a whole branch of philosophy is dealing with the question of how societies might, despite their profound and ubiquitous disagreements, find forms of association or institutional arrangements that are superior to a 'mere modus vivendi.' These theories have in common that they are 'second-order theories' and that they are attempting to find a way out of modus vivendi. Let me illuminate what

I have in mind here. First, it is helpful to distinguish between first- and second-order theories. "First-order theories," as Amy Gutmann and Dennis Thompson explain, "seek to resolve moral disagreement by demonstrating that alternative theories and principles should be rejected."[6] To simplify the matter: First-order theories are concerned with establishing *who is right*. Utilitarianism, perfectionism, libertarianism, egalitarianism and communitarianism are the most well-known members in that line of business. The development of second-order theories can best be understood as a response to the failure of first-order theories to come to a consensus – both in theory and in practice. While there is no immediate necessity to resolve these questions in the ivory tower, this is exactly what the real world expects. Second-order theories are primarily "about other theories in the sense that they provide ways of dealing with the claims of conflicting first-order theories."[7] In a nutshell, second-order theories inquire whether we can find an inter-subjectively justified order, despite our first-order differences. We can further distinguish between second-order theories that regard such an inquiry as predominantly an academic endeavor, from a subset of second-order theories that are primarily concerned with solving real-world issues. In this essay, I am, for the most part, interested in the second class of second-order theories. These theories are trying to find political orders that are feasible, stable and inter-subjectively justified. Typically, these theories pay much more heed to the epistemic and psychological constraints of human nature. Furthermore, they are much more concerned with issues of feasibility and stability. Important contributions in this area are John Rawls's *A Theory of Justice*, James M. Buchanan's work on constitutional economics and the various writings that can be summarized under the umbrella term 'deliberative democracy.'[8] Although all three approaches are very influential, they nevertheless, as we will discuss later, fail to deliver a convincing solution to the problem of modus vivendi. In this essay, I will argue that these approaches fail because they attempt to institutionally tame and hedge existing instrumental and evaluative diversity.

The goal of this essay is to construct and present a new approach for solving the problem of modus vivendi. I want to call this concept 'polycentric democracy.'[9] In contrast to the traditional approaches, polycentric democracy is based on utilizing rather than hedging existing instrumental and evaluative diversity. Building on the work of Paul Dragos Aligica, I define polycentric democracy as an institutional arrangement involving a multiplicity of polities acting independently, but under the constraints of a democratically supervised framework for institutional competition.[10] A well-regulated competition between polities should achieve three outcomes that are especially interesting from a normative perspective.

1 **Discovering new heights:** Since institutional competition is a discovery process, a political polycentric system should constantly find new and better 'ways of living together' or simply better 'modus vivendi arrangements.'
2 **Reducing shallow disagreement:** Much disagreement in political philosophy is most likely due to our disagreement on non-normative facts.

In a polycentric system, a larger number of socio-economic claims can be tested than is possible in our current democratic systems; this should reduce disagreement.

3 **Defusing deep disagreement:** It is highly likely that at least some of our reasonable political disagreements are best explained by fundamental disagreements about the right and the good. In a polycentric system, people who reasonably disagree with each other are allowed to enter into polities with more like-minded people. This might reduce moral tensions in society.

However, the goal of this essay is not simply to make a case for polycentric democracy based on the likely advantages that a well-regulated polycentric democracy could yield. In this essay, I want to defend a more specific normative claim, which I call the 'Domination Claim.' Simply put, the claim states that for a very diverse set of reasonable political factions, choosing polycentric democracy over our current modus vivendi would be rational. Since this is the case, escaping our current modus vivendi arrangements should be feasible.

The approach, which I will develop in this essay, is strongly influenced by scholars who emphasize the necessity of trial and error in political philosophy: John Stuart Mill, with his emphasis on "experiments in living," and Karl Popper and Friedrich August von Hayek, with their emphasis on social learning processes, come to mind.[11] To this list, I also need to add Michael Polanyi, who coined the term 'polycentricity.'[12] Furthermore, James M. Buchanan's discussion of ideal federalism as well as Robert Nozick's idea of a libertarian meta-utopia have influenced my approach to a large extent.[13] There are, though, important differences. The most important difference is that these scholars touch upon the idea of institutional competition and its sister concept ideal federalism only in passing.[14] In the work of these scholars, we find only scattered insights into the workings and the advantages of political polycentrism. Unfortunately, neither of these scholars has provided an integrated account of a polycentric political order. Another difference, which is important from a normative point of view, is that these thinkers are typically interested in institutional competition as a natural outgrow of a property rights regime that emphasizes negative rights. In discussions between these scholars, the benefits of institutional competition are then primarily important in order to justify – or to add additional plausibility to – classical liberal or libertarian principles. In this essay, I attempt to systematize the insights of these scholars with respect to the advantages of institutional competition *without adopting their normative priors*.

An overview

Can modern societies – despite their pervasive disagreements – do better than settling for modus vivendi arrangements? The goal of this essay is to develop an innovative answer to this age-old question. In the first part of this essay (Chapters 1–5), I will start out by laying some groundwork and by expanding on various parts of our conundrum. Most importantly, I will give a definition for 'modus vivendi'; and explain what counts as a successful escape from modus vivendi. For that reason, I construct a specific jury device, the 'representatives of comprehensive doctrines'-test or in short the 'RoCD Test.' A proposal for fixing our current modus vivendi will pass the RoCD Test only if the representatives of comprehensive doctrines are convinced that a given proposal is better than our current modus vivendi. I will then proceed by reviewing three prominent philosophical answers to our question: John Rawls's theory of justice (Chapter 2), deliberative democracy as presented by Gutmann and Thompson (Chapter 3) and constitutional economics with a focus on James M. Buchanan (Chapter 4). Chapter 5 summarizes the results of the first part.

The goal of the first part is to vindicate three claims: (a) I want to show that the most important political philosophies of our day hold that we are currently living in a 'modus vivendi,' that is, a state of affairs that is morally wanting and presents a mere accommodation between disputing parties (Modus Vivendi Hypothesis). (b) I aim to show that these political philosophies claim that, in order to move to a mutually justified state of affairs, we need to hedge (rather than unleash) our evaluative and socio-economic disagreements (Dangerous Diversity Hypothesis). (c) I argue that not one of these major philosophies manages to convincingly show a way out of our current democratic modus vivendi (No Escape Hypothesis).

In the second part of this essay (Chapters 6–8), I will propose a philosophical U-turn. While standard second-order theories have been searching for a solution to the problem of modus vivendi mainly in terms of taming diversity, I want to set out in the opposite direction. The second part of this essay asks what we can gain from diversity and how we might do so. In the politico-philosophical literature, we find two main approaches for how to make use of our instrumental and evaluative diversity: the deliberative approach and the polycentric approach.[15] Consequently, I will spend most of the second part in discussing and comparing both approaches. The focus here will be on the problem-solving capacity of both approaches with regard to hard problems. I conclude that the polycentric approach is, both empirically and analytically, especially well-suited to allow us to profit from evaluative and instrumental diversity.

In the third part (Chapters 9–10), I develop the idea of a polycentric democracy – a political order that thrives on evaluative and instrumental diversity. In Chapter 9, I will be concerned with outlining the institutional grid of polycentric democracy. Since there are a number of options for implementing the ideal of polycentric democracy, I will discuss various options for implementation and in the end select one that seems most promising given the normative goals of this essay.

In Chapter 10, I will present a normative argument for polycentric democracy. I shall defend the following claim: From the perspective of reasonable political factions, a polycentric democracy is a Pareto improvement over the familiar, centralized modus vivendi arrangements of the West. The case for a polycentric democracy rests on two pillars: the Amelioration Argument and the Unblocking Utopia Argument. These two claims are meant to organize the main arguments for a political polycentric system developed in this essay as well as those found in the history of political philosophy and economics. The two arguments can be summarized in this fashion:

1 **The Amelioration Argument**: Polycentric democracy ameliorates the problem of subjugation by improving public discourse, mitigating the democratic principal–agent problem and defusing deep disagreement.
2 **The Unblocking Utopia Argument:** Social innovators need space to demonstrate the value of their ideas, to generate the evidence that is necessary to convince the 'lukewarm supporters' and eventually the skeptics. By giving every reasonable political doctrine space to generate additional and maybe decisive evidence for its own principles, a polycentric democracy will discover better institutional solutions – and maybe even 'utopia' if it exists.

The first claim is original foremost in organizing classic arguments for polycentrism and institutional competition in a new and hopefully illuminating fashion. The second claim, on the other hand, might be understood as a truly original contribution to the discussions of polycentrism and political theory in general. The last section also reviews questions concerning stability and provides some replies to a number of important objections. Chapter 11 concludes the essay by summarizing its core ideas and arguments.

Fast track

Time is scarce and books, there are many. You, therefore, might wonder whether there is a way to fully appreciate the argument of this essay without reading everything. To put it differently, is there a smart way to cut corners? There is! To appreciate the main argument, you should start by reading Chapter 1: The key concepts here are the 'representatives of comprehensive doctrines' (RoCD device) and the notions of 'shallow' and 'deep disagreement.' It makes sense to read the summary chapter (i.e. Chapter 5) of the first part and the introductory chapter (i.e. Chapter 6) of the second part to get a better appreciation of the trajectory of the arguments to follow. To appreciate the epistemic value of polycentrism, you have to read Chapter 7, Section 7.2 on the epistemic limits of deliberation, then Chapter 8, Sections 8.1 and 8.3. The latter develops two core notions, the notion of 'hidden champion' and 'sequential persuasion.' Chapter 9, Section 9.2 spells out the ideal of polycentric democracy in institutional terms. The ideal of polycentric democracy can be implemented in various ways. Since none of the existing concepts for implementing the ideal of polycentric democracy can hope to pass the RoCD Test, I introduce the

'Free-City Approach,' which should meet with less resistance. Finally, Chapter 10 develops the core argument in favor of polycentric democracy. Naturally, you should not skip any of that. The last chapter, Chapter 11, summarizes the core ideas and arguments of the essay.

Notes

1 Gaus (2011c, p. 319).
2 Of course, what Benni regards as justified might depend itself on what other people see as justified, but this does not have to be the case.
3 Gray (2000, p. 5).
4 Rawls (2005b, p. 145).
5 Williams (2008, p. 2, fn2).
6 Gutmann and Thompson (2004, p. 13).
7 Gutmann and Thompson (2004, p. 13).
8 Brennan and Buchanan (2000), Buchanan (2000), Buchanan and Tullock (1999), Gutmann and Thompson (2004), Habermas (1996), Rawls (2005a). Amartya Sen's social choice approach to political philosophy might also fall into this category, Sen (2009). Furthermore, it can be argued that recent contributions in nonideal theory also belong to this field of study, e.g. Wiens (2012), Farrelly (2007), etc.
9 The term has been used occasionally in papers mostly outside of political philosophy. However, the term does not yet denote any specific approach in political theory or philosophy.
10 Aligica and Tarko (2013, p. 727).
11 Hayek (1945), Hayek (2012), Hayek (2002), Mill (1989), Popper (2002a), Popper (2002b).
12 Polanyi (1998).
13 Buchanan (1996), Nozick (1999).
14 Other important clues for starting to think about institutional competition as a potential means to solve problems in political philosophy stem from Aligica and Boettke (2009), Aligica and Tarko (2012), Aligica and Tarko (2013), Aligica (2014), Ostrom (2005), Ostrom (1991), Ostrom (1997), Ostrom *et al.* (1961), Tiebout (1956), Tocqueville (2002), Vanberg (2008), Vanberg and Kerber (1994), Vaubel (2008), and Wohlgemuth (2008).
15 In the second part I will be concerned with epistemic qualities of deliberation, while in the first part I am concerned with the justificatory elements of deliberation.

Part I

Escaping modus vivendi

1 The model

Debating friends

In this chapter, I want to expand on some of the basic concepts I touched upon in the introduction and bring into play an additional set of tools that will accompany us throughout this essay. First of all, I need to define in some more detail what I mean by 'modus vivendi arrangements' (Section 1.1). Furthermore, I want to explicate why modus vivendi arrangements obtain. To do this, I will present a novel taxonomy of political disagreement (Section 1.2). I will close this chapter by conceptualizing a jury device that allows us to identify what counts as a 'successful escape' (Section 1.3).

1.1 What is a modus vivendi?

In this section, I want to give a very short account of modus vivendi arrangements and some of their implications. Modern democratic societies are marked by profound instrumental and evaluative disagreement. Disagreement breeds friction and friction easily leads to conflict. Modus vivendi arrangements can be understood as social machinery for the settling of conflicts and for ensuring peaceful cooperation. In modern democratic countries, this machinery encompasses important governmental institutions, such as the constitution, democratic elections and decisions, the judiciary and so on. We can further distinguish between 'modus vivendi arrangements' and 'modus vivendi bargains.' In modus vivendi arrangements new *modus vivendi bargains* are negotiated all the time. While the modus vivendi arrangements are relatively stable, modus vivendi bargains shift over time as new governments introduce new legislation and the judiciary changes its interpretation of the law. The political process within a modus vivendi arrangement consists of negotiations, "bargaining, compromise, persuasion, a measure of give and take, cobbling together policies that may be effective but whose intellectual coherence is doubtful, strategies of avoidance, exploiting ambiguity, and so on."[1]

Modus vivendi arrangements are, furthermore, accepted[2] as a second-best by the parties to such an arrangement. Accepting a modus vivendi as a second-best has two sides to it. First, the parties agree to a modus vivendi arrangement because it secures some benefits for them.[3] A modus vivendi is thus mutually beneficial for the parties. At the same time, every party to a modus vivendi would persuade the other parties to accept an alternative set of institutions, if it could[4], meaning that none of the parties is fully satisfied with the arrangement, typically for both moral and non-moral reasons. Although the parties are dissatisfied with the institutions, they are dissatisfied for different reasons. Mia for instance might deem a particular modus vivendi arrangement unjustified because there is too much inequality, while Philipp might judge the same modus vivendi as unjustified because there is too much redistribution. In short, modus vivendi arrangements entail both *mutual benefit* and an *overlapping dissatisfaction.*

Let me add two comments here about the notion of 'justification' that this essay employs and the relation between 'X being judged as a second-best' and 'X being judged as justified.' In this essay, I am not concerned with the standards of justification. This essay is about the question of whether a diverse set of reasonable people, relying on diverse notions of justification, can conceive and concurrently agree on a social order that is better than the current modus vivendi arrangement. In this sense, I employ the notion of justification in a descriptive sense. A social order X is justified for the reasonable agent A, if the reasonable agent A judges that it is justified. Accordingly, a social arrangement is inter-subjectively justified, if every reasonable agent in the arrangement judges that, from her or his point of view, it is justified.[5]

Let us then take a closer look at the relations of 'X being judged as a second-best' and 'X being judged as justified.' Imagine this: A group of settlers has just arrived on an uninhabited island. Since they need to organize life in the new settlement, they begin to discuss different social arrangements. After a while, the set of proposals boils down to five. Mia orders the proposals like this: $S_b > S_c > S_d > S_a > S_e$. First of all, you should not assume that S_b, Mia's favorite option, is the only one she deems justified. It might very well be the case that every proposed social arrangement is justified from Mia's perspective. It might equally be the case that she only sees S_b and S_c as justified or, for that matter, that she sees none of the proposals as justified. This means: 'X being justified to Mia' and 'X being Mia's best option' are two different things. Mia might grudgingly agree to any one of these proposals, since, under these circumstances, accepting some proposal is better than outright conflict, but she might judge nevertheless that the order is unjustified. We might imagine, for instance, that not one of these proposals allows women to hold an office and that all the proposals which allow women to hold an office are infeasible given the distribution of power in the new settlement. In this sense, from Mia's perspective, all available proposals would fall into the categories of 'unjustified' and 'second-best.' Summarizing, we can then state that *all* proposals that A judges to be unjustified are second-bests, but not all second-bests are necessarily unjustified.

Let me add a final comment. Whether Mia views the social order as justified or not is not only relevant from a normative perspective, but also from a functional perspective. In general, if Mia sees a law or a social order as unjustified, the only reasons she has to honor its prescriptions and to punish digressions seem to be prudential ones. If Mia, on the contrary, views a law as justified, this gives her an additional reason to honor it and punish digressions by third parties.[6] An example will be sufficient to illuminate this point: If Mia does not deem the tax code to be justified, her only reason not to cheat on her taxes seems to be prudential. This implies that Mia will cheat on her taxes as long as there are no countervailing prudential reasons (e.g. the fear of punishment). If Mia, on the contrary, deems the tax regime just, she would presumably have additional (moral) reasons to abstain from cheating.[7] We can then tentatively conclude that there is a positive correlation between the stability of a social order and the degree to which it is viewed as justified.

1.2 Why does a modus vivendi obtain?

In this section, I attempt to answer the following question: Why does a modus vivendi obtain in the first place? Why do we, as human beings, not pull together, but instead waste so much of our time and energy in political tugs of war? I cannot attempt to give an exhaustive answer to this question since it involves a host of very intricate issues. Nevertheless, it is important for this essay to understand what sets people apart in the political sphere. In this section, I want to unearth some of the root causes of our *political disagreements*. My discussion about the root causes of political disagreement is a discussion about the disagreement between good reasoners. It is thus about people who are willing to think about a question and try to honor the rules of good reasoning. I am here and throughout the whole essay only concerned, unless I indicate otherwise, with 'good reasoners' and 'reasonable disagreement.' My understanding of reasonable disagreement is very similar to the definition by Christopher McMahon, who defines reasonable disagreement as "disagreement that survives the best efforts of a group of reasoners to answer a particular question – that is, to find a unique answer that is required by reason."[8] I am decidedly not concerned with pig-headed people, since pig-headed people are often not willing to honor the rules of good reasoning. Popper rightly notes:

> Even a logical proof cannot alter the fundamental situation that only he who is prepared to take these things seriously and to learn about them be impressed by ethical (or any other) arguments. You cannot force anybody by arguments to take arguments seriously, or to respect his own reason.[9]

Since I will touch on different aspects of disagreement throughout this essay, I will confine myself here to two categories of reasonable disagreement: shallow and deep disagreement.

1.2.1 *Lazy, shallow and deep disagreement*

Let me start off by distinguishing three kinds of disagreements: lazy, shallow and deep disagreement. Most disagreement – especially about political matters – might correctly be classified as lazy. A disagreement is lazy if the reason that two people disagree is simply that at least one of them has either failed to take into account the available evidence or has failed to process the information correctly. In a case of lazy disagreement then, two people disagree about a certain matter even though the available evidence is sufficient to establish the truth of that matter beyond reasonable doubt. Thus, to resolve lazy disagreements, all it takes is for all parties to the disagreement to correctly aggregate the available knowledge. Lazy disagreement is simply based on ignorance and thus unreasonable.

Even though ignorance is certainly one of the major reasons why people disagree about politics, in this essay I am not concerned with lazy disagreements for the most part. This essay is mostly concerned with shallow and deep disagreement. So what is shallow disagreement?

Shallow disagreement occurs in situations in which there exists a truth about a certain matter, but our existing stock of knowledge is not sufficient to establish the truth of the matter beyond reasonable doubt. In cases of shallow disagreement, people evaluating the same evidence, the same body of knowledge, or the same set of claims with regard to a specific question come to different conclusions without committing any demonstrable mistakes. This is a common occurrence in the social sciences as well as in the humanities. In economics, for instance, experts on minimum wage disagree about its impact on poverty. The reason for their disagreement has to do with the fact that establishing the truth about this question is hard and the evidence inconclusive. The same is of course true for many questions in philosophy. For instance, philosophers theorizing peer disagreement disagree about how a rational agent/person should revise her belief about a certain proposition if she comes to know that her peer holds the opposite belief. Again, there might be a truth about what the proper response is, but reasonable people, currently, can disagree about what the right response is to peer disagreement. The evidential basis, broadly understood, remains inconclusive.[10]

For the purposes of the essay, I want to distinguish between two kinds of shallow disagreement. First, there is shallow disagreement that is based on disagreement about (non-moral) facts.[11] Take this case: Gabriel and Mia both agree that the basic structure of society should confirm to Rawls's two principles of justice. The only problem for Gabriel and Mia is that they cannot agree on which institutional set best realizes 'justice as fairness.' Gabriel, for instance, might agree with Rawls that democratic socialism will realize the two principles of justice, while Mia thinks that the two principles will be best realized under a small state.[12] Gabriel and Mia, evidently, base their respective judgments on very different sets of socio-economic theories. Many persisting disagreements in politics can be, in the same fashion, explained by persisting disagreements about the relevant facts. Frankena writes:

> A large part of the debate about what to do about drugs, pollution, or a war arises because we are ignorant of much of what bears on these problems. On these issues and on many others, most of us would probably be clear about what should be done if only we knew all the relevant facts.[13]

However, not all our shallow disagreements are based on reasonable disagreement about facts. Let me now turn to the second case: shallow disagreements that are based on a disagreement about value. To get a sense of the second kind of shallow disagreements, I want first to say a few things about non-moral value judgments. Sometimes a reasonable person simply misjudges what he or she likes and dislikes. Think about Benni. Since he graduated from high school, Benni has always gone for all-inclusive holidays and consequently has spent all of his leisure time by a pool slurping margaritas. Now imagine Benni has a new girlfriend who pressures him to spend the next vacation with her in Rome instead of on Ibiza. After a while Benni grudgingly agrees and both visit Rome. Much to his own surprise, Benni discovers that he really enjoys visiting all the art galleries, and the beautiful plazas and ruins of Rome. While climbing the Colosseum, Benni thinks to himself that an educational vacation is better than expected and actually beats all-inclusive trips to Ibiza. What is important here is that Benni did not change, but was simply *mistaken* about his preferences. Compare this with the case in which Benni has been going on beach vacations in the summer and on educational trips during the winter for five years, because his girlfriend urged him to. During all these years, Benni has judged that he likes beach vacations a lot more than educational vacations. But two years later, Benni begins to enjoy his summer vacations less and less. A little later, he finally judges that he really does not like beach vacations anymore and thus decides to go on educational trips only. In the first case, Benni made an evaluative mistake and consequently learned something about his own preferences, while in the second case Benni simply changed his preferences. Distinguishing these two cases is important also when it comes to genuine moral judgments. Moral judgments as any kind of judgment is subject to error. Gerald A. Cohen agrees with this fallibilist view of moral judgments, writing:[14]

> It is typically in and through experience that people form and adjust their principles [. . .]. Suppose some person, having observed the toils of unwanted pregnancy suffered by some of her friends, consequently believes that abortion is morally acceptable, at any rate at early stages of fetal development. She then herself becomes pregnant and comes to think otherwise, and thereby changes her principles. She comes to believe that it is wrong to kill a living human fetus, however young that fetus is. She has come to believe that it is wrong to take human life, as such, and she has come to believe this as a result of the experience of not being able to take (or direct the taking of) a human life herself.[15]

If we sometimes struggle with relatively straightforward moral issues, it is plausible to assume that we might also be wrong with regard to more complex moral judgments that are based on difficult value trade-offs between diverse political values (such as freedom, equality, security, economic well-being and so on). Consider Mia, who is an ardent egalitarian. Let us imagine a case in which Mia succeeds in changing her village into an egalitarian utopia. An account of how such an egalitarian utopia might look like can be found in Nietzsche's *Zarathustra*:

> They abandoned the regions where it was hard to live [. . .]. One still loves one's neighbor and rubs up against him: for one needs warmth. Becoming ill and being mistrustful are considered sinful by them: one proceeds with caution. A fool who still stumbles over stones or humans! A bit of poison once in a while: that makes for pleasant dreams. One still works, for work is a form of entertainment. But one sees to it that the entertainment is not a strain. One no longer becomes poor or rich; both are too burdensome. Who still wants to rule anymore? Who still wants to obey anymore? Both are too burdensome. No shepherd and one herd![16]

It is at least conceivable that Mia, after living in this community for a certain time, might judge that an egalitarian utopia is unbearably boring and that she was actually mistaken about the value of egalitarianism. Let me get a little bit more technical, to get a better understanding of what I am talking about here. When Benni wants to evaluate a state of affairs that he has not experienced before (e.g. a social world, the taste of an unknown fruit, an unknown tourist destination), he needs to first mentally construct the state of affairs and then evaluate the different facets of his construal.[17] Benni thus essentially creates a hypothesis in t_1 about how he will evaluate a state of affairs when he actually experiences it t_2. When Benni is in t_2 and experiences the state of affairs he just imagined before, he will confirm or refute his initial hypothesis. Laurie A. Paul explains, in slightly different lingo: "Having the experience for the first time involves a kind of revelation."[18] Only once we have had the new experience, Paul notes further, can we "assign the experience a subjective value."[19] I take this to mean that Benni beforehand just had a vague hypothesis about how he would actually experience a particular state in t_2. However, after experiencing the state in t_2, he has gained somewhat reliable knowledge for the first time. It should be noted that Paul's thesis is even stronger than mine. While I am stating that Benni might evaluate a state of affairs that he has never experienced wrongly, Paul thinks that, at least in some cases, there is an epistemic limitation so that Mia "can't know what it is like to have new experiences."[20] David Lewis seems to hold an equally strong view when he writes:

> There's truth to this. If you want to know what some new and different experience is like, you can learn it by going out really having the experience. You can't learn it by being told about the experience, however thorough your lessons may be.[21]

I will be content here with the weaker and less controversial claim that at least sometimes we might be wrong when imagining states of affairs that we have not experienced before.

Coming back to the example, we might say that in acting under uncertainty, Benni first needs to establish an evaluative hypothesis about the choiceworthiness of a certain state and then establish an instrumental hypothesis about how he can achieve this state of affairs. What is important here is that Benni can be wrong with regards to both these hypotheses. If Gabriel and Benni share a preference ordering – judged from a god's eye perspective – and Gabriel wrongly evaluates a state of affairs, Gabriel and Benni will face shallow disagreement that is caused by a wrong evaluation. Gabriel and Benni might also face a shallow disagreement if at least one of them is mistaken about the means to achieve a certain state of affairs.

Thus, much of our disagreement might be due to the fact that some of us are mistaken with regard to factual or evaluative judgments. Before I move on to discussing deep disagreements, let me say a few words about my terminology here. I have talked in a rather loose way about errors in evaluative and moral judgment. This cannot be avoided here since there is simply not enough space to unfold a proper theory of rational valuation and moral epistemology. Nevertheless, let me at least say a few words about what I mean by an evaluative or moral judgment being mistaken. In epistemology, a familiar distinction is the one between a rational and a warranted belief. As it is well known, these things can go apart: A belief might be rational to hold but nevertheless wrong from an objective point of view. Typically, a rational person will come to a wrong conclusion about a certain matter if the evidence is misleading. Now, as I said in the beginning, I am mainly concerned with reasonable disagreement, thus with disagreement between people who form their beliefs about moral and non-moral issues in a rational way. To go back to our earlier example, Benni's prior belief that he prefers an all-inclusive vacation over an educational trip was rational; it was rational because his beliefs were in coherence with his own experiences, with his external evidence (for instance with what friends and family believe about him) and thus with his entire self-knowledge.

Nevertheless, I stated that his belief was wrong in some sense. But in what sense was it wrong? I cannot hope to given exhaustive answer here, but the idea is the following: One prominent approach in moral epistemology states that it is rational to believe a certain proposition given a certain evidence base only if it is also rational to believe that "the total evidence would continue to support the proposition"[1] Depaul (1993, p. 165).

In the same vein, we might think that it is rational to believe a certain evaluative or moral proposition only if it is also rational to believe that the "judgment will remain firm in the face of all enriching formative experience."[22] Given this account, a rational belief always entails some kind of prediction – a prediction about the judgment being firm in the face of more evidence or more enriching (as opposed to corrupting) experience. What is important for my purposes is that this prediction is subject to falsification in the ways described earlier. Looking back, Benni thus rationally might come to the conviction that his prior assessment of his own preferences was rational (given the available evidence) but wrong; in the same vein Mia looking back might come to the conclusion that her prior moral assessment of what values should govern the basic structure of a society was rational, but wrong. The standard of wrongness employed here is, therefore, an internal one. The judgment that a certain belief was wrong, on this account, is issued by a rational agent looking back, continuing to bring his or her beliefs into a reflective equilibrium through a process of "balance and refinement."[23] From this vantage point, then, shallow disagreements are disagreements that can be resolved by generating more evidence or enriching experience. It should be noted that while we can often judge with confidence that a certain disagreement about facts is shallow (and will thus be resolved upon generating the necessary evidence), the case is different for moral disagreement. Whether a moral disagreement is shallow or deep will usually only be evident ex post – that is, after the relevant parties have gone through the particular enriching experiences.

What about deep disagreements, then? On the one hand, it is plausible to assume that if we knew all the relevant facts about psychology, economics, sociology, biology and so forth, the set of reasonable disagreement would shrink dramatically. Further, if rational agents were able to go through all the relevant, enriching and formative experience necessary for a fully informed judgment about political matters, we might reasonably assume that the set of disagreement would shrink even more. On the other hand, even if rational agents were to go through all these motions, it is reasonable to believe that the set of disagreement would not be empty. Nicholas Wolterstorff writes:

> For many, if not most existing or seriously proposed pieces of coercive legislation in [. . .] society, there are some citizens of that society who, if they were fully informed and rational, would regard the law as a good thing, and others who, if they were fully informed and rational, would not regard it as a good thing. That is because disagreements among fully informed and rational persons [. . .] are a fundamental feature of our human condition. Rationality does not typically yield consensus.[24]

This residual disagreement I call 'deep disagreement.' A disagreement between agents is deep if it remains stable even after the agents (a) have accessed the maximal set of knowledge possibly to be gained, (b) have made the full set of enriching experiences possibly to be had and (c) have brought their beliefs into a reflective equilibrium through the method of balance and refinement.[25] As I pointed out earlier, one of the important things to keep in mind is that it is often not clear at the outset what the nature of a particular disagreement is. While it might often be relatively straightforward to tell whether a disagreement is lazy, it will often be ex ante hard if not impossible to tell whether a disagreement is shallow or deep.

This concludes my taxonomy of disagreement. I have distinguished between three kinds of disagreement: lazy disagreement, shallow disagreement and deep disagreement. In the later parts of this essay, I will come back to all three variants of disagreement. However, the focus of my discussions, in particular in the last chapter, will be on shallow disagreements and what it takes to resolve them.

1.3 What counts as a successful escape?

The goal of the first part of this essay is to review some classical approaches for escaping modus vivendi arrangements. Later on, I will discuss my own approach, which is based on utilizing rather than hedging instrumental and evaluative diversity. But before we can engage in any of these exercises, we first need to know *what counts as a successful escape*.

First of all, in the Rawlsian tradition, I am looking for a solution at the level of institutions. I am thus interested in finding a 'basic structure' that is better than our current democratic modus vivendi arrangement. I will accept two kinds of solutions. The first solution is a Pareto improvement over our current modus vivendi arrangement.[26] Although a Pareto improvement is not what philosophers usually aim for, it is maybe the best thing we can realistically hope for.[27] The second solution is a basic structure that is not simply a better modus vivendi, but an inter-subjectively, or publicly justified institutional structure. A publicly justified order is an order that every reasonable agent, given his or her evaluative standards, deems justified. To put it differently, a particular political order and its corresponding

> exercise of political power is justified only if it is justifiable to all those subject to it, that is, only if it is acceptable to all suitably rational and moral individuals without them having to give up the religious or philosophical doctrine they reasonably espouse.[28]

Both the 'Pareto-improvement' and the 'public-justification' route imply that we somehow need to model a jury and its collective judgment. As is well known, there are different approaches in modeling such a jury. In modeling the participants and the debate of a jury, we need to keep in mind the goal of our work. In the contractarian and contractualist tradition, such juries have been employed for a diverse set of tasks. Thomas Hobbes and John Locke use the jury, or contract devices, to solve questions of (political) 'authority.' In Rawls the jury is used to come up with 'principles of justice' and the social and political institutions of the 'basic structure.'[29] Buchanan uses a jury to develop an appropriate constitution and collective choice rules[30] and Gerald Gaus to justify moral rules.[31]

In this essay, I have a theoretically much more humble goal. The aim is to inquire whether we can conceive of a political order that might be judged superior to our current modus vivendi arrangements from a very diverse set of normative viewpoints. The jury device in this essay should be understood as a proxy for what kind of proposals a diverse but reasonable group of real-world agents could agree on. Moreover, the jury employed is not interested in purely academic discussions, but finding a better and workable social order.

It is thus no use to staff the jury with agents who possess full knowledge including both normative and non-normative facts, since reasonable agents are not in command of such epistemic resources. At the same time, we also cannot staff our jury with copies of randomly selected individuals, say a representative sample of a Western democracy. Without a doubt, such a group would not (if asked individually) converge on any conclusion. As I have already mentioned, pig-headed people do not deliberate in accordance with rules of good reasoning. We would like the jury to represent a group of well-meaning, reasonable people who subscribe to a very diverse set of socio-economic and normative theories. To do this, I want to staff the jury with representatives of what Rawls calls *comprehensive doctrines*.[32] The notion of comprehensive doctrines in Rawls comprises religious doctrines, like Catholicism, as well as moral and political doctrines like libertarianism, Marxism, perfectionism and utilitarianism.[33] I understand this concept here in an equally extensive way, even though I will mainly focus on genuinely political approaches for reasons of brevity. The 'representatives of comprehensive doctrines' (RoCD) accordingly should be thought of as a group of individuals that represents all major factions in our philosophical and political landscape. Focusing on representatives of the leading schools of political philosophy and existing political factions has the additional advantage that it keeps the author of this essay honest and the results meaningful. Philosophers are prone to overestimate the reasons and arguments dearest to themselves while undervaluing the arguments of their opponents – so much so that we often wonder what results in political philosophical are sold to us as 'in the interest of all' or as fulfilling the criterion of 'unanimous consent.' Staffing the jury with representatives of existing philosophical factions at least raises the bar for presenting the results of our inquiries as 'in the interest of all.' Ideally, I would present the final judgment of every comprehensive doctrine in the RoCD Test. Since this would seriously infringe on the readability of this essay, I will just give voice to a subset of political philosophies in the RoCD Test. To guarantee a certain representativeness of existing political factions, I will staff the jury with the following core members: utilitarians, egalitarians, deliberative democrats, realists, classical liberals and natural rights libertarians.[34]

We can envision that the RoCD will each in turn suggest a political order that is in his or her view likely to be a candidate for being a viable escape out of modus vivendi. After every presentation, the other parties to the deliberative process will be given the opportunity to judge whether the proposal can be considered feasible, stable and justified *from their own perspective*. If this is not the case, the RoCD will judge whether the proposal might be considered as a Pareto improvement over our existing democratic modus vivendi arrangements. Before we go in medias res, let me reiterate that we should imagine our representatives as reasonable, sincere, real-world agents, who have come together because they are all, for various reasons, dissatisfied with the current modus vivendi arrangement.

Let us now turn to the proposals. The proposals we want to discuss are all second-order proposals.[35] Returning to our background story, we can imagine that the discussion among the RoCD has already passed the point where first-order proposals could be discussed as possible options for escaping modus vivendi. Since no first-order proposal has persuaded the RoCD, the representatives are now debating second-order proposals. Unfortunately, within the limits of this essay, it is not possible to discuss all second-order theories and proposals, so I can present only a window into this debate. Put differently, we need to be content to review a small subset of second-order theories. In choosing a subset, I want to make sure that I represent at least the most important philosophies and at the same time also cover a range of different political philosophies. As I have already discussed in the introduction, I have decided here to review Rawls's theory of justice, deliberative democracy as defended by Gutmann and Thompson, and constitutional economics as outlined by Buchanan.

Notes

1 Horton (2010, p. 441).
2 I use 'acceptance' here in a rather weak sense. We do not accept a modus vivendi arrangement simply by taking part in the game. I am agnostic in how far the acceptance of a modus vivendi arrangement might create moral obligations. Different parties to a moral modus vivendi might have different views on what moral obligations come with living in (i.e. accepting) or consenting to a modus vivendi arrangement.
3 Wendt argues convincingly that the parties can have moral and purely prudential reasons to agree to a modus vivendi arrangement (Wendt 2015).
4 Wendt (2015).
5 Again, it might very well be the case that most of the conceived standards of justification or accounts of morality that are employed in academic discussions and in society are wrong from a god's eye perspective. From a god's eye perspective, a social order that is deemed inter-subjectively justified might indeed be unjustified. I am then also not claiming that inter-subjective agreement is a truth-maker of any kind.
6 It is very difficult to make any general statement with regard to the relation of reasons for action and their justification across many different moralities and political philosophies. It is therefore prudent to emphasize the tentative nature of this paragraph.
7 Of course the moral reasons do not have to be conclusive.
8 McMahon (2009, p. 2). For are similar account of reasonable disagreement, see Gaus (2011c, chap. 14) and Larmore (1996, p. 64).
9 Popper (2002a, p. 583).
10 For reasons of brevity, I will refer to the set of considerations that speak in favor of a specific claim as evidence.
11 For reasons of readability, throughout the text I will use the word 'facts' to denote non-moral facts, that is facts about the empirical world.
12 Kofman (2012, p. 249).
13 Frankena (1973, p. 13).
14 Cohen thinks that there are fact independent ultimate principles. But this is importantly, as he himself points out, a claim about the "structure of normative beliefs, and not about their genesis."
15 Cohen (2003, p. 232).
16 Nietzsche (2006, p. 10).
17 I follow Mantzavinos here (2001, pp. 46–49).
18 Paul (2014, p. 13).
19 Paul (2014, p. 13).
20 Paul (2014, p. 13).

21 Lewis (2004, p. 77).
22 DePaul (1993, p. 166).
23 DePaul (1993).
24 Wolterstorff (2007, pp. 146–147).
25 Note that the definition of deep disagreement is compatible with various metaethical positions. It is coherent with pluralism understood as a metaethical theory about the realm of value, but it is also coherent with a metaethical position that combines value monism with a pessimistic epistemological view about the ability of rational agents to discover the true order of value. Moreover, it seems to me that this view can also be made consistent with various anti-realist positions in metaethics.
26 Following Hausman and McPherson, a state of affairs X is a Pareto improvement over Y if no party prefers state Y to X and at least one party prefers X to Y (Hausman and McPherson 1996, p. 43). To put it less technically: given a certain status quo, a Pareto improvement makes at least some – if not all – better off, while making no one worse off.
27 In political philosophy, especially contractarian theories build on the Pareto criterion: Buchanan (2000), Gauthier (1986), Moehler (2014), Lütge (2015).
28 Lister (2010, p. 151).
29 Rawls (2005a).
30 Buchanan and Tullock (1999).
31 Gaus (2011c, p. 271).
32 Rawls (2005b, p. 13).
33 Rawls (1999b, p. 424).
34 Both deliberative democracy and classical liberalism are rather broad schools of thought that feature first-order versions and second-order versions of their core concepts. In the jury, we will find representatives of the first-order version of this theory.
35 A second-order proposal is a proposal that is based on a second-order theory.

2 Rawls

Property-owning democracy

The first approach I want to review is described in *A Theory of Justice* by John Rawls. Rawls is undoubtedly one of the most famous philosophers of the twentieth century. He is well known for reviving political philosophy, and contract theory in particular. In this chapter, I want to inquire whether we can find an answer to the problem of modus vivendi in Rawls. The focus of this inquiry will be mainly on Rawls's theory of justice.[1] The choice for *A Theory of Justice* (TJ) over *Political Liberalism* (PL) comes down to reasons of exposition. One of the core goals of this and the following review chapters is to get an overview of various ways in political philosophy to cope with the fact of reasonable disagreement about facts and norms. Since I am interested here in presenting an overview of devices for dealing with diversity, the goal is to present three distinctive mechanisms of dealing with diversity.[2] An important way in which second-order theories differ is on how much they deem it necessary to normalize diverse perspectives about facts and norms in their roadmaps for escaping modus vivendi. Reviewing Rawls's first opus magnum is a natural choice because the proposal developed in TJ, as opposed to PL, relies on a full normalization of perspectives and thus clearly demarcates one end of the normalization scale. Later, I will argue that one of the advantages of polycentric democracy – the approach developed in this essay – is that it is situated on the polar opposite of the scale in that its potential success relies on there being a diversity of perspectives rather than on ironing them out.

In Chapter 1, Section 1.1, I called attention to the fact that although there is an overlapping dissatisfaction with the current modus vivendi, the parties usually cannot agree on a shared problem description. This is the case because what an agent views as a problem depends on his or her normative standards. In reviewing the second-order theories, I want to reflect this insight. I will divide this and the following review chapters into three parts. The first part of each chapter has two goals: first, to demonstrate that each of the second-order theories views the political status quo in democratic countries as a modus vivendi arrangement; and second, to give an account of how the respective second-order theory *interprets* the problem of modus vivendi. To put it differently, the first section in every review chapter will illuminate how the problem of modus vivendi presents itself from the perspective of the respective second-order theory. In the second section, I will outline how the theory intends to *solve* the problem of modus vivendi. Here I will, as explained, focus especially on the institutional recommendations of each approach. In the third and final section of each chapter, I will apply the RoCD Test to the institutional solutions suggested by the respective theory.

2.1 Interpreting modus vivendi

In the first chapter of TJ, Rawls writes that in "existing societies" "what is just and unjust is usually in dispute."[3] According to Rawls "men disagree about which principles should define the basic terms of their association."[4] The overarching goal of both TJ and PL is in a sense to solve this problem and to show "how a reasonably just and well-ordered democratic society might be possible."[5] Although Rawls never calls our current state of affairs a modus vivendi, it becomes apparent from these quotes that Rawls thought that Western democracies are wanting from a normative standpoint. In the introduction, I distinguished two kinds of second-order theories. First, there are theories that are concerned with real-world problems and real-world solutions, and second, there are theories that are concerned with normative questions that are primarily interesting from an academic point of view. Rawls was decidedly concerned, even though some critics deny this, with solving a real-world issue. Samuel Freeman confirms: "The overriding concern in Rawls's account of justice, early and late, is to describe how, if at all, a well-ordered society in which all agree on a public conception of justice is realistically possible."[6] The concern for a real-world solution, according to Freeman, also explains "Rawls's concern for the stability of justice as fairness."[7] The Rawls specialist continues: "All along, Rawls aims to describe the conditions under which a 'social contract' – general agreement upon principles of justice among free and equal persons with a sense of justice – can be achieved as a real possibility in the world."[8]

The question then might be raised whether Rawls sees our current democratic arrangements as modus vivendi arrangements. It is interesting to note that Rawls uses the term 'modus vivendi' in PL. For Rawls a modus vivendi is a treaty or contract that will be adhered to by all sides as long as it is in the interest of all parties. In general, though, the parties "are ready to pursue their goals at the expense of the other, and should conditions change they may do so."[9] Furthermore, a modus vivendi arrangement according to Rawls is a "social consensus founded on self- or group interests, or on the outcome of political bargaining."[10] In a modus vivendi arrangement – and thus in "the absence [. . .] of agreement on what is just and unjust,"[11] according to Rawls "distrust and resentment" threaten to "corrode the ties of civility, and suspicion and hostility tempt men to act in ways they would otherwise avoid."[12] If I want to answer the question of whether Rawls views the current democratic arrangements as modus vivendi arrangements, I need to distinguish his usage of the term from the definition that I employ. The difference between the definition of modus vivendi employed by Rawls and the definition that I employ is mainly that I think that people agree to such arrangements usually for both moral and non-moral reasons.[13] To my knowledge, Rawls never explicitly calls our current democratic arrangements modus vivendi arrangements. Hence, it remains a matter of interpretation as to how he himself conceived of our democratic arrangements. As I stated in the beginning, Rawls viewed our current order as wanting. Furthermore, he clearly states in *Justice as Fairness* that capitalist welfare states do not reflect the two principles of justice. According to Rawls, a "property-owning democracy," would satisfy the two principles of justice.[14] To conclude, it is not clear whether the Rawls of TJ viewed the current capitalist welfare states as a modus vivendi (according to the PL definition). At the same time there is good reason to believe that Rawls viewed capitalist welfare states as 'second-best' of sorts and thus as modus vivendi arrangements in my sense.

Let us then turn to Rawls's own approach of tackling the problem of persistent disagreement. Rawls develops his argument for the principles of justice in two parts. In the first part, Rawls employs the veil of ignorance to establish what "free and rational persons concerned to further their own interests would accept in an initial position of equality as defining the fundamental terms of their association."[15] In the second part, Rawls wants to show that the principles that were crafted behind the veil of ignorance can be stable under favorable circumstances. I will discuss Rawls's answer against the background of the questions of this essay.

2.1.1 *Justice*

In many ways, John Rawls's TJ can be understood as a philosophical refinement of the earlier work in the contract tradition. "My aim," Rawls writes, "is to present a conception of justice which generalizes and carries to higher level of abstraction the familiar theory of the social contract as found, say, in Locke, Rousseau, and Kant."[16] Rawls asks which principles of justice free and equal people would agree on. The immediate problem when thinking about this question is that reasonable people disagree about the answer to this question. According to Rawls, our disagreement stems at least in parts from the fact that when discussing these issues, individuals have problems taking up a disinterested point of view and casting aside considerations about what would be in their own interest, in the interest of their friends, or in the interest of their faith.

The central question of contention, in the eyes of Rawls, is the question of distribution. While everybody profits from commerce and from the division of labor, and thus has a general interest to take part in society, the question of how the fruits of society shall be divided is a thorn in society's side. Rawls writes:

> There is conflict of interests since persons are not indifferent as to how the greater benefits produced by their collaboration are distributed, for in order to pursue their ends they each prefer a larger to a lesser share.[17]

Since those considerations very easily tend to cloud our judgment when it comes to moral questions, and thus lead to moral dissent, Rawls envisioned a device that would help us put aside all considerations that should not, in his view, influence moral deliberation. To make this question more tractable, Rawls introduces the veil of ignorance. People behind the veil of ignorance don't know their "place in society, their class position or social status," their "fortune in the distribution of natural assets."[18] They do not know which abilities they have; neither do they know about their "strength" or "intelligence."[19] In addition, they are oblivious to "their conceptions of the good or their special psychological propensities."[20] More generally, the "parties must not know the contingencies that set them in opposition."[21] On the other side, the parties in the original position know all important socio-economic facts. They thus "understand political affairs and the principles of economic theory."[22] Two important sets of knowledge that the parties in the original position possess are worth highlighting. The people behind the veil of ignorance know about the "laws of human psychology,"[23] which importantly include the laws about moral psychology. This entails that the people behind the veil of ignorance appreciate that people are no saints and that their commitment to principles of justice in the face of stresses has certain limits. Therefore they consider what Rawls calls, "the strains of commitment"[24]:

> They cannot enter into agreements that may have consequences they cannot accept. They will avoid those that they can adhere to only with great difficulty. Since the original agreement is final and made in perpetuity, there is no second chance. In view of the serious nature of the possible consequences, the question of the burden of commitment is especially acute.[25]

Another aspect of the original position that needs to be highlighted is that the parties are aware of what Rawls calls the "circumstances of justice."[26] The circumstances of justice have two important properties. First, Rawls concedes that

> men suffer from various shortcomings of knowledge, thought, and judgment. Their knowledge is necessarily incomplete, their powers or reasoning, memory, and attention are always limited, and their judgment is likely to be distorted by anxiety, bias, and a preoccupation with their own affairs.[27]

While some of these defects stem from genuine moral error, Rawls explains, most of them are grounded in the *conditio humana*.

The second important property of the "circumstances of justice" is the fact of moderate scarcity and a certain mutual disinterest between individuals.[28] From this it should become clear that, although Rawls's theory of justice is an effort in ideal theory, Rawls nevertheless tries to establish principles of justice for people as they are, in a world plagued by scarcity and human fallibility. Rawls's theory of justice is often criticized as not being "adequately fact-sensitive."[29]

The exposition to this point paints a different picture. Rawls himself emphasized that contract theory agrees with utilitarianism in "holding that the fundamental principles of justice quite properly depend upon the natural facts about men in society."[30] As I have pointed out, "This dependence is made explicit by the description of the original position: the decision of the parties is taken in the light of general knowledge."[31] The original position is best understood as a device that allows us – at any time – to reach normative conclusions that are in accordance with how free and equal persons would judge.

> The idea [of the original position] is simply to make vivid to ourselves the restrictions that it seems reasonable to impose on arguments for principles of justice [. . .]. Thus it seems reasonable and generally acceptable that no one should be advantaged or disadvantaged by natural fortune or social circumstances and the choice of principles. It also seems widely agreed that it should be impossible to tailor principles to the circumstances of one's own case.[32]

It is possible for us at any time to enter the original position "simply by following a certain procedure, namely, by arguing for principles of justice in accordance with these restrictions."[33] Further, the original position is a device to make progress in reaching a reflective equilibrium. Reaching reflective equilibrium, for Rawls, is the preeminent aim of political philosophy. Reaching reflective equilibrium can be understood as a process in which we try to mutually adjust normative principles and our considered judgments in a coherent form. Consequently, reflective equilibrium is reached when all "our principles and judgments"[34] coincide. The reflective equilibrium is in turn a guiding methodological principle that informs both the construction of the original position and the discussion within the original position.

We are now at a point, where we can press further and ask what terms of cooperation free and equal persons in the original position would choose. According to Rawls's analysis, free and equal persons would choose his two principles of justice under fair conditions:[35]

1 **First principle:** Each person is to have an equal right to the most extensive total system of basic liberties compatible with a similar system of liberty for all.
2 **Second principle:** Social and economic inequalities are to be arranged so that they are both (a) to the greatest benefit of the least-advantaged, consistent with the just savings principle, and (b) attached to offices and positions open to all under conditions of fair equality of opportunity.[36]

The two principles of justice are ordered lexically. This means that the fulfillment of the first principle takes priority over the fulfillment of the second. This priority ranking also applies to the second principle internally. Here, the principle of fair opportunity (2b) takes priority over the difference principle (2a).[37] The two principles of justice in turn provide us with a distinctive standard to choose from the set of all feasible institutional sets. Members of this set include laissez-faire capitalism, the welfare state, different forms of pure socialism, democratic socialism, property-owning democracy and, we might imagine, many more. In *Justice as Fairness: A Restatement* Rawls argues, as I noted earlier, that the principles of justice would most likely be met by democratic socialism or a property-owning democracy.[38]

2.1.2 Stability

One of the central questions that motivate Rawls's work is to find principles of justice that under favorable circumstances could be stable in spite of the circumstances of justice. Two kinds of problems endanger the stability even of initially just societies. Only if these two problems can effectively be prevented can "the hazards of the generalized prisoner's dilemma"[39] be removed.

Generalized prisoner's dilemma

At the heart of every democratic state, according to Rawls, lies a simple prisoner's dilemma endangering the stability of society. This dilemma can be depicted from different angles. First, we can depict it from the angle of the citizen's contribution to the state, or to put it differently, as a problem of provision. Let us take the case of paying taxes, as Rawls notes: "From a self-interested point of view each person is tempted to shirk doing his share."[40] The reason behind this is simple. If Jon cheats on his taxes, the provision of a good (e.g. public health care) will not be diminished in any tangible form. While his defection of not paying taxes actually hurts no one, he himself profits significantly from shirking. Now he can afford to buy his mother the veranda she always wanted, pay more money to his favorite charity and work less in the following year and thus spend more time with his family. As Rousseau notes:

> his share of the wrong done to the public seems nothing to him when compared to the exclusive advantage that he intends to take for himself. Except for this private advantage, he has on his own behalf as strong a desire as anyone else for the public good.[41]

The second aspect from which the hazards of the generalized prisoner's dilemma arise is the problem of law provision. Again, from the self-interested viewpoint, a society regulated by the two principles of justice might be a very pleasant place to live in, but an even better society from the self-interested viewpoint is a generally just society in which an additional set of privileges favors him or her exclusively.

The problem that Rawls is hinting at is that if everybody in a democratic society uses the democratic mechanism to advance his or her personal conception of the good or right, we will end up in a "generalized prisoner's dilemma" (Table 2.1).

Table 2.1 Prisoner's Dilemma 1

	A: Cooperates	*A: Grabs privilege*
B: Cooperates	Just society	Just society + A's privilege/ B's cost
B: Grabs privilege	Just society + B's privilege / A's cost	Generalized prisoner's dilemma

A just democratic society thus faces – prima facie – the same problems as a normal democracy. Rawls judges that "these tendencies arising from self-interest lead to instability."[42] This sort of instability is called "instability of the first kind."[43] In Rousseau, we find this very vivid description of a democratically hedged war of all against all:

> When the social tie begins to loosen, [. . .] when particular interests begin to make themselves felt, and smaller groupings influence the greater one, then the common interest no longer remains unaltered, but is met with opposition, the votes are no longer unanimous, and the general will no longer the will of all; contradiction and argument arise, and the best opinion is not accepted without dispute. Finally [. . .] when the crudest self-interest insolently adorns itself with the sacred name of the public good, then the general will falls silent; the motives of all are kept secret, their votes are no more the votes of citizens than if the state had never existed, and the decrees that are falsely passed, under the name of laws, have private interests as their only aim.[44]

The solution to the generalized prisoner's dilemma is relatively straightforward in TJ. Rawls assumes that in a well-ordered society (WOS) – that is, a society regulated by the principles of justice – people would generally develop a *sense of justice*. Rawls sketches a three-stage process of moral development that every child in a WOS goes through. The first stage of moral development is called "The morality of authority." On this basic level, the child learns the normative precepts and norms from his parents. The child might at first take these precepts as arbitrary sanctions of his or her behavior, but since the parents "love the child and are worthy objects of admiration," they arouse in the child a "sense of his own value" that in turn stirs up a desire in the child to emulate the parents.[45] When a child becomes older, he or she will enter the second stage of moral development by taking up school and joining more and more associations, like sports clubs or guilds of multiplayer online games. All these associations have their own formal and informal social rules, which include "common sense rules of morality."[46] Through interaction in these diverse groups the common sense rules of morality "are impressed upon him by the approval and disapproval of those in authority."[47] Furthermore, participation in due time allows teenagers to develop the capacities for "fellow feeling" and "friendship" if they are members of associations in which these ideals are realized.[48] The third stage is called "the morality of principles."[49] Up to the third level the teenager cares mainly for the moral rules that are embedded in the diverse practices of associations and family life. He or she aspires to live up to the common sense rules of these social unions, but the "motive for complying with them [. . .], springs largely from his ties of friendship and fellow feeling for others."[50] Importantly, the teenager's reason for compliance is thus not yet "justice as fairness," but, for the most part, the "approbation of the wider society."[51] Rawls tells us that the "conception of acting justly [. . .] comes to have an attraction analogous to that possessed before by subordinate ideals."[52] We first acquire the conception of acting justly by being part of associations, which in turn are regulated by the principles of justice and are in any case, in the WOS, well known. For example, while in the first stage, Philipp learned about the basic values of family and common sense morality, he internalized ideals of friendship and fellow feeling in the second stage. In the third stage, Philipp will develop a "desire to act from a conception of right and justice."[53] Furthermore, the fully developed sense of justice "gives rise to a willingness to work for [. . .] the setting up of just institutions, and for the reform of existing ones when justice requires it."[54] Rawls in summary then assumes "that the sense of justice is acquired gradually by the younger members of society as they grow up" in a WOS.[55]

Coming back to the original prisoner's dilemma, we can now appreciate how a fully developed sense of justice prevents the dilemma from arising in the first place. Since everybody in the WOS organizes the desires, ideals and moral values under his or her sense of justice, Philipp has no inclination not to pay taxes or to vote for some special privilege. It is for this reason that Rawls calls his institutional system "inherently stable."[56] Nobody has a decisive desire to bend the rules of the society in his or her favor. Compare this strategy of avoiding a prisoner's dilemma with the Hobbesian strategy of solving the prisoner's dilemma. The Hobbesian solution is disincentivizing defection by punishment. This means counteracting the initial desire to defect by punishment and thus changing the pay-off matrix. The Rawlsian approach, on the contrary, does not need to disincentivize defection, because there is no desire for defection in the first place. Two comments might be in place here. First, traditionally, there are two ways of solving normative problems: to change human motivation, and to change the rules of the game and thereby the payoffs. Rawls, this seems clear now, belongs in the first camp. In Chapter 4, I will discuss a more Hobbesian approach to solving the generalized prisoner's dilemma.

The second comment relates to the problem of law provision in general. Since law provision itself is a public good, there are actually no (or at least very few) coercive means a democratic state that can employ to prevent the generalized prisoner's dilemma. Since there are no coercive means to prevent the dilemma, we might think that changing the attitudes of persons is actually the *only* effective means to prevent the hazards of the generalized prisoner's dilemma. I will come back to that point later. For the moment, I shall simply note that Hobbes solves this problem by instituting a Leviathan; thus he does not even attempt to solve the *democratic* collective action problem of law provision.

The mutual assurance problem

As we have seen the prevention of the generalized prisoner's dilemma is predicated on everybody in the WOS possessing and adhering to his or her sense of justice. The sense of justice in Rawls is, as I explained, to a huge degree a result of nurture, not nature. Since the sense of justice is at least in part something artificial, the citizens within the WOS can in principle decide for or against their sense of justice. An analogy might be helpful. Let's take the case of Philipp, who grows up in a very religious household. In his childhood, he learns and adopts, for the most part unconsciously, the various religious precepts, rituals, routines and ethical standards of his parents. After he graduates from high school, he comes to question the standards of his parents and his own moral feelings. In the end, he decides that the religious ideals of his parents are quite parochial and that their social and moral rules are not only antiquated, but wrong. Subsequently, he chooses to live by new rules. Over the following weeks, he often has a bad conscience and feels a numbing pain as he throws his 'holy book' in the trash. Since he knows that there is a certain time lag between a conscious decision for or against certain moral standards and the transformation of our gut response, he chooses to ignore these emotions, and, with time, his moral feelings adapt to his new moral standards.

Coming back to Rawls's discussion of the sense of justice, the question is whether the people in the WOS usually will affirm their sense of justice or discard it as we would do with an oppressive ideology. Rawls takes this problem rather seriously and spends the entire third part of TJ on coping with it. In summary, Rawls attempts here to establish that everybody has decisive reasons to affirm his or her sense of justice even from the viewpoint of self-interest. In Rawls's words: "What is to be established is that it is rational (as defined by the thin theory of the good) for those in a WOS to affirm their sense of justice as regulative of their plan of life."[57] To achieve this, Rawls must show that there is a "congruence" or a "match" between goodness and justice.[58] Further, only if Rawls can show that the congruence claim holds can he show that people in the WOS would affirm their sense of justice, which in turn, is a necessary condition for stability. Paul Weithman recently delivered a prolonged study of the stability arguments in both TJ and PL. In this section I will follow Weithman's excellent and meticulous analysis of Rawls's argument in support of the congruence claim. To demonstrate that the congruence claim holds, Rawls needs to show that from the viewpoint of self-interest, based on the "thin theory of the good,"[59] the members of the WOS have decisive reason to affirm their inherited sense of justice. Rawls then, according to Weithman's reconstruction, has to demonstrate the following claim:

> $[C_T]$[60]: Each member of the WOS judges, from within the thin theory of the good, that her balance of reasons tilts in favor of maintaining her desire to act from the principles of justice as a highest-order regulative desire in her rational plans.[61]

Weithman, though, rightly believes that this is too strong of a claim. The reason for this is that the claim implies that each person would affirm his or her sense of justice and act accordingly "*regardless* of how he is treated by institutions and by other people."[62] What Rawls needs to show, according to Weithman, is the somewhat weaker claim that each person, judging from within the thin theory, has sufficient reason to affirm his sense of justice, *as long as his or her fellow citizen's actions are similarly guided.* Weithman calls this the Nash Claim:

> C_N: Each member of the WOS judges, from within the thin theory of the good, that her balance of reasons tilts in favor of maintaining her desire to act from the principles of justice as a highest-order regulative desire in her rational plans *when the plans of others are similarly regulated.*[63]

This claim reflects that Rawls wants to know whether *a person who lives* in a WOS – a society that is effectively regulated by the principles of justice – has sufficient reason to affirm his or her sense of justice. What Rawls then has to solve is essentially an assurance problem. Since the assurance problem hinges critically on what Philipp judges from within Rawls's thin theory of the good, we should examine this theory a bit more closely. The thin theory of the good, as it turns out, is neither particularly thin nor particularly close to what we would usually associate with a self-interested perspective (or a thin theory of the good). Furthermore, as Gaus notes, the thin theory of the good even "goes far beyond the theory of primary goods employed in the first stage of the argument from the original position."[64] In Weithman's reconstruction of Rawls's thin theory of the good, the main components of the theory can be reformulated as four claims[65]:

1 All members of the WOS think of themselves, at least implicitly, as natural free, equal, and rational persons, and want to express their nature as such.
2 All members of the WOS want to avoid the psychological costs of hypocrisy and deception.
3 All members of the WOS want ties of friendship.
4 All members of the WOS want to participate in forms of social life that call forth their own and others' talents.[66]

In reviewing these desires, it is helpful to recall under which circumstances the desires underlying these claims are developed. These desires, according to

Rawls, develop in people who grow up in a WOS, that is, a society in which all "social values – liberty and opportunity, income and wealth and the bases of self-respect – are [. . .] distributed equally unless an unequal distribution of any, or all, of these values is to everyone's advantage."[67] This means that these desires are important for people who have already fulfilled more than their basic needs. Rawls explains the desires with reference to the so-called Aristotelian principle and companion effect.[68] The Aristotelian principle states that "other things equal, human beings enjoy the exercise of their realized capacities (their innate or trained abilities), and this enjoyment increases the more the capacity is realized, or the greater its complexity."[69] Rawls qualifies the principles as a principle of motivation[70] and considers it to be a "psychological law."[71] The companion effect that is part of the Aristotelian principle runs like this:

> As we witness the exercise of well-trained abilities by others, these displays are enjoyed by us and arouse a desire that we should be able to do the same things ourselves. We want to be like those persons who can exercise the abilities that we find latent in our nature.[72]

These fundamental psychological laws explain that the members of the WOS (a) want to express their nature as free, equal and rational persons; (b) avoid the psychological costs of hypocrisy and deception; (c) want ties of friendship; and (d) participate in forms of social life that call forth their own and others' talents.

In TJ there are two main arguments from the thin theory that support the congruence claim. The first one is called the *argument from love and justice*. The argument draws on the claims (b), (c) and (d). Rawls makes the argument that the best way for the members of a WOS to satisfy the three desires – *psychological integrity, friendship* and *participation in association* – is essentially for them to hold on to their sense of justice as long as everybody else does.[73] Thus, the sense of justice is not only a means of achieving first-order stability, but also of fulfilling everybody's wants according to the thin theory of the good. The first argument, though, has its clear limitations. While it is unquestionable that just actions will in many cases be instrumental to important goals such as *friendship* and *participation in associations*, it is undoubtedly also true that sometimes acting justly will set back our good. In summary, this means that the *argument from love and justice* shows only that members of the WOS have good – but clearly not conclusive – reasons to affirm their sense of justice. What Rawls has to show is that "just action *as such* is congruent with our good."[74]

The *Kantian congruence argument* attempts to show exactly this. Rawls argues that "the desire to act justly and the desire to express our nature as free moral persons"[75] are actually the same desire under different descriptions. The only way to satisfy this desire is "by acting on the principles of right and justice as having first priority."[76] In Weithman's schemata the argument then draws on desire (a), the desire "to express our nature as a free and equal rational being."[77] Notice the distinctly Kantian element here. A desire for expressing our nature as free, equal and rational beings essentially means that we have a desire to live according to the principles of justice. To simplify, the principles of justice are the principles that our rational selves would choose. In this sense, the members of a WOS have a desire to follow the rules that they have given themselves.

If the two arguments – the argument from 'love and justice' and the argument from 'Kantian congruence – go through, Rawls would show that judging from the thin theory of the good, the members of the WOS have decisive reason to affirm their sense of justice as long as others do so. Since in a WOS people affirm their sense of justice, everyone who comes to reflect on his or her sense of justice has decisive reason to affirm it. In summary: If Rawls's argument is correct, he would show that a WOS can successfully hedge the hazards associated with the generalized prisoner's dilemma.

2.2 Solving modus vivendi

In the first part of this chapter, I reviewed John Rawls's defense of justice as fairness. Rawls's goal was not merely to present and defend another set of desirable principles. His aim was to formulate a set of normative principles that can – despite our disagreements – secure their own uptake and generate their own support.[78] The question that arises then is: What kinds of institutional changes are recommended by justice as fairness? Or to put it differently: In which direction do we need to alter our current democratic institutions to escape modus vivendi?

Before we engage with this question, let me add a few strokes to the picture of the Rawlsian project. Although there is undoubtedly a realistic pull to justice as fairness, Rawls himself has never spent much ink on questions of implementation. In TJ, we find the distinction between ideal and nonideal theory. Ideal theory is about forging and defending desirable principles that "characterize a well-ordered society under favorable circumstances."[79] Nonideal theory, on the contrary, asks how the goals, defended by ideal theory, can be brought to fruition, or put into practice.[80] Rawls writes:

> Nonideal theory asks how this long-term goal might be achieved, or worked toward, usually in gradual steps. It looks for courses of action that are morally permissible and politically possible as well as likely to be effective.[81]

The main focus of the Rawlsian project – as he himself emphasizes in TJ – is on ideal theory.[82] In neither TJ nor PL does Rawls discuss the institutional structure of a WOS in much detail.[83] It is only in his last treatise, *Justice as Fairness: A Restatement,*[84] that he finally discusses what kind of institutional system would best fit his approach. In this work, Rawls distinguishes between five social systems: laissez-faire capitalism, welfare-state capitalism, state socialism with a command economy, property-owning democracy and liberal democratic socialism.[85] Without much discussion, Rawls rejects laissez-faire capitalism and state socialism. Although he seems to have some sympathies for liberal democratic socialism, Rawls surprisingly never spends more than a few words on this social system. The main focus of Rawls's rather short discussion of social systems lies clearly on differentiating the concept of a property-owning democracy from welfare-state capitalism. While Rawls rejects the latter approach – and thus our current social system – he thinks that the first concept has a good chance of securing fair cooperation over time.

The first occasion on which Rawls clearly rejects welfare-state capitalism in favor of a property-owning democracy is in the preface of the French translation of TJ.[86] Here, he writes that one of the shortcomings of the original version of TJ is that he has not distinguished "more sharply the idea of a property-owning democracy [. . .] from the idea of a welfare state."[87]

Let us then get a clearer picture on what a property-owning democracy is and why Rawls believes it to be superior to a capitalistic welfare state. As I noted, Rawls did not spend much time on nonideal theory. Furthermore, even in the few instances Rawls engaged with nonideal theory, his remarks remain sketchy, as he himself acknowledges, and his arguments are mostly "rough and intuitive."[88] This is also true for Rawls's definition of a property-owning democracy or rather the lack thereof. Rawls writes:

> Both a property-owning democracy and a liberal socialist regime set up a constitutional framework for democratic politics, guarantee the basic liberties with the fair value of the political liberties and fair equality of opportunity, and regulate economic and social inequalities by a principle of mutuality, if not by the difference principle.[89]

Unfortunately, again, Rawls neither tells us much about the institutions that regulate economic and social equality, nor about the constitutional framework for democratic politics. The deciding institutional factor that distinguishes a liberal socialist regime, a property-owning democracy and a welfare state is economic in nature and relates to the distribution of the means of production. In a socialist regime, the means of production are "owned by society," while in a property-owning democracy the "economic power is dispersed among firms."[90] In contrast, according to Rawls, welfare-state capitalism permits the concentration of economic assets up to the point where "a small class" has a "near monopoly of the means of production."[91] Freeman, then, seems to be essentially right in defining the Rawlsian property-owning democracy "as one that puts into the hands of citizens generally, and not in the hands of a few, the productive means and equal political power needed to make them fully cooperating members of a democratic society."[92]

To get a more nuanced view of Rawls's preferred system of social cooperation, it is worthwhile to get a deeper understanding of the reasons that motivated his choice. In order to properly evaluate the two systems we need to compare them along two criteria:[93] first, we need to assess whether a certain system confirms to the two principles of justice; second, we need to analyze whether a certain system could be "effectively designed to realize its declared aims and objectives."[94] To fulfill the second criterion, a social system needs to generate sufficient support from the citizens and "the tasks assigned to offices and positions would prove simply too difficult for those likely to hold them."[95] Although Rawls acknowledges explicitly the need for a feasibility check in this chapter, he decides to skip the second check entirely.[96] Instead, Rawls's comparative analysis between a property-owning democracy and a capitalistic welfare state focuses solely on this question: "What kind of regime and basic structure would be right and just, *could* it be effectively and workably maintained?"[97] This means that Rawls compares both social systems with regard only to how well they are faring in fulfilling the two principles of justice. In particular, he asks to what extent both systems are compatible with regard to securing the basic liberties (specifically *equal political liberties*) and guaranteeing *fair equality of opportunity,* and are in line with the *difference principle.* Rawls argues that a welfare state performs worse in regard to all three standards.[98] In a nutshell, he argues that in welfare states, tolerated inequalities in economic power "enable those better situated to exercise a larger influence over the development of legislation."[99] In particular, Rawls fears that an economically powerful elite will have too much "weight in settling social questions"[100] to the disadvantage of the worst-off. In a property-owning democracy, on the contrary, the steady diffusion of productive means and therefore economic power – is thought to counteract inequality of political power. Securing equal political liberties (i.e. equal political influence or power) then seems to be akin to a necessary condition for securing both fair equality of opportunity and the application of the difference principle.

Furthermore, a property-owning democracy at the very outset seems to reflect the idea of a fair system of cooperation between free and equal citizens much better than does its rival. A property-owning democracy, by defusing property rights, puts "all citizens in a position to manage their own affairs on a footing of a suitable degree of social and economic equality."[101] The hope here is that – Rawls is quite explicit about this – in a property-owning democracy, there is no underclass and the citizens encounter each other in both the political as well as the economic arena as equals.[102] A welfare state, on the contrary, merely secures a certain minimum and protects its citizens against the gravest misfortunes and accidents.

Freeman further highlights a central difference between both systems that harks back to our discussion of diversity. He writes that "by focusing its attention primarily on the level of welfare of members of society, the welfare state does not encourage its citizens to *take control of their lives* and be actively productive and equal participants in social and political life."[103] While a welfare state is primarily concerned with welfare, a property-owning democracy "is oriented to *realizing the freedom, independence, and active participation* of equal citizens in economic and political life."[104] A property-owning democracy thus secures not only formal, but also real opportunities for individuals to follow their diverse goals. Implementing the two principles of justice defuses the hazards of diversity by allowing everybody a great space to follow his or her own moral and religious goals and realize the goods that he or she deems worthy. In contrast to a pure system of natural liberty (like laissez-faire capitalism), a property-owning democracy does not only formally guarantee a space in which individuals can decide for themselves and follow their own aims, but also guarantees the necessary means for individuals to realize these goals. Above that it secures equal political liberties that give individuals the opportunity to make sure that their interests are properly represented and respected on a political level. From this perspective, the two principles of justice can be viewed as devices for coping with persistent diversity itself. The two principles of justice solve the problem of disagreement by giving individuals both the right and the means to strive for their own good.[105]

To sum up: Rawls essentially uses two devices to cope with diversity. The first device is the veil of ignorance. This device allows us to pick out principles of justice that all can agree with. These principles of justice – if implemented – secure and guarantee each contractor a huge sphere of freedom in which she or he is allowed to strive for what she or he sees as her or his own good. Although the contractors cannot agree on substantive issues (the good, moral and religious question), they nevertheless agree on a device, a system of liberties, that allows everyone to some extent to live his or her life according to his or her own moral and religious outlook and conception of the good. Rawls's second device for solving or at least defusing the hazards of disagreement is then *disaggregation,* or as Fred D'Agostino calls it, "commensuration via separation."[106] I will return to the disaggregation response to disagreement on several occasions in this essay. Most prominently, I discuss this approach in Chapter 10, Section 10.3.2.[107]

2.3 RoCD Test

In this final section, I want to explore whether Rawls's argument can reasonably hope to convince the RoCD (see Chapter 1, Section 1.3). As is well known, one of the deepest objections to TJ was raised by Rawls himself. In later years, he became convinced that: "The fact of a plurality of reasonable but incompatible comprehensive doctrines – the fact of reasonable pluralism – shows, that as used in *Theory*, the idea of a well-ordered society is unrealistic."[108] Rawls continues: "This is because it is inconsistent with realizing its own principles under the best foreseeable conditions."[109] Despite Rawls's own rejection, I want to see whether TJ can persuade the RoCD to adopt its principles and its political implementation: a property-owning democracy.[110] As I have outlined in Chapter 1, Section 1.3, the RoCD Test comprises two questions: (a) is the proposal inter-subjectively justified? (b) Can the proposal be seen as a Pareto improvement over the current modus vivendi arrangements? For reasons of brevity,

I will not discuss both questions separately for each RoCD, but just present a short statement from which the answer to both questions can be easily inferred. Let us now turn to the judgment of the jury.

Utilitarians: Utilitarians are usually not convinced of the lexical ordering of the principles of justice.[111] While it is clear that utilitarians would not deem a society in which principles of TJ are properly implemented just, it is not clear whether they might choose such a society over our current modus vivendi. Most likely, there would be no agreement on the later question between utilitarians.

Classical liberals: Classical liberals cannot accept TJ, because it does not properly protect economic liberties.[112] For classical liberals and libertarians, implementing the principles of justice would seem like a move in the wrong direction. Thinkers in that direction would see such a society surely not even as a Pareto improvement over our current arrangements. In addition, classical liberals disagree on an instrumental level. Classical liberals such as Pennington argue that normative goals similar to the ones in TJ would be best achieved by a small state.[113]

Deliberative democrats: Deliberative democrats are of the opinion that even fundamental rights need to be subject to public discourse.[114] It is to be assumed, though, that many deliberative democrats would, nevertheless, choose an arrangement in which the principles of justice are implemented over the current modus vivendi arrangements.

Realists: Realists criticize that the principles are not fine-grained enough to adjudicate most of the real-world issues that arise in a democracy.[115] Realists are a heterodox group, too, so, most likely, there would not be a unanimous vote.

Egalitarians: For some egalitarians, Rawls's proposal is in a sense not radical enough. However, it might be very well the case that egalitarians would choose a society that is regulated after the principles outlined in TJ over our current modus vivendi.[116]

Natural rights libertarians: Defenders of natural rights, like Robert Nozick, reject Rawls's proposal because it violates rights. Since Rawls favors a more comprehensive state than the current welfare state, natural rights theorists surely will not endorse TJ over our current modus vivendi.[117]

Having collected these statements, I can now proceed to a conclusion: While there is no doubt that parts of the RoCD would welcome a move from our current modus vivendi arrangements to a political arrangement that implements Rawls's two principles of justice, it is certain that many parties would not. There is no doubt that many parties to the RoCD convention would emphatically resist a move from our current modus vivendi arrangements to a *democratic socialism* or a *property-owning democracy* that is regulated by Rawls's two principles of justice.

Notes

1 I will base my argument on his original statement from 1971.
2 For a recent discussion about different readings of PL and the relation between PL and TJ, compare Gaus (2013), Weithman (2010) and Freeman (2007b, chap. 6). This is not to deny that there are also other important differences between both approaches. Rawls's PL is especially interesting for a first understanding of the similarities and differences (Rawls 2005b, chap. 9).
3 Rawls (2005a, p. 5).
4 Rawls (2005a, p. 5).
5 Rawls (2005b, p. lviii).
6 Freeman (2007b, p. 4).
7 Freeman (2007b, p. 4).
8 Freeman (2007b, p. 4).
9 Rawls (2005b, p. 147).
10 Rawls (2005b, p. 147).
11 Rawls (2005a, p. 6).
12 Rawls (2005a, p. 6).
13 Rawls seems to hold that modus vivendi arrangements are an outcome of a contract that is based on purely prudential reasons. For a similar view compare Wendt (2015).
14 Rawls (2001, pp. 135–140). For an in-depth discussion of Rawls's preference for a property-owning democracy see Freeman (2007a).
15 Rawls (2005a, p. 11).
16 Rawls (2005a, p. 11).
17 Rawls (2005a, p. 4).
18 Rawls (2005a, p. 12).
19 Rawls (2005a, p. 12).
20 Rawls (2005a, p. 12).
21 Rawls (2005a, p. 137).
22 Rawls (2005a, p. 137).
23 Rawls (2005a, p. 137).
24 Rawls (2005a, p. 176).
25 Rawls (2005a, p. 176).
26 Rawls (2005a, p. 127).
27 Rawls (2005a, p. 127).
28 Rawls (2005a, p. 128).
29 Farrelly (2007, p. 845).
30 Rawls (2005a, p. 159).
31 Rawls (2005a, p. 159).
32 Rawls (2005a, p. 18).
33 Rawls (2005a, pp. 19, compare also: 139).
34 Rawls (2005a, p. 20).
35 The parties behind the veil of ignorance compare different principles in a pairwise fashion. This means that there is not a single argument for the two principles of justice. The argument for the principles of justice is always an argument that relates to a pairwise

comparison. In TJ, Rawls only simulates the comparison of a very limited set of principles. He mainly compares the principles of justice to utilitarian standards (Rawls 2005a, §28, §30).
36 Rawls (2005a, p. 302).
37 It should be noted that Rawls presentation in this earliest version of the two principles might be misleading, since 2b actually takes priority over 2a.
38 Rawls (2001, pp. 135–140).
39 Rawls (2005a, p. 577).
40 Rawls (2005a, p. 336).
41 Rousseau (2009, p. 135).
42 Rawls (2005a, p. 336).
43 Rawls (2005a, p. 336).
44 Rousseau (2009, p. 135).
45 Rawls (2005a, p. 465).
46 Rawls (2005a, p. 467).
47 Rawls (2005a, p. 467).
48 Rawls (2005a, p. 470).
49 Rawls (2005a, p. 472).
50 Rawls (2005a, p. 473).
51 Rawls (2005a, p. 473).
52 Rawls (2005a, p. 473).
53 Rawls (2005a, p. 476).
54 Rawls (2005a, p. 474).
55 Rawls (2005a, p. 462).
56 Rawls (2005a, p. 498).
57 Rawls (2005a, p. 567).
58 Rawls (2005a, p. 399).
59 Rawls (2005a, pp. 395–399).
60 Weithman calls this Claim C_6 since it is elaborated on in Chapter 6. I renamed it for reasons of convenience: C_T = Claim on the basis of the *thin* theory of the good.
61 Weithman (2010, p. 63). Italics in the original.
62 Weithman (2010, p. 63). Emphasis added.
63 Weithman (2010, p. 64).
64 Gaus (2013, p. 239).
65 In contrast, Gaus counts at least six elements (2013, pp. 239–240).
66 Adopted from Weithman (2010, p. 64).
67 Rawls (2005a, p. 62).
68 Rawls (2005a, pp. 424–433).
69 Rawls (2005a, p. 426).
70 Rawls (2005a, p. 427).
71 Rawls (2005a, p. 427).
72 Rawls (2005a, p. 428).
73 Compare Weithman (2010, p. 182).
74 Gaus (2013, p. 242). Italics in original.
75 Rawls (2005a, p. 572).
76 Rawls (2005a, p. 574).
77 Rawls (2005a, p. 574).
78 D'Agostino (2004, p. 350).
79 Rawls (2005a, p. 245).
80 For an extensive discussion of ideal and nonideal theory as it applies to Rawls, see Simmons (2010).
81 Rawls (1999c, p. 555).
82 Rawls (2005a, p. 245).
83 In TJ, there are some brief remarks about the institutions that should secure distributive justice Rawls (2005a, chap. 43). Rawls distinguishes here in broad strokes between four

branches of government – the allocation branch, the stabilization branch, the transfer branch, and distribution branch – that together should stabilize the social system in a way "the resulting distribution is just however things turn out." Rawls (2005a, p. 275).

84 Rawls (2001).
85 Rawls (2001, p. 136).
86 Rawls (1999a). Originally published in 1987.
87 Rawls (1999a, p. 419).
88 Rawls (2001, p. 135).
89 Rawls (2001, p. 138).
90 Rawls (2001, p. 138).
91 Rawls (2001, p. 139).
92 Freeman (2007a, p. 104).
93 Rawls actually counts four criteria, but two of the criteria can legitimately be viewed as subcategories.
94 Rawls (2001, p. 136).
95 Rawls (2001, p. 136).
96 In my earlier discussion, I noted that Rawls argues that the principles of justice are fully justified only if the principles generate enough uptake under beneficial circumstances so as to create stable long-term cooperation. For that reason, it is also important to "trace out [. . .] the institutional content of the two principles of justice" (Rawls 2001, p. 136). Before we have no reasonable clear picture of the institutional workings of a society that is regulated by justice as fairness, according to Rawls, we cannot even provisionally endorse the principles of justice (Rawls 2001, p. 138). That Rawls decides at this important stage to skip the feasibility check casts a shadow over his appraisal of a property-owning democracy. Furthermore, it raises the question of whether Rawls in this section truly engages in nonideal theory, as I stated before.
97 Rawls (2001, p. 137). Emphasis added.
98 Rawls (1999a, p. 419).
99 Rawls (2005a, p. 225).
100 Rawls (2005a, p. 225).
101 Rawls (2001, p. 139).
102 Rawls (2001, p. 140).
103 Freeman (2007a, p. 108). Emphasis added.
104 Freeman (2007a, p. 108). Emphasis added.
105 For a similar view, see D'Agostino (2004).
106 D'Agostino (2004, p. 358).
107 In short, the disaggregation response says that, in the face of disagreement, it is sometimes the best solution to economize on collectively binding decisions and instead partition the decision space so that everyone can decide an issue according to his or her preferences or normative standards.
108 Rawls (2005b, p. xvii).
109 Rawls (2005b, p. xvii).
110 There is, of course, dispute about what institutions would best realize the two principles. For reasons of brevity, I will trust Rawls's judgment here and assume that his principles are best realized by a property-owning democracy.
111 Harsanyi, for instance, defended the more specific claim that the parties behind the veil of ignorance would choose to maximize their subjective expected utility (Harsanyi 1975).
112 Tomasi (2012a).
113 Pennington (2011).
114 Habermas (1995). This critique obviously focuses on PL, but there is no doubt that it is even more true for TJ.
115 Wiens (2015), Wiens (2012).
116 Cohen (2008).
117 Nozick (1999).

3 Gutmann and Thompson

Deliberative democracy

In the last chapter, I presented the Rawlsian approach as a second-order theory. The key idea of Rawls's approach to disagreement is to *simulate* a discourse about different principles of justice under certain idealized conditions. In this chapter, I want to present a second-order theory that emphasizes *actual* rather than simulated discourse. As Gutmann and Thompson write, philosophers in the deliberative camp "do not consider the hypothetical justifications proposed by some social-contract theories as sufficient."[1] According to deliberative democrats, the justification for principles of justice or certain bodies of law can be sketched in advance by philosophers, but must be in some sense actualized by real deliberation between the affected parties. To put it differently, from the viewpoint of deliberative democracy, philosophers and academics create normative hypotheses. These hypotheses "must survive the test of actual deliberation" in order "to ground laws that bind citizens."[2]

Deliberative democracy, as is well known, is a rather broad church. I will focus here in particular on the approach of Amy Gutmann and Dennis Thompson. There are two reasons for this choice. First of all, the coauthors develop their particular approach as a philosophical response to moral disagreement. Disagreement is thus the starting point for their philosophical contemplation. The importance of disagreement for both theorists is also reflected by the title of one of their best-known books: *Democracy and Disagreement*.[3] Furthermore, the deliberative approach by Gutmann and Thompson is theoretically rather thin. Since in ethics and metaethics most concepts are contested, thin approaches seem to have a better chance of securing agreement between diverse factions. For that reason I choose Gutmann and Thompson's approach over the more comprehensive deliberative theories such as Jürgen Habermas's discourse ethics.[4]

You might ask if deliberative democrats actually share my initial assumption that we are currently living in a modus vivendi. After all, don't we live – at least in Western societies – in *democratic* societies, where public deliberation already plays a huge role in daily life? Journalists and experts discuss the moral value of particular laws in TV shows; ordinary people post and discuss news on Facebook and various internet sites. In addition, we have professional media that inform us about every aspect of politics and try to uncover fraud and corrupt practices. Nonetheless, as will become clear in this chapter, deliberative democrats are in no way satisfied with the status quo. A quip by Rousseau against British democracy may catch the gist of the deliberative democrat's stance towards our current political situation.

> The people of England believes itself to be free; it is quite wrong: it is free only during the elections of Members of Parliament. Once they are elected, the people is enslaved, it is nothing.[5]

The deliberative democrat is not content with a state of affairs where the democratic electorate makes a few crosses every four years, but in the meantime has very limited power to influence political decisions. A great deal of legislation in current democracies is simply the outcome of bargaining processes between special-interest groups behind closed doors. Since deliberative democrats dismiss purely procedural modes of democracy (i.e. the idea that a majority vote is sufficient for justification) they take issue with much of the current political process. Deliberative democrats, then, agree that the current modus vivendi is a second-best and thus share the dissatisfaction with our current arrangements.

This chapter, again, is divided into three parts. In Section 3.1, I will develop the normative theory of deliberative democracy. This will give us a clearer picture of what aspects and facets of our current political order seem to be problematic from the perspective of deliberative democracy. In Section 3.2, I will outline the escape route out of modus vivendi that deliberate democracy has in store for us. In Section 3.3, I will check whether the deliberative approach is able to convince the RoCD.

3.1 Interpreting modus vivendi

From the viewpoint of deliberative democracy, modern democracies are marked by profound disagreement. Gutmann and Thompson, though, are not concerned with just any kind of disagreement, but with a particular set of disagreement – that is, with *moral disagreement*. Disagreement, according to them, counts as moral when it is based on conflicting moral claims or arguments. To count as a moral claim, a claim has to fulfill certain formal criteria. Both thinkers rely on a particular interpretation of the classical criteria of generality, universality and publicity. Since these criteria are open to diverse interpretations, it is useful to briefly sketch how Gutmann and Thompson interpret these criteria. Moral claims or judgments are general in the sense that they apply not to particular persons, but to everyone who is similarly situated. They are thus not about what Gabriel should or should not do in a particular situation, but about what everybody in Gabriel's place should do. Moral claims are universal in the sense that they are based on values or principles that are generally intelligible and "that are shared or could be shared by fellow citizens."[6] Furthermore, moral claims and arguments are always raised in certain contexts, against certain premises and are addressed to particular people. What makes moral claims public, according to Gutmann and Thompson, is that "claimants reach out to find principles or perspectives that others can accept."[7] Although in moral argument, we reach out to find some common ground like a shared perspective on a given moral problem, we often fail in this endeavor. Whenever we are failing, the result is moral disagreement.

Both philosophers point out that moral disagreement is not only ubiquitous between different first-order theories like utilitarianism, libertarianism, or egalitarianism, or between political factions, but also *within* first-order theories and political factions. Utilitarians, for instance, agree that the social order should maximize social welfare, while at the same time they are "disagreeing among themselves about what it means and how it should be done."[8] Gutmann and Thompson do not present a detailed analysis of the root causes of moral disagreement, but instead are content with pointing to four important *sources* of moral disagreement. Following Rawls in reviving David Hume, both thinkers point to "limited generosity" and "scarcity" as continual sources of moral disagreement.[9] One of the major sources that motivate moral disagreement is essentially the fact that we cannot satisfy all our desires with the limited resources available to us. On top of this, Gutmann and Thompson recognize – as I did in Chapter 1 – that there is also persistent moral disagreement between well-meaning and benevolent people. They write:

> These moral conflicts can be understood and experienced by one person taking a moral point of view, appreciating the competing claims of more than one fundamental value, and therefore struggling internally to resolve the conflict.[10]

Gutmann and Thompson attempt here to abstain from a first-order judgment about the nature of value and thus avoid taking a position in the meta-ethical discussion about value pluralism. They simply note that, descriptively, reasonable people are not able to persuasively resolve value conflicts.[11] The last source of disagreement that the coauthors point out relates to our "incomplete understanding" of particular situations. Gutmann and Thompson explain: "Even if everyone were completely benevolent, some may reasonably give different weight to the many complex factors, moral and empirical, that affect the choice of public policies."[12] The two last sources for moral conflict are very similar to what Rawls calls "the burdens of judgment." There is also some resemblance to my own discussion of shallow and deep disagreement (see Chapter 1, Section 1.2).

The goal of every second-order theory is to appropriately deal with moral disagreement. Or to put in the words of Gutmann and Thompson: "The fundamental problem confronting all democratic theorists is to find a morally justifiable way of making binding collective decisions in the face of continuing moral conflict."[13] The approach of Gutmann and Thompson is developed against the background of two rival democratic theories: procedural and constitutional democracy. Briefly outlining both approaches will allow us to get a better understanding of how Gutmann and Thompson interpret the current modus vivendi arrangements. At the same time, it will allow us to better appreciate the conceptual particularities of deliberative democracy.

Procedural democracy essentially attempts to resolve conflict by majority vote. Under procedural democracy, the members of a society agree "to be governed by the will of a majority or their accountable representatives."[14] Joshua Cohen distinguishes procedural, or aggregative, democracy and deliberative democracy in the same fashion:

> According to an aggregative conception of democracy [. . .] decisions are collective just in case they arise from arrangements of binding collective choice that give equal considerations to – more generically, are positively responsive to – the interests of each person bound by the decision. According to a deliberative conception, a decision is collectively just in case it emerges from arrangements of binding collective choice that establish conditions of free public reasoning among equals who are governed by the decisions.[15]

Within procedural democracy, we can distinguish between two schools. The first brand, pure proceduralism, understands democratic decision-making as a procedure that is morally transformative in the sense that its decisions are morally binding. In this first reading, pure proceduralism overrules the substantive principles of first-order theories through public vote. The second brand is more modest. This approach views procedural settlements as instrumental to secure important ends like stability and legitimacy.[16] Furthermore, such an approach does not overrule first-order theories, it is agnostic towards foundational questions. This approach thus seems to be very akin to the modus vivendi conceptions of Gray and John Horton.[17] Under purely procedural arrangements, the modus vivendi bargains shift as majorities change. All conflicts are settled only provisionally, and any bargain might be revised at a later point in time. In this weak version of pure proceduralism, collective decisions are not seen as morally transformative but rather as prudent provisional settlements.

Gutmann and Thompson take issue with both versions of procedural democracy, yet they mostly focus on the strong version. The objections to this approach are well-rehearsed. Viewing popular vote as morally transformative is problematic. If everybody simply voted with his or her self-interest in mind, there would be no reason to believe that the result of democratic decisions is in the best interest of all. On the contrary, if democratic results were just the aggregate of individual preferences, popular voting would look like a modern version of *might makes right*. In addition, even if everybody were to vote on a mixed bag of motivations, this would still not prevent outcomes that infringe on the rights of minorities. Imagine that in a country there is a small majority voting in accordance with its Christian *moral* beliefs. The consequence might be a curtailing of religious freedoms, religious constraints on what can be taught in public schools, a prohibition to work on Sundays (as for instance in Germany) and so forth. Many people in that society would view such rules as unjust and unjustified. Thus, it is hard to see why factions, following diverse normative standards, should always view majority decisions as morally binding. There might be good prudential reasons for factions to act in accordance with rules that are arrived at by majority vote, but it is again hard to see why majority decisions should be accepted as morally binding. Pure procedural democracy seems to be unfit because it hopes to resolve disagreement of first-order theories by substituting a multitude of first-order theories by its own approach "and therefore turns out to be a first-order theory itself."[18] Viewed from this angle, pure procedural theories become competitors of first-order theories and thus stop to function as second-order theories, since they "simply reproduce [. . .] the substantive disagreement that created the problem of disagreement in the first place."[19] The advantage to the weak version of pure proceduralism is, then, that it does not aim at resolving moral conflict, but rather at producing settlements. It does not try to challenge first-order theories on their own turf. At the same time, Gutmann and Thompson think that such a theory is normatively too thin, because it has no normative resources to critically engage with the results of majority rule.[20] Although Gutmann and Thompson do not discuss philosophical modus vivendi theories, it is safe to assume that their critical assessment of weak proceduralism also applies to modus vivendi theories as sketched by Gray and Horton.

The second competitor of deliberative democracy is constitutional democracy. Constitutional democracy has the salient advantage that it guarantees certain inalienable basic rights and goods for every citizen by restricting procedural democracy. It thus has sufficient normative resources to critically assess particular majority decisions. Furthermore, the difference between variants of democratic theory is not, as it is often thought, that constitutional democracy in contrast to procedural democracy guarantees rights. Procedural democracy indeed also needs to secure some rights that are necessary for its own functioning. The decisive difference between both variants is that constitutional democracy secures "rights that are external to the democratic process and not necessary for its fair functioning."[21]

To Gutmann and Thompson, the paradigmatic constitutional democrat is Rawls. Deliberative democrats usually take issue with the normative foundation of principles that are supposed to constrain democracy. Gutmann and Thompson, on the contrary, mainly focus their critique on another soft spot of constitutional democracy. They criticize the principled approach to democracy, because it is unable to do what it is supposed to: overcome normative disagreement by presenting normative principles that guide democratic decision-making. Principles like the ones provided by Rawls, in Gutmann and Thompson's view, secure at best a shallow agreement:

> The substantive standards they offer seem compelling when stated abstractly: who would deny that majorities should not violate the vital interests of their fellow citizens? But the abstraction purchases reasonable agreement

on the principles at the price of reasonable disagreement about their interpretation.[22]

This is, of course, an issue not only with Rawls's principles of justice, but with constitutionally guaranteed rights in general. They are always subject to interpretation and thus again produce disagreement. With regard to the problem of moral disagreement, constitutional democracy is mainly – if at all – able to conceal disagreement. The shallowness of agreement becomes visible the moment diverse factions attempt to employ the standard in hope of settling moral disagreement. Rawls, for instance, calls for implementing "the most extensive basic liberty compatible with a similar liberty for others."[23] Gutmann and Thompson reply that we are tempted to agree with such a standard, but whenever it comes to hard problems, "such as legalizing violent pornography, prostitution, and abortion,"[24] Rawls's principles seem to be open to many reasonable interpretations and thus are not able to secure agreement. We could also put it in a different way: Since we are facing deep disagreement, we need to be cautious about which substantive principles we want to add to a given second-order theory. Adding substantive principles to a second-order theory – under conditions of profound disagreement – makes the theory prima facie *more* contestable. Thus, adding substantive principles should come with a clear gain, for instance, an improvement in dealing with disagreement. Gutmann and Thompson seem to imply that the gains do not outweigh the costs when it comes to incorporating substantive (i.e. non-provisional) principles into a democratic theory.

Let us turn to Gutmann and Thompson's approach: deliberative democracy. The theorists define deliberative democracy as "a conception of democratic politics in which decisions and policies are justified in a process of discussion among free and equal citizens or their accountable representatives."[25] In this approach, deliberation, not majority vote, does the main justificatory work. While in some deliberative theories, deliberation does all the justificatory work, Gutmann and Thompson's concept is somewhat richer. The core principle of this approach is that "citizens owe one another justifications for the laws they collectively impose on one another."[26] From this core substantive principle of reciprocity Gutmann and Thompson derive a set of *provisional principles* that should guide and regulate the conditions and the content of deliberation.[27] They expand: "Reciprocity, publicity, and accountability are the chief standards that regulate the conditions of deliberation. Basic liberty, basic opportunity, and fair opportunity are key components of the content of deliberation."[28] In a deliberative democracy these principles are *morally* provisional in the sense that they are open for discussion and revision. Furthermore, the political outcome of the deliberative process – the laws and decisions – are politically provisional in the sense that they are revisable. The only unrevisable part is the core notion of reciprocity itself. This means that moral discourse and political process might reinterpret the principle of reciprocity. However, the core idea of reciprocity as mutual moral justification cannot be rejected. Deliberative democrats, the coauthors explain, "can welcome criticism of any of their principles, but they cannot sanction the general rejection of moral reasoning to justify binding political decisions."[29]

The core difference between deliberative democracy, pure procedural democracy and constitutional democracy is the emphasis on deliberation. Gutmann and Thompson suggest that strengthening the deliberative processes and the institutions that facilitate and enable deliberation presents a way out of our current modus vivendi arrangements, or at least an efficient means of smoothing the rough edges of our current democratic practices. Let us then look a bit deeper into their conception of deliberation. As I have already mentioned, the core principle of deliberative democracy is reciprocity. Reciprocity in the context of deliberation means that the parties should seek "agreement on the basis of principles that can be justified to others who share the aim of reaching reasonable agreement."[30] Thus, reciprocity essentially entails a process of reason-giving between reasonable people. Translating the principle of reciprocity into a political context, Gutmann and Thompson describe deliberative democracy

> as a form of government in which free and equal citizens (and their representatives), justify decisions in a process in which they give one another reasons that are mutually acceptable and generally accessible, with the aim of reaching conclusions that are binding in the present on all citizens but open to challenge in the future.[31]

Let us for a moment zoom in on the kind of discourse they envision here. Thompson and Gutmann propose that in deliberating about laws, we should in general rely on "mutually acceptable" and "accessible reasons" for purposes of justification. The question is what they mean by acceptable and accessible reasons. In *Why deliberative democracy* we find that the process of public justification should be open for any kind of reason that is mutually "comprehensible,"[32] and "the source of those reasons, even if accessible, is irrelevant to their mutual justification."[33] I should note here that Gutmann and Thompson in this passage give a nod to the public justification debate in political philosophy. One of the central questions in that debate is the question of what kinds of reasons are eligible in public discourse. If we want to justify a law to someone, are we allowed to proceed with reference to all our reasons (even religious ones), or only with reference to a set of reasons that we could all (given a certain amount of idealization) agree to? This is a very complex debate that I cannot go into right now. What should be noted here, however, is that there are two ends to the continuum. On one end, there are theorists like Rawls[34] who argue that in the process of public justification we should only refer to a limited set of reasons that are shared by all. At the other side of the spectrum there are theorists like Gaus[35] who argue that in the process of public justification, we are allowed to base our judgments on the more extensive set of all our reasons, as long as they are intelligible.[36] When it comes to the question about which reasons are allowed in public debate, Gutmann and Thompson seem to stand in stark opposition to Rawls and in agreement with Gaus.

The initial statement of the accessibility requirement of reasons is elaborated further by Thompson and Gutmann. I find three additional criteria that comprehensible reasons need to fulfill: They need to be moral,[37] respectful,[38] and revisable.[39] With the morality requirement, Thompson and Gutmann want to block people from basing their proposals on purely self-interested reasons. The criterion of mutual respect "requires a favorable attitude toward, and constructive interaction with, people with whom one reasonably disagrees when those persons are similarly willing and able to adopt such an attitude."[40] Let us then turn to the third qualification. Gutmann and Thompson write that "a fundamental feature of deliberative reasoning is that its conclusions are morally revisable over time."[41] Further, they explain that deliberators must take seriously the possibility that in hindsight their own moral reasons turn out wrong, while the "opponents' moral reasons" turn out right.[42] Gutmann and Thompson's view of public justification thus seems to have certain similarities with that of Gaus. Highlighting the difference between both theories allows us to shed additional light on Gutmann and Thompson's theory. The crucial difference between both approaches consists in Gaus's 'presumption for liberty' which reads:

> For a law to be acceptable to a member of the public, it must be a net improvement on liberty. Consulting her own standards, each must hold that the law, in comparison to a condition of liberty, brings more benefits than costs. If a condition of liberty – no law at all – would be better, given her evaluative standards, then she has no reason to accept the law. Self-legislating such a proposal would be manifestly irrational: it would create net losses as judged by her evaluative standards.[43]

Let us exemplify the difference. In Gaus's proposal a law against pornography has no chance, because there are reasonable persons who – although they understand the moral reasons of their fellow citizens to prohibit pornography – will nevertheless conclude that this will impose an overall cost on them and thus veto the proposal. The presumption for liberty essentially reduces the set of eligible rules dramatically and gives Gaus's proposal a classical liberal, if not libertarian, tilt. Without this criterion, the eligible set from which democracy needs to choose is vast. Because there are comprehensible reasons for banning pornography that everybody understands – endangering youth, for instance – a ban on pornography might be a justified result according to deliberative democracy. Note further that such a conclusion can be reached by a majority voting under circumstances of respect – and under the additional criterion of a general awareness of the provisionality of reasons.

Since we are now in a better position to understand the concept of Gutmann and Thompson, let us again consider how we can interpret our current modus vivendi arrangements through the lens of deliberative democracy. From the perspective of deliberate democracy there is a host of political proposals for almost all political problems that could be inter-subjectively justified. Take, for instance, public schooling. Each representative of a comprehensive doctrine (e.g. Catholicism, perfectionism, and libertarianism) has at least one proposal for how to organize public education. Since all these doctrines (or first-order theories) are reasonable, all their proposals for organizing public education – if selected by public vote – would represent justified ways of organizing education. For reasons of clarity, we could thus define a set of rules that contains all proposals, which could become a justified point of agreement. Let us call this the Eligible Set of Deliberative Democracy (ES_{DD}). This set contains all proposals of all first-order theories for organizing health care, public education, taxation, redistribution, and so forth. From the viewpoint of deliberative democracy, our current modus vivendi democracy is unjustified if and in so far as it picks laws that are outside $ES_{DD.}$ Thus, all laws that are the outcome of pure self- or group-interest are certainly not in the eligible set. Legislation that was not reached in line with the standards that regulate the conditions of deliberation is also unjustified. That means not only that legislation needs to pick out the right laws, but that the process of selecting the laws also needs to go through the right motions (i.e. a process of actual reason giving and taking).

Before I tackle the question of how deliberative democracy wants to ensure institutionally that democratic decisions become more deliberative and pick from ES_{DD} more frequently, I want to summarize a few advantages of deliberative democracy. Although deliberative democracy is not neutral with regard to first-order theories,[44] it does not overrule particular first-order theories as some pure procedural theories do. Furthermore, deliberative democracy as a political philosophy has the means to criticize the results of a popular vote. It "has no problem saying that what the majority decides, even after deliberating, need not be right."[45] Gutmann and Thompson expect that an increase in real deliberation might increase the legitimacy of legislated law in the eyes of the constituents. They write quite persuasively:

> Even among policies with which we disagree, we should take a different attitude toward those that are adopted after consideration of the relevant conflicting moral claims, and those that are adopted after only calculation of the relative strength of the competing political interests.[46]

While deliberation and reason giving might ameliorate disagreement that arises mainly from the fact of scarcity, both theorists hope that deliberation might also be able to increase our 'limited generosity.' The idea is here that we get a broader view on the range of reasonable perspectives through deliberation with people who hold different first-order theories. This is thought to make us more inclined to consider reasons apart from our own and give weight to the good of others as well. Gutmann and Thompson's approach is anchored in reality, thus both theorists do not think that deliberation will turn its participants into public-spirited citizens. Their expectations are more limited and their judgment is comparative in nature when they write:

> all we need to assume is that citizens and their representatives are more likely to take a broader view of issues [. . .] in a process in which moral arguments are taken seriously than in a process in which assertions of political power prevail.[47]

In addition, they hope that deliberation will help to clarify existing moral disagreement, reduce shallow disagreement and uncover which conflicts are truly based on deep disagreements. In particular, they hope that deliberation might help to "sort out the self-interested from the public-spirited claims, and among the latter helps identify those that have greater weight."[48] Very closely related to that point, deliberative democrats also hope that collective deliberation over time might mirror collective trial-and-error learning processes in which "citizens can learn from each other, come to recognize their individual and collective mistakes, and develop new views and policies that are more widely justifiable."[49]

3.2 Solving modus vivendi

Gutmann and Thompson's approach is in many ways more hands-on than a Rawlsian approach. When it comes to fixing our current modus vivendi arrangements, their proposals stay true to a more pragmatic approach. Two basic classes of proposals can be distinguished. The first class of proposals is concerned with fixing the background conditions – the basic structure – so that every faction has a real opportunity and capability to voice and discuss their concerns. The second is concerned with reforming the institutions of democracy in such a way that decisions in the government and important democratic institutions are taken in light of the moral questions at stake and not primarily on the basis of power. I will look at both in turn.

3.2.1 Fixing background conditions

Many deliberative democrats think that meaningful collective deliberation processes are possible only against the background of a more egalitarian society. Consequently, they not only call for more deliberation, but also for changes with regard to the institutional background of society. Harvard Professor Archon Fung, for instance, argues that societies need to become "dramatically more egalitarian"[50] before we can hope for meaningful deliberative processes. One of the big problems from the standpoint of deliberative democrats is that many groups in society have no effective power to address their problems and moral standpoints. The problem of exclusion is mainly addressed by demanding better education for the least well-off, as the education system must prepare citizens for an active role in politics. Therefore, many deliberative democrats think that educational reform is one of the most pressing issues.[51] Furthermore, political participation is itself not without cost. Getting informed and participating in the various deliberating processes requires both time and sufficient financial resources. For that reason, deliberative democrats emphasize that the government needs to supply the least well-off with enough means so that they have actual opportunity to participate and make their voices heard. Jack Knight and James Johnson defend an even stronger claim, arguing that "deliberation presupposes equality of resources"[52] for two reasons. First, a more equal distribution is necessary "to ensure that an individual's assent to arguments advanced by others is indeed uncoerced."[53] Here the coauthors seem to have in mind something like the leveling of bargaining power. Fung agrees when he writes that the playing field needs to be leveled, since a difference and inequality in resources "enable wealthier parties to improperly displace communicative power by mounting threats, purchasing compliance, drowning out other perspectives, mobilizing many forms of support, or simply privatizing some area of concern out of the domain of public deliberation."[54] Second, Knight and Johnson argue that a more equal distribution of resources is needed because "deliberation requires equal capacity to advance persuasive claims."[55]

The theorists of course differ in their assessment in how far the background inequalities prevent successful deliberation. Gutmann and Thompson are relatively silent on this question. As I noted earlier, though, their conception of deliberative democracy includes the principles of "basic opportunity" and "fair opportunity."[56] These two principles demand that citizens should have "adequate health care, education, security, work, and income."[57] In general, deliberative democrats are not very explicit about what changes in our basic structure would be necessary to make meaningful deliberation possible. Most theorists, though, seem to be in agreement with James Bohman when he concludes that institutions need to correct for the current disparities in resources and capabilities and that "these disparities are quite large today."[58]

3.2.2 Extending the sphere of deliberation

Deliberative democrats want to not only equalize the playing field, but also reform our current institutions in such a way that they will leave more room for actual deliberation and reason-giving. This requires that officials in their public statements "justify their actions in public" and give reasons that are "accessible to citizens."[59] According to the coauthors, the requirement for public justification would necessitate that politicians and experts find better ways "to explain their recommendations in public forums."[60] The requirement "would also rule out some secret or confidential processes of policy making that now take place."[61] While deliberative democrats emphasize that government officials and offices need to better communicate their decisions, deliberative democrats' actual attention is more concerned with institutional reform in the strict sense. Johnson writes that many political theorists "lament the absence or the demise of deliberation within U.S. political institutions."[62] Consequently, the aim of deliberative democrats is to refurnish existing institutions so that they are more open for actual discussion. Deliberative democrats have in mind forums in which citizens engage in actual discussions "rather than the kind of forums that are now more common, in which citizens merely express their views to government."[63] Deliberation, the coauthors press, should not be restricted to "ordinary legislation," but should also include "constitutional questions."[64] As a remedy, they propose that congressional hearings should not "merely be [. . .] a procession of interest-group representatives giving testimony," but should at least include "panels of citizens" who engage in actual debate.[65] While there is agreement among deliberative democrats that society needs more deliberation, there is disagreement about the scope of institutions that should adopt a more deliberative approach. Gutmann and Thompson think that implementing deliberative democracy calls for reform of both political and social institutions: "Many institutions in which citizens work and with which they interact – corporations, hospitals, the media – should provide opportunities for constructively engaging moral disagreement."[66]

In general, deliberative democrats belong to one of a small number of philosophical schools that put much thought into the question of implementation. In particular, deliberative democrats have begun to think about how the Athenian ideal of deliberation can be transferred to or reinterpreted under the conditions of modernity. Robert E. Goodin gives a good overview about the work done in this field.[67] Some deliberative democrats focus on the question of how "conventional institutions of government" can be reformed, while others place their hope on web-solutions and so-called mini-publics. Goodin explains: "[Mini-publics] are designed to be groups small enough to be genuinely deliberative and representative enough to be genuinely democratic – although they rarely meet standards of statistical representativeness."[68]

Such mini-publics can take various forms, such as deliberative polls, planning cells, consensus conferences and citizens' juries.[69] The goal of these devices is to encourage collective moral reasoning as opposed to self-interested collective bargaining processes. Deliberative democrats emphasize that the design of institutions must itself prevent incentives systems that put a "premium" on "interest group bargaining" at the "expense of moral persuasion."[70]

Although some deliberative democrats are optimistic when it comes to reinventing the Athenian model of public deliberations, others do not share their optimism. Goodin, for instance, concludes that "in any large and complex community, deliberation cannot realistically take place in the agora (or its electronic equivalent)."[71] Other deliberative democrats look for alternatives to plug the deliberation gap that will most likely persist in any modern society even under advantageous conditions. A common move here is to emphasize the importance of the public sphere and its connectedness to the political institutions. Habermas's *Between Facts and Norms* can be viewed as an exercise in thinking of how the informal and formal discursive channels of society can relieve individuals from cognitively unmanageable tasks such as participating in every political decision that concerns them. Habermas describes the way of how public concerns find their way through the media into the realms of politics as follows:

> Moving in from this outermost periphery, such issues force their way into newspapers and interested associations, clubs, professional organizations, academies and universities. They find forums, citizen initiatives, and other platforms before they catalyze the growth of social movements and new subcultures. The latter can in turn dramatize contributions, presenting them so effectively that the mass media take up the matter. Only through their controversial presentation in the media do such topics reach the larger public and subsequently gain a place on the "public agenda." Sometimes the support of sensational actions, mass protests and the incessant campaigning is required before an issue can make its way via the surprising election of marginal candidates or radical parties, expanded platforms of "established" parties, important court decisions and so on, into the core of the political system and there receive formal consideration.[72]

Although deliberative democrats are constantly criticized for having too lofty ideals, they are working hard to find ways of implementing and testing their various methods of pushing the democratic decision process in the general direction of ES_{DD}.

3.3 RoCD Test

Let me start out here with a few general comments. In the introduction to *Democracy and Disagreement*, Gutmann and Thompson state that in modern democracies citizens and their representatives already engage in deliberation. Deliberative democracy, according to the coauthors, then "simply asks that they do so more consistently and comprehensively."[73] This initial statement of deliberative democracy seems relatively uncontroversial. It says: *Let us engage in a bit more deliberation. In that process we might indeed correct a few errors and become a little more sympathetic to other views.* At the same time, as we learned, the deliberative process is pretty liberal with regards to the moral reasons that are allowed to enter into the public debate. This creates a vast eligible set of possibly justified laws. To understand why the comprehensibility criterion lets the set of justified legislation explode, it is fruitful to ask which laws could not pass under this criterion. Since deliberative democracy is usually thought to tend towards egalitarianism – so much so that John Tomasi recently asked whether deliberative democracy "can only make left turns"[74] – we might expect that Gutmann and Thompson's account would block libertarian proposals. But libertarians for sure can give intelligible moral reasons for their favorite laws. So if libertarians happen to be in the majority in a society, a thorough libertarian constitution would be within Gutmann and Thompson's eligible set. We can easily see that, for the very same reasons, a more egalitarian society would also be in the eligible set. All that is needed is that egalitarians find a suitable interpretation of those six provisional principles of deliberative democracy that hold for any political competitor (see Section 3.1).

At first glance, then, deliberative democracy seems relatively uncontroversial, as it is not unfairly blocking any important first-order theory. In addition, a little bit more deliberation here and there would not hurt anybody, and it might sometimes improve the results of our current modus vivendi arrangements. At the same time, in this reading, deliberative democracy also looks stale and uninspiring – to such an extent that we might reasonably ask whether there is any actual difference between deliberative democracy and what we already have.

Deliberative democracy, though, also lends itself to another reading. Fung recently began one of his articles with the words: "Deliberative democracy is a revolutionary political ideal."[75] Fung argues that deliberative democracy is a radical ideal because it "calls for fundamental changes in the bases of political decision making, scope of those included in decision-making processes, institutions that house these processes, and thus the very character of politics itself."[76] Let me then attempt to present a second reading of deliberative democracy. In this reading, I will take more seriously some of the proposals that I discussed in Section 3.2. As a consequence, deliberative democracy will emerge as a more radical approach.

According to this reading, deliberative democracy comes with a reformation of the education system and necessitates a huge amount of redistribution of wealth. Furthermore, not only our political, but also most of our *social institutions* will be transformed in a deliberative fashion. The social institutions that Gutmann and Thompson have in mind are corporations, hospitals, the media and certainly also universities.

The result of this approach – prima facie – will be a much more politicized society. Since every principle (except the foundational principle of reciprocity) is seen as provisional, every building block of society is up for debate. Although this opens up the possibility for making society more just – since injustices at every level of our society can be more readily addressed – such politicization also comes at a cost. To get a better grasp of the results of such increased politicization, consider this example: Imagine that in your particular social environment, twenty groups attempt simultaneously to renegotiate the structure of your university, the menu plan of your favorite restaurant, the terms and conditions of the sauna in your gym, and the working conditions of your workplace.

Let us now turn to the RoCD Test. I have presented a strong and a weak reading of deliberative democracy. Since the strong reading is far more interesting, for reasons outlined earlier, I will apply the test to the strong reading.

Utilitarians:	There will be no agreement between utilitarians whether a move towards deliberative democracy will, overall (or on average), maximize utility. Whether a utilitarian will expect an increase or decrease in utility from a move towards deliberative democracy, depends on her or his socio-economic beliefs.

Classical liberals:	Classical liberals will oppose a move towards deliberative democracy on many grounds. First of all, classical liberals view rights as an important mechanism to partition the moral decision space and thus as an important way of ameliorating disagreement.[77] A move towards more deliberation seems to be a move that weakens rights and thus will result in more conflict. Second, classical liberals will oppose a move towards deliberative democracy on epistemic grounds. Substituting a multitude of diverse decision centers with a deliberative decision might lead to worse outcomes from an epistemic point of view.[78]
Realists:	Realists are in general skeptical of the malleability of human behavior. For that matter, realists should be expected to be very skeptical with regard to any sweeping reform of the education system that promises to raise the average citizen's capability to reason by a huge margin. Walter Lippmann laconically comments that "every optimistic book on democracy written for one hundred and fifty years" will eventually turn to education and educational reform.[79] Realists hold that we should not expect that large numbers of the public will ever reason at a sufficiently high level and, therefore, fear that increased politicization might destabilize society.
Egalitarians:	The deliberative ideal is certainly most attractive to egalitarians. The result of deliberative democracy on a social level seems to be very close (at least in the strong reading) to the egalitarian's first-best option. We could thus imagine that a move towards a deliberative democracy is both a Pareto improvement from the perspective of egalitarians as well as a fully justified solution to the problem of modus vivendi.
Natural rights libertarians:	Defenders of libertarian natural rights will surely oppose a move from the current status quo to a deliberative democracy. Natural rights libertarians usually share the socio-economic background theory of classical liberals and thus oppose deliberative democracy from not only an ethical, but also an economic and epistemic point of view.

In conclusion, I can state that deliberative democracy as a second-order theory cannot convince the RoCD. Deliberative democracy, from the standpoint of the RoCD, is neither a Pareto improvement over our current modus vivendi, nor does it represent an inter-subjectively justified alternative to our current arrangements.

Notes

1 Gutmann and Thompson (2000, p. 176).
2 Gutmann and Thompson (2000, p. 176).
3 Gutmann and Thompson (1996).
4 Habermas (1990).
5 Rousseau (2008, p. 127).
6 Gutmann and Thompson (1995, p. 88).
7 Gutmann and Thompson (1995, p. 88).
8 Gutmann and Thompson (2000, p. 163).
9 Gutmann and Thompson (1995, p. 90).
10 Gutmann and Thompson (1995, pp. 90–91).
11 With a nod to Isaiah Berlin, they note, though, that "the sources of moral disagreement lie partly within morality itself." Nevertheless, they try to avoid taking a substantive stance in this debate (Gutmann and Thompson 1995, p. 91).
12 Gutmann and Thompson (1995, p. 91).
13 Gutmann and Thompson (2000, p. 161).
14 Gutmann and Thompson (1995, p. 92).
15 Cohen (1998, p. 186). Italics deleted.
16 Gutmann and Thompson (2000, p. 166).
17 Horton (2010), Gray (2000).
18 Gutmann and Thompson (2000, p. 165).
19 Gutmann and Thompson (2000, p. 165).
20 Gutmann and Thompson (2000, p. 166).
21 Gutmann and Thompson (1995, p. 99).
22 Gutmann and Thompson (1995, p. 100).
23 Rawls (2005a, p. 60).
24 Gutmann and Thompson (1995, p. 100).
25 Gutmann and Thompson (2000, p. 161).
26 Gutmann and Thompson (2000, p. 161).
27 Gutmann and Thompson (2000, p. 167).
28 Gutmann and Thompson (2000, p. 167).
29 Gutmann and Thompson (2000, p. 175).
30 Gutmann and Thompson (2000, p. 167).
31 Gutmann and Thompson (2004, p. 7).
32 Gutmann and Thompson (2004, p. 144).
33 Gutmann and Thompson (2004, p. 145).
34 Rawls (2005b, part 4 in particular).
35 Gaus (2011c).
36 For an accessible overview about this debate, see Gaus (2011a) and Vallier and D'Agostino (2014).
37 Gutmann and Thompson (2004, p. 147).
38 Gutmann and Thompson (2004, p. 151).
39 Gutmann and Thompson (2004, p. 156).
40 Gutmann and Thompson (2004, p. 151).
41 Gutmann and Thompson (2004, p. 156).
42 Gutmann and Thompson (2004, p. 156).
43 Gaus (2010, p. 249).
44 As I mentioned earlier, deliberative democracy contains some provisional moral principles: for instance, the "principle of basic opportunity." This principle "calls for giving individuals the capacity to make choices among good lives by providing them with the basic opportunities that give them such a capacity." This means that, in the view of deliberative democracy, the state has a pro tanto obligation to guarantee health care, security, education, work, and income (Gutmann and Thompson 2000, p. 170).
45 Gutmann and Thompson (2000, p. 169).

46 Gutmann and Thompson (1995, p. 107).
47 Gutmann and Thompson (1995, p. 107).
48 Gutmann and Thompson (1995, p. 108).
49 Gutmann and Thompson (1995, p. 108).
50 Fung (2005, pp. 397–398).
51 Gutmann and Thompson (2004, p. 61).
52 Knight and Johnson (1997, p. 281).
53 Knight and Johnson (1997, p. 281).
54 Fung (2005, p. 397).
55 Knight and Johnson (1997, p. 281).
56 Gutmann and Thompson (2000, p. 170).
57 Gutmann and Thompson (2000, p. 170).
58 Bohman (1997, p. 346).
59 Gutmann and Thompson (1995, p. 110)
60 Gutmann and Thompson (1995, p. 110).
61 Gutmann and Thompson (1995, p. 110).
62 Johnson (1998, p. 161).
63 Gutmann and Thompson (1995, p. 110).
64 Gutmann and Thompson (2004, p. 60).
65 Gutmann and Thompson (1995, p. 110).
66 Gutmann and Thompson (1995, p. 110).
67 Goodin (2008).
68 Goodin (2008, p. 11).
69 For an overview compare Grönlund *et al.* (2013) and Fung (2011). For a critical assessment, see Lafont (2015).
70 Gutmann and Thompson (2004, p. 150).
71 Goodin (2008, p. 256).
72 Habermas (1996, p. 381).
73 Gutmann and Thompson (1996).
74 Tomasi (2012b, p. xxvii).
75 Fung (2005, p. 397).
76 Fung (2005, p. 397).
77 Gaus (2007), Constant (1988).
78 Pennington (2010). I will discuss this point in much detail throughout Chapters 7–8.
79 Lippmann (1982, p. 147).

4 Buchanan

The neoliberal state

Since the most well-known second-order theories failed to show a way out of modus vivendi, to make progress we might wish to look for other possibilities. One of the central alternatives to the political philosophies we discussed is constitutional economics. There are two overlapping notions of constitutional economics. Narrowly defined, constitutional economics refers to a research program pioneered by Buchanan and Gordon Tullock that extends economic scrutiny to the field of institutional analysis.[1] Buchanan, however, not only contributed to economics, but also created his own politico-philosophical approach around his research program. In this essay, 'constitutional economics' shall therefore accordingly refer to his encompassing philosophical approach.

Buchanan's political philosophy is influenced by two philosophical traditions. On the one hand, his thought is deeply influenced by contractarian thinkers like Hobbes and Baruch Spinoza.[2] On the other hand, as a political economist and classical liberal, Buchanan is deeply influenced by Adam Smith, Ludwig von Mises, Frank Knight and Hayek.[3] Despite their differences, both traditions – contractarianism and classical liberalism – have a common denominator: They attempt to accomplish social progress without relying (too much) on moral reasons and moral motivation. In both traditions, talk about moral reasons is usually substituted with talk about benefits and incentives.[4] This, of course, makes traditional political philosophers highly skeptical of constitutional economics – but the suspicion is mutual. Buchanan writes:

> Political economists and social philosophers] have felt themselves obligated to propose changes that are derived from external ethical criteria, changes that are presumably to be imposed on the existing structure. This sort of discussion has tended to distract effort and attention from the less romantic but more productive approach involved in working out possible compromise modifications that would be agreeable to large numbers of persons in the community.[5]

In presenting Buchanan's political philosophy, we can emphasize the contractarian or the classical liberal elements. Both parts are, of course, in many ways interwoven; nevertheless, all writing that sets out to outline Buchanan's work has to choose which aspects to emphasize. In this essay, I will emphasize the classical liberal element in Buchanan's thought. I will thus treat 'constitutional economics' as an extension and refinement of classical liberal thought.[6]

For reasons of symmetry, I will discuss Buchanan's constitutional economics in three parts. In Section 4.1, I will outline how constitutional economics understands and frames the problems of our current modus vivendi arrangements. For that matter, I will inquire which normative standards are at work when Buchanan criticizes the ongoing democratic processes. In Section 4.2, I will talk about some solutions that constitutional economics has to offer. In Section 4.3, I will again apply the RoCD Test.

4.1 Interpreting modus vivendi

In comparison to the other second-order approaches that I have reviewed in this essay, constitutional economics has less demanding normative goals. Essentially, constitutional economics just aims at creating a *better modus vivendi arrangement*. Nonetheless, Buchanan voices his dissatisfaction with the current political arrangements more forcefully than do his philosophical peers:

> Descriptively, we live in what might be called 'constitutional anarchy,' where the range and extent of federal government influence over individual behavior depend largely on the accidental preferences of politicians in judicial, legislative, and executive positions of power. Increasingly, men feel themselves at the mercy of a faceless, irresponsible bureaucracy, subject to unpredictable twists and turns that destroy and distort personal expectations with little opportunity for redress or retribution.[7]

The intellectual descendant of Smith argues, in a nutshell, that society can be constitutionally set up to produce a diverse set of modus vivendi arrangements and that some setups are generally more choice-worthy than others, which seems to be a relatively uncontroversial claim. Surely, almost every reasonable person would agree that the current institutional setup of Germany or Sweden is much superior to the communist setup of North Korea. The more controversial claim that Buchanan and many of his intellectual ancestors defend is that not only are some political arrangements better than others, but also that one relatively specific modus vivendi arrangement is, judged from a diverse set of individual perspectives, superior to its rivals. This modus vivendi arrangement is the 'small state.' The goal of the next two sections will then be to explain why constitutional economists think that a 'small state' – a state in which the hands of the legislature are tied constitutionally, while almost all social problems are solved through the market mechanism – is the best political arrangement we can hope for.[8]

4.1.1 Normative standards

Buchanan views the political process as a complex exchange process between individuals.[9] In politics, Buchanan writes, individuals "seek to secure collectively their own privately defined objectives that cannot be efficiently secured through simple market exchanges."[10] The aggregate result of these ongoing bargaining processes is in Buchanan's framework mainly a function of the rules of the game. Whether the constant stream of modus vivendi bargains (to use my terminology) is on average to advantage of everyone or not is a result of the constitutional setup of politics. As becomes obvious from the earlier quote, Buchanan seems to have no faith in our current institutional setup. Buchanan writes that, in "many areas of modern politics," our political arrangements – on average – produce "zero-sum and negative-sum" results.[11] Buchanan thinks that we can do better. As I pointed out, Buchanan claims that a *constitutionally restrained democracy* would be better from *the viewpoint of everybody* than the kind of democratic modus vivendi we enjoy in Western societies. From a philosophical point of view, this raises three questions. The first question is this: If a restrained democracy, or a small state, is truly better from the viewpoint of everybody, why do modern democracies feature extensive regulation and a comprehensive welfare state? Second, what is meant by the 'viewpoint of everybody'? The third question regards the notion of a 'constitutionally restrained democracy.' Since we already live in a constitutionally restrained democracy, we might ask what it is that distinguishes Buchanan's ideal political arrangement from our current modus vivendi arrangements. I will tackle the first question immediately, then come back to the second question in Section 4.1 and the third in Section 4.2.

Let me begin with the first two questions. It should be immediately clear that the phrase 'from the viewpoint of everybody' cannot be meant literally. If an overwhelming majority, under a democratic modus vivendi arrangement, wants something, they will usually get it. Now, as Buchanan and other classical liberals realize, there is actually almost no demand in modern democracies to return to a 'small state.' In most modern democracies, classical liberal or libertarian parties are rather small. So, classical liberal thinkers surely mean something else. A quotation by Hayek will shed light on our problem:

> The principles that plead for the self-limitation of the power of the majority are not proved wrong if democracy disregards them, nor is democracy proved undesirable if it often makes what the liberal must regard as the wrong decision. He simply believes that he has an argument which, when properly understood, will induce the majority to limit the exercise of its own powers and which he hopes it can be persuaded to accept as a guide when deciding on particular issues.[12]

The key term here is "properly understood." Hayek seems to say the following: If people would just consider the arguments, we would essentially all agree to restrict the democratic process more stringently than we already do. The economist's argument then relies on abstracting from the alleged economic ignorance of the electorate. The economist's abstraction strategy can be compared with the abstraction strategy philosophers employ. We have already seen that philosophers in the contract tradition abstract from certain common human properties – such as moral biases or knowledge deficiencies – to reach their respective conclusions. Remember Rawls's veil of ignorance, behind which people are essentially endowed with an encyclopedic memory like Wikipedia that includes all the relevant knowledge about economics, social science, psychology and so on. What is important here is that philosophers usually normalize both the moral outlook *and* the epistemic capabilities of their (idealized) assemblies. The constitutional economist, in contrast, uses Occam's razor and proposes that we could make huge progress (in the sense of a Pareto improvement) if we could just get the economic and the social facts right. In a sense, Buchanan thus urges us to pick the low hanging fruit first, since it is surely easier to get agreement on non-moral facts than on moral facts – assuming for a moment that moral facts exist in the first place.

The argument of constitutional economics can be formalized in the following way. First of all let me define the idealized members of society (M_i) that the constitutional economist works with. M_i has two important properties: First, M_i is endowed with full economic knowledge. Second, M_i is sane. This shall mean that he or she is not sadistic and interested in human suffering. Further, let D_{MV} stand for our current democratic modus vivendi arrangements understood as a set of substantive laws and privileges, CL for constitutional liberalism (a constitutionally restrained democratic small state) and I_i for the social ideal of the respective idealized member, his or her first-best. Now, the hypothesis of Buchanan – and of the adherents of classical liberalism more generally – is that the following preference order obtains for every M_i: $I_i > CL > D_{MV}$.[13] Every M_i favors his or her personal ideal over CL, but favors CL over D_{MV}. The interesting move is this: If we imagine a collective choice between constitutional arrangements, I_i is not in the choice set, since it is a first-best option. The reason for this is basically that in a diverse society, there are too many I_is, so that none of the instantiations of I_i is backed up by a sufficiently large group of people. Institutional choice in a diverse society, from the viewpoint of the constitutional economist, is almost necessarily a choice between different second-best alternatives, that is, between different modus vivendi arrangements.

The question then becomes why everybody should prefer CL over D_{MV}. The idea here is that M_i can choose between a market-based modus vivendi in which nobody has a privilege (CL) and a market-based modus vivendi in which everybody uses the political process to grab some special privilege (D_{MV}). It is important to note that privilege needs be understood here in a rather broad sense. Thus, using the political process to secure special protection for animals, subsidizing the arts or lobbying for a mandatory health insurance are all cases that fall under the rubric of 'politics as taking.'[14] Constitutional economists believe that they can show, mainly by relying on economic arguments, that CL has a comparative advantage over D_{MV} in a wide range of areas that are important to every reasonable citizen. Buchanan, as a classical liberal thinker, takes for granted that a small state would be better than D_{MV} in raising overall living standards, reducing poverty, providing health care, protecting nature and keeping peace, raising educational levels and so on.[15] Theorists in the classical liberal tradition believe that, by means of comparative institutional analysis, they can make a good case that a small state outperforms our current modus vivendi arrangements with regard to all reasonable standards of good living.[16]

One of the obvious objections to this whole approach is that there might be people for whom I_i and D_{MV} are equivalent. A constitutional economist might respond to this challenge by replying that D_{MV} describes actual democracies with all their problems of exclusion, lobbyism, corruption and public debt. Such a state of affairs is surely not ideal from anyone's perspective.

4.1.2 Explaining ignorance

Let us now turn to the second question: If a small state is so much better than our current modus vivendi arrangements, why have people not picked up on that idea? This problem has been plaguing liberal thinkers for at least three generations. In this section, I want to review some of the responses to this question by liberal thinkers such as Buchanan. In reviewing their responses we will get a deeper understanding of how constitutional economics interprets the current modus vivendi.

From the viewpoint of the political economist, the essential reason why we are stuck in the (inferior) current modus vivendi arrangements is that people do not have sufficient incentives to form reasonable[17] judgments when it comes to politics. In this section I will give an account of why economists think that most voters do not form reasonable judgments about most political matters. Political economists in the classical liberal tradition are committed to methodological individualism. This means, among other things, that social macro phenomena – like the outcomes of our political process – need to be explained as the outcome of individual actions. The choices that an individual makes are – in the world of the economist – a function of the individual's initial preferences and the set of incentives and disincentives which the individual faces in a certain situation. When it comes to choice, the first question a political economist might ask is, 'about what kind of good?' Institutional economists usually distinguish between four kinds of goods: private goods, toll goods, public goods and common-pool resources (Table 4.1).

Table 4.1 Four Basic Types of Goods[18]

		Subtractability of use	
		Low	*High*
Difficulty of excluding potential beneficiaries	*Low*	Toll goods	Private goods
	High	Public goods	Common-pool resources

Both the constitution as well as legislated law are, from the economist's point of view, public goods.[19] Public goods have two important properties: (a) low subtractability of use and (b) high difficulty of excluding potential beneficiaries. 'Low subtractability' means that the usage of a good does not diminish its capacity to satisfy others. For example, Anna's enjoyment of the sun does not subtract sunlight from Betty. Contrast that with a piece of bread. If Anna eats the whole piece, there is nothing left for Betty. 'High difficulty' of excluding potential beneficiaries means that it is very difficult to exclude anybody from the benefit of a good – radio waves, for instance. The same is true for the law with respect to the citizens of a state. The law applies to everyone in the state in an identical fashion. As is by now widely known, the production of public goods poses problems of collective action. The collective problem of producing public goods can be best illustrated by a large-scale prisoner's dilemma. In a large-scale prisoner's dilemma of law production, it is rational for every single individual to stay ignorant with regard to politics regardless of the actions of everybody else. Since nobody, from a self-interested point of view, has sufficient reasons to educate himself or herself about current policies, the economist expects that voters will usually not be well informed, or even ignorant, when casting their ballot.

There are three main reasons why Benni might be motivated to cast an informed vote, even in the face of the outlined incentive structure of the prisoner's dilemma: (a) Benni has countervailing external incentives to cast an informed vote, (b) Benni is intrinsically interested in politics and (c) Benni acts for his own moral reasons.[20] Let us quickly review the three options. We could think of many countervailing incentives that lead Benni to cast an informed vote; here I will talk about two options. The state could oblige voters to inform themselves about current political affairs and fine voters who will not inform themselves. Alternatively, the state could preclude anyone who is not properly informed from voting.[21] Evidently, though, in current democracies, voters are neither required by law to inform themselves, nor is there any form of formal punishment for remaining ignorant about political matters. Informal social sanctioning mechanisms might also provide countervailing incentives. Elinor Ostrom, for instance, shows that small communities are able to efficiently provide collective goods because they are able to establish and enforce informal social rules against free riding. This means that members of a social group who do not chip in for the provision of a collective good are punished by their community. Unfortunately, securing common goods by relying on informal social rules and social enforcement has its clear limitations for reasons of transaction costs. Informal sanctioning mechanisms usually work only in face-to-face communities.[22] In current democracies, which are marked by anonymity, it is hard enough to get 70 percent of the electorate to cast their vote on the day of election. Public shaming for casting an uninformed ballot does not seem to be a viable option for getting an informed electorate. We are thus left with the alternatives. Let us then turn to (b). A second reason that might lead Benni to become educated about political matters is simply genuine interest. In this case, Benni would generally cast informed ballots as a side effect of his interest in politics. Now, whether the public in general is deeply interested in political matters is simply an empirical question. It is common knowledge, though, that in every generation only a, very miniscule part of society is deeply interested in politics. This leaves us with an interesting result at the very outset. The only reason why the average person might inform himself or herself about political matters is a moral one. Benni might think that he – qua being a citizen – has an obligation to educate himself. He might also think that democratic elections are in and by themselves something valuable that he needs to respect by informing himself.

A constitutional economist could stop his or her explanatory endeavor at this point and simply summarize that voters are generally ignorant when it comes to politics, because they have only moral reasons for getting properly informed (given that they are not inherently interested in politics), and moral reasons are empirically not known to be heavy lifters (i.e. they usually constitute a rather weak motivational force). Many public choice economists indeed stop at this point. Constitutional economists, on the contrary, do not rely on the model of purely self-interested agents in their explanatory activity and thus attempt to make a stronger argument.

Political economists in the classical liberal tradition view knowledge as a scarce good – scarce in the sense that it is costly both in terms of money and time to acquire and process new knowledge. Individuals always face trade-offs in deciding how they want to invest their scarce resources. This is not only true when it comes to consumption activities, but also when it comes to moral questions. Let us illuminate this point with an example. During election, Anna is confronted with the question of how she should spend the next two hours. She has two options: She could read up on the health care reform or she could write a letter to her sick mother. Spending an extra two hours reading about health care reforms will not in any way change the probability of the outcome of the election. However, if Anna writes a letter to her sick mother she might really make her mother better off. Anna thus faces a trade-off between two moral values: her obligations as a citizen and her obligations as a child. This example highlights that having a moral reason and having a conclusive moral reason are not the same thing. Even if a person recognizes that she or he has a moral reason to get informed about current political affairs, she or he might reasonably judge that the overall balance of moral (and non-moral) reasons obliges her or him to abstain from getting informed about politics.

Furthermore, economists emphasize how costly it is to arrive at reasonable judgments in politics: The moral and non-moral opportunity costs of getting informed might be too high even for those who are generally inclined to act on their moral reasons. Let me briefly point out why economists think that getting an informed view about political matters is costly. They emphasize that anticipating the outcomes of new laws and legislation is oftentimes really difficult even for experts, as changes in rules have counterintuitive outcomes and are inherently hard to grasp. Although economists often talk as if preferences are just given, they realize that evaluating outcomes is not without cost. First, we need to get a relatively firm grip on the essential features of a state of affairs, then assign values to these different features and in the end come up with an all-considered judgment. We all know how difficult, time- and energy-consuming our everyday consumption decisions sometimes are. Buying a new mobile phone or deciding on a new internet provider sometimes takes weeks. But such decisions are in many respects cognitively much easier than arriving at a well-informed decision about a piece of legislation. A related issue that increases the costs of getting informed is that controlling politicians in democracies is in itself cognitively very taxing. Ideally, we would need to have a complete overview about the decisions a politician made and compare them with counterfactuals to see in how far a certain politician was really representing our own preference or ethical stance.

In summary, a constitutional economist can argue that casting an informed ballot is very expensive in terms of time and thus has huge non-moral and moral opportunity costs. Cumulatively, this makes it even more unlikely that people who are not inherently interested in politics will be sufficiently motivated by their moral reasons to cast an informed ballot. This in turn increases the likelihood that citizens might actually be badly informed when it comes to *particular policies* and *alternative political arrangements*. While traditional political economists like Hayek, Mises, Joseph Schumpeter and Buchanan relied only on their personal experience with voters to confirm their economically educated judgments about the general information level of voters, political scientists and experimental economists have gathered an immense data set that essentially confirms the predictions of constitutional economists. In the next section, I want to give a very short review of some of the most relevant results.

Ignorance and biased judgment

By now there is a rather extensive literature on the question of how good – or rather how bad – the knowledge of the average citizen is with regard to basic economic questions. A sustained overview about this literature and a discussion about the methodological advantages and disadvantages of certain studies would surely lead us too far astray at this moment. I will thus be content with summarizing the results of Bryan Caplan's extensive meta-study. Based on empirical results Caplan distinguishes four types of economic biases.[23]

1 The 'antimarket bias' denotes the tendency of citizens to underestimate the economic advantages of the market order. The main reason for that is that the working of the price mechanism is in general poorly understood by citizens.
2 The 'antiforeign bias' denotes the tendency of citizens to underestimate the economic advantages of global trade, migration and outsourcing. According to Caplan, this bias is rooted in the general lack of knowledge with regard to the theory of comparative advantage. The theory of comparative advantage says that trade between two parties is mutually advantageous even if one of the countries is more efficient in producing all of the goods (thus has an absolute advantage).

3 The 'make-work bias' denotes the tendency of citizens to underestimate the social advantages of economizing on labor. A common example of this might be people's fear that machines will eventually substitute all simple human labor, leaving whole strata of society unemployed. The citizens in Caplan's argument overlook the fact that machines are a necessary condition of economic progress.[24]

4 The 'pessimistic bias' denotes the tendency of citizens to underestimate the economic progress in the past and the present. This in general leads citizens to overestimate the impact of current events and crises.[25]

All these biases may lead a citizen to construe political decisions incorrectly. Incorrect construal of options in turn will lead to incorrect evaluations of options. This is of course very relevant for all kinds of political decisions. If Anna subscribes to the argument that politicians should help the worst-off, and that the minimum wage raises the income of the worst-off, she has reason to conclude that politicians should introduce minimum wage laws. Consequently, we will expect that Anna will vote for the party or the candidate that promises to introduce a minimum wage law. The problem is, of course, that if the second premise is empirically wrong and the minimum wage in reality hurts the poor, then Anna would from her own perspective be wrong in voting for a politician who promises to introduce a minimum wage law. Unfortunately, we need to understand the basic workings of the price mechanism to decide under which circumstances a minimum wage law could hurt or benefit the worst-off – but as Caplan tells us on the basics of his statistical analysis, citizens in general have a very dim understanding of the price mechanism.

Let me close this section by reviewing a common counterargument against the view that citizens in general are badly informed about which policies in particular and modus vivendi arrangements in general would best suit them. It is often discussed whether or not the media could in some ways plug the epistemic hole that I have described. After all, isn't it the job of the media to critically discuss political propositions, summarize political track records and keep checks on lobbyists? Furthermore, we might question whether it is at all necessary that citizens are well informed about political issues. More to the point, we could argue that it is the job of pundits to explain the consequences of different political proposals, so that voters just need to evaluate the outcomes according to their liking. There are, we could argue, many social – both formal and informal – institutions that ease the epistemic problem for the voter to a point where picking the policies that we prefer is as easy as choosing the right ice cream variety in the summer.

The constitutional economist might answer that, while certain media formats certainly ease the epistemic burden, the individual still needs to choose between watching such formats and all the other TV programs that compete for his or her attention. The real problem, of course, is that different TV pundits will make different forecasts and recommend different policies. This in turn opens up the question of how trustworthy pundits and their predictions are.

After all, pundits are not paid in accordance with their track record of true predictions, but often in relation to their entertainment value broadly defined. The political psychologist Philip E. Tetlock paints a bleak picture of "experts in demand."[26] According to Tetlock, those pundits that are especially liked by wide audiences are also the ones that are particularly unreliable.

> [Citizens] rely on low-effort heuristics that prize attributes of alleged specialists, such as institutional affiliation, fame, and even physical attractiveness, that are weak predictors of epistemic quality. Indeed our data – as well as other work – suggests that consumers [. . .] often rely on low-effort heuristics that are negative predictors of epistemic quality.[27]

Overall, Tetlock has very little trust in citizens when it comes to distinguishing good from bad pundits. This result is congruent with the constitutional economist's prediction that the general lack of motivation to get informed about politics will also lead to a rather weak motivation to check the track record of any particular pundit.

Summary

In this section we have seen that, from the perspective of constitutional economics, the main problem of our current modus vivendi arrangements is the problem of ignorance. People have little incentive to get properly informed about current political issues, to keep a track record of elected politicians or think about the incentives of the political game itself. The argument of political economists in the classical liberal tradition is that *if we could come to grips with the problem of ignorance, we could drastically improve the living conditions of everyone*. Constitutional economics, then, presents a very different analysis of the modus vivendi problem. The allure of this approach can be summarized like this: Traditional philosophical first- and second-order approaches usually single out egoism, moral failure and unjustified moral disagreement as the main causes of modus vivendi. Consequently, the only solution to social betterment in their books is *moral change*. Rawls's solution to the problem of modus vivendi, as outlined in Chapter 2, requires that the absolute majority of society accept the two principles of justice and act in accordance with the sense of justice. Constitutional economists, on the contrary, present a solution to the problem of modus vivendi that does not rely on moral change, but simply on curbing ignorance.

In the next section, I will show that constitutional economists not only came up with an alternative interpretation of modus vivendi but also devised a new set of strategies to ameliorate the dangers of modus vivendi.

4.2 Solving modus vivendi

Constitutional economics offers many quite heterogeneous proposals for improving our current modus vivendi arrangements. As we would expect, many of these proposals concern small changes in the tax code, and reforming the health care or education system. In this essay, I am mainly interested in more sweeping reforms, that is, systematic alternatives to our current modus vivendi arrangements. For that reason I will especially focus on one proposal. As we have seen, constitutional economists believe that we could all improve our living conditions if we moved from D_{MV} to CL. Unfortunately, there is very little reason for each of us individually to think deeply about the political issues at hand, and even less reason to think about deeper political questions, such as the political system as a whole. For that matter, most people are not aware that a move to CL would actually be a Pareto improvement. Therefore, constitutional economists do not view the actual voting behavior of the electorate as a particularly good indicator of what people really want.[28] Hayek affirms: "Majority decisions tell us what people want at the moment, but not what it would be in their interest to want if they were better informed."[29] Not only has the individual very little reason to care for politics, but also politics is epistemically very demanding. Jeffrey Friedman summarizes our discussion about the epistemic and moral demands of democracy like this:

> [In politics] we need to be good metaphysicians to recognize that we are employing hypotheses about cause and effect that require testing, but that cannot be tested post hoc ergo propter hoc. We need to be good logicians to test those hypotheses counterfactually, in the laboratories of our minds. We need to be good epistemologists to recognize the cultural and genetic biases that may taint our reasoning, and to avoid cynically attributing other theorists' biases to evil motives or simple self-interest. We need to be able to recognize our instinctive resistance to the likes of Hayek as possibly originating in misleading intuitions and cultural indoctrination, and then have the patience to work through the theories of such "reactionaries" with open minds. In short, we need to be the paragons of self-critical rationality embodied in the normative interpretation of Popperian fallibilism.[30]

Constitutional economists argue that although piecemeal engineering through democratic decisions might be possible in principle, in reality piecemeal engineering is cognitively too taxing for the electorate. Thus, if a modern democracy engages in piecemeal engineering despite widespread public ignorance, that society will in the long term destroy more value than it gains through legislative tinkering. While Hayek emphasizes that nobody in society has the knowledge to coordinate production more efficiently than the market, the previous argument is weaker. It emphasizes that some people (most likely in academia) might have good solutions for social problems, but it is very unlikely that voters, due to their ignorance, will divert to those experts (or groups of experts) that provide the golden bullet. A prominent contemporary exponent of this view is Michael Huemer, who writes:

> Voters, activists, and political leaders of the present day are in the position of medieval doctors. They hold simple, prescientific theories about the workings of society and the causes of social problems, from which they

> derive a variety of remedies – almost all of which prove either ineffectual or harmful. [. . .] Unsatisfying as it may seem, the wisest course for political agents is often simply to stop trying to solve society's problems.[31]

But a lack of knowledge on the side of voters, activists and politicians does not only lead to bad policies, but also creates more openings for special interest groups to further their private interests at the expense of everybody else – or the common good. The economic logic behind this is quite simple: Any increase in political complexity (more agencies, more laws, more tax regulations) makes it more difficult for a citizen to fulfill his or her obligations in controlling politicians and casting an informed ballot. If the time a citizen spends on political education is fixed, and he or she spends equal time on every subject, then every additional topic on the political agenda decreases the average time he or she can spend on a single item. It is again worth pointing out that constitutional economists do not believe that all politicians or even the majority of them are pure egoists. It is only that those (few) self-serving political actors will have an easier time to get away with policies that solely benefit certain interest groups. Furthermore, when it becomes obvious that democracy has increasingly become a vehicle for furthering private interests at the public's expense, more and more people might gradually abandon their previous moral restraints and succumb to rent-seeking behavior. Buchanan writes in a passage that resembles certain parts in Rousseau's *Social Contract*:

> As laws and regulations have multiplied, competing group interests have been promoted. [. . .]. Observing this, citizens have become more disillusioned with governmental processes and are more and more attracted to assume roles as moral anarchists.[32]

The general idea of classical liberals is, then, that the current modus vivendi arrangements produce (with some necessity) modus vivendi bargains with cumulative effects that in the long run undermine democracy itself.

> It is not the least part of this liberal argument that to disregard those limits will, in the long run, destroy not only prosperity and peace but democracy itself. The liberal believes that the limits which he wants democracy to impose upon itself are also the limits within it can work effectively and within which the majority can truly direct and control the actions of government.[33]

The question for constitutional economics is thus how we can prevent democracy from destroying itself. Traditionally, constitutional economists have always emphasized the necessity of a more thorough economic education of the electorate. The biases that Caplan listed, for instance, could be significantly reduced with a better understanding of economics. At the same time, constitutional economists attempt to promote a multilateral 'political disarmament.' As Mises writes:

> A free man, must be able to endure it when his fellow men act and live otherwise than he considers proper. He must free himself from the habit, just as soon as something does not please him, of calling for the police.[34]

I take Mises's metaphor to mean that democratic societies must learn to resolve their differences in a nonpolitical manner and in the end be more tolerant of diversity. Mises basically suggests a principle of live-and-let-live, like this: I will not push for a prohibition of drugs, if you do not push for a prohibition of crucifixes in schools. I will not lobby for subsidizing the arts, if you do not lobby for subsidizing the metal industry. The equilibrium that liberals like Mises aim at is an equilibrium that is based on reciprocity. *I don't go for privileges as long as you don't go for privileges*. It should be noted that this principle of reciprocity is based on purely prudential reasons, not on foundational values like mutual respect or negative rights. The point here is simply that it would be better for everyone, if everyone would abstain from 'politics as taking.'

This equilibrium, at the very outset, seems very fragile. Each new election offers every voter in society a new chance to get her or his set of privileges right now, while any kind of retribution for defecting from the no-privilege equilibrium depends on changing majorities and thus lies in the future. Furthermore, what counts as defection might be hard to ascertain. Whether a certain set of policies already constitutes a privilege or is within the bounds of what a small state allows will often be subject of dispute. Disputes about these questions might easily lead to distrust and preemptive defection and counter-defection. Constitutional economics views democratic elections as a big cookie jar. It is just too tempting for a voter to cast his or his ballot in accordance with easily available intuitions and heuristics that are badly adapted to the political world. To remove temptations, Buchanan proposes to put the cookie jar on top of the kitchen cabinet, so that urges for something sweet will not result in eating an additional cookie. In the same way, a stable classical liberal order needs to be reinforced by a constitution that makes it more difficult for the electorate to reach the cookie jar. At the same time, the cookie jar metaphor suggests that a classical liberal equilibrium is not only fragile, but it is also very dubious that we would ever reach it through a piecemeal democratic decision process. Buchanan thus believes that the whole endeavor of fixing the epistemic and strategic problems of Western democracies through piecemeal engineering might in the end be fruitless: For every small change in the right direction, there might be two steps in the wrong direction. Instead, the economist says that what we need is a 'constitutional revolution.' To Buchanan, a constitutional revolution is a series of "non-incremental changes in the structural order of the community, changes in the complex set of rules that enable men to live with one another, changes that are sufficiently dramatic to warrant the label 'revolutionary'."[35] In his *Limits of Liberty*, Buchanan summarizes that such revolution is of importance, because the "existing legal order may have lost its claims to efficiency or [. . .] legitimacy."[36] Ten years later, in *The Reason of Rules*, Geoffrey Brennan and Buchanan restate the necessity of such a revolution:

> We are asking no less than that the basic rules of the socioeconomic-political game be changed, rules that have been in place for decades, and that these changes be made peacefully while the game continues to be played under the old rules. This order is a tall one indeed, and we should be under no delusion that a constitutional revolution will simply emerge, in revolutionary fashion, without a conscious investment of effort.[37]

David Reisman explains that an actual constitutional revolution between self-interested people should be understood as a "coordinated multilateral disarmament," where, in a process of reciprocity, everyone dispenses with his or her privileges: "My tariff for your subsidy, my tax-deduction for your selective exemption,"[38] Buchanan also thinks that such a constitutional revolution will likely entail a huge, onetime redistribution of wealth. He writes:

> Ultimately the hope for some 'improvement' must lie in the mutual consent of the special interests themselves for constitutional changes which will act so as to reduce the excessive costs that discriminatory legislation imposes on all groups over time. It is in seeking such changes in the organizational rules themselves that genuinely enlightened self-interests of these groups may be expressed.[39]

Although Buchanan has emphasized the necessity for a new constitutional moment, he has never given a full exposition of the content of such a constitutional revolution. In his books and articles, we can find certain mechanisms that he thinks would likely be agreed on in a constitutional moment. One essential part of such a new constitution could be to set in place a super-majority rule that puts brakes on special interests and stabilizes the new constitutional equilibrium. Under such a regime, every piece of legislation would require not only a simple majority, but a qualified majority – for instance, a two-thirds or four-fifth majority. There is also a host of very particular proposals, such as 'earmarked-taxation,' or a tax reform that would set certain limits on both the tax rate and tax base that Buchanan deems likely to be implemented.[40] There seem to be at least two reasons why Buchanan never outlined a perfectly efficient constitution. The first reason is that the content of such a constitution is to a huge degree a function of the preferences, risk attitudes and bargaining powers of the people. In *Limits of Liberty* Buchanan explains: "My natural proclivity as an economist is to place ultimate value on process or procedure, and by implication to define as 'good' that which emerges from agreement among free men, independent of intrinsic evaluation of the outcome itself."[41] In this statement, it becomes again apparent that constitutional economics is a second-order theory – a theory that starts from the premise of profound diversity. Although constitutional economics comes to very similar results from an institutional point of view as libertarianism, this statement again underlines the different normative stances of both theories. In constitutional economics, the small state emerges as a second-order solution to the bargaining process of economically informed persons with diverse normative standards and preferences, while in the libertarian picture, the minimal state emerges as a result of agents that find themselves in agreement about fundamental normative questions such as individual rights. The difference between constitutional economics and libertarianism at the same time also crystallizes institutionally. In both Hayek's and Buchanan's view such a new constitution will be unlikely to be akin to a minimal state:

> We find it unquestionable that in an advanced society government ought to use its power of raising funds by taxation to provide a number of services which for various reasons cannot be provided, or cannot be provided adequately, by the market [. . .] even if there were no other need for coercion [. . .] there would still exist an overwhelming case for giving the territorial authority power to make the inhabitants contribute to a common fund from which such services could be financed.[42]

Although Buchanan has never fully fleshed out the details of a constitutional revolution, it is safe to assume that the 'principle of generality' might be an essential element of a new constitutional contract. Buchanan and Hayek have independently argued that the *principle of generality* would ameliorate the *generalized prisoner's dilemma* or, as Buchanan called it, "politics as taking."[43] To understand the importance of this principle for both thinkers, it is worth noting that Buchanan's last monograph, *Politics by principle not by interest,* is basically entirely about the generality principle. In the epigraph of this essay, we find a telling quote by Hayek.

> [The First Amendment] ought to read, "Congress shall make no law authorizing government to take any discriminatory measures of coercion". The principle essentially prohibits all "[d]ifferential treatment and the operation of the law, say, on the basis of gender, age, race, religion, class, location, or political access".[44]

A good example for this principle can be found in Buchanan's discussion about taxation. Most people would find it outrageous if the legal system were to tax them according to their skin color, sex, weight or religion. Such a form of taxation would surely be against the principle of generality. However, as Buchanan notes, right now "tax rates can be varied over a wide set of economic characteristics: income and wealth classes, occupations, professions, and industrial categories."[45] For instance, under our current modus vivendi arrangements, "race horse breeders, real estate developers, and resort operators can secure special treatment without constitutional challenge."[46] A consequent application of the generality principle would not allow such differential treatment. Buchanan grounds the principle on prudential reasons.[47] The more discretionary power governments have in making special rules for special classes of people, the more time citizens need to spend on controlling them. The point in case here is the following: Under the current modus vivendi arrangements, most people will hardly notice if the government grants a small tax exemption to a certain group of companies. Compare that to the case where *all* companies would be taxed according to a general rule. If such a rule changes, many people will be affected at the same time, and public discussion would surely take up the topic. But the taxation example is also interesting, because it shows the limitations of the principle. The generality principle can be interpreted in many ways and applied to different levels of granularity. Let me consider the first case in relation to income taxation. The criterion of generality lends itself to many interpretations when it comes to income taxes. For instance, we can argue that everybody paying a fixed amount annually would surely fall under the criterion of generality (head tax). But, of course, everybody paying the same tax rate, say 20 percent, would also fall under the generality principle (proportional tax). Another problem with the principle is that it could be applied to different levels of granularity. For instance, we could demand that 'all companies' must be taxed an amount x, or that a certain subgroup, say, 'all health care related companies,' should be taxed an amount x or, for that matter, that a subgroup of a subgroup 'all pharmaceutical industry companies' should be taxed an amount x. All these three statements seem to fulfill the requirement of generality. If we apply the principle of generality on the lowest granularity, 'pharmaceutical industries,' there is again plenty of leeway for practically all kinds of discriminatory taxation.

Let me finish this section with a last comment about the generality principle. Although it has some interesting epistemic features and can work against discrimination in cases where groups try to gain privileges or impose costs on others, the generality principle is not a safeguard against all kinds of discrimination. It cannot prevent a majority from laying down laws that they themselves are prepared to follow. For instance, a prohibition against cars, drugs or alcohol is fully in accordance with the generality principle. Of course, Buchanan sees that as well, and comments: "The intrusiveness or nonintrusiveness of law is not addressed by the generality [. . .] principle, as such."[48]

Against the background of the second-order theories that we have reviewed so far, we can conclude that in his brand of classical liberalism Buchanan comes to a very different set of recommendations than Rawls or Gutmann and Thompson. This is, in a sense, good news, since neither Rawls's nor Gutmann and Thompson's approach could convince the RoCD.

4.3 RoCD Test

Undoubtedly, there is a certain attraction to the proposal of constitutional economics. "Life in the here and now," writes Buchanan, "may be more brutish than need be, and certainly more nasty."[49] Constitutional economics promises that, although we cannot agree on principles of justice or standards of legitimacy, we could nevertheless all live a much better life if we were to have a 'constitutional revolution' that essentially locks society in a classical liberal small state. The allure of the argument is, then, that if we could just agree on the facts (i.e. the constitutional economist's theory of the market) we could escape our current modus vivendi. This approach has two salient advantages. First, the claim that if only people were fully informed about economics, they would agree on the institutions of a small state, is essentially empirical one and thus, prima facie, falsifiable. The second and related advantage is that it solves the question at hand with a much more limited set of abstractions. It normalizes only the agents' socio-economic beliefs, while a theory such as Rawls's theory of justice normalizes both socio-economic and moral beliefs. But the same feature that makes this approach attractive also makes it vulnerable to objection. A first problem relates to the feasibility of this approach. We might ask how the transition from people as they are to our idealized members of society could be imagined. It is a bit surprising that economists, who usually emphasize the rigidity of preferences and the unwillingness of the electorate to engage in deep political questions, imagine that such a transition can be feasible. Jeremy Shearmur makes a very similar point:

> It is not clear how citizens will be able to match up the disadvantages of such institutions with the benefits that they obtain from them. While this is information that might be possessed by a social theorist, it is not clear how it is supposed to be accessible to citizens.[50]

While it might be true that Buchanan's main argument is falsifiable, I have to be clear about the fact, that, in the meantime, I have strong disagreements about that very conjecture and the socio-economic theory it is derived from. Many social scientists, philosophers and economists believe that the market is inherently unstable and produces all kinds of moral and social atrocities. Based on the theory that a market order is unstable and continuously produces moral ills, these theorists think that a proactive government is vitally important to the very stability of a market society. Any attempt to tie the hands of the government from that perspective looks very dubious or outright dangerous. The problem for constitutional economics is, then, that it is based on a socio-economic theory that is not only rejected by most of the non-academic electorate, but also by great parts of academia itself. This is, of course, a point that Buchanan himself was well aware of. In the introduction to *The Reason of Rules*, Brennan and Buchanan write defiantly: "Basic 'constitutional illiteracy' extends to and includes both the learned and the lay."[51] Furthermore, I should note that constitutional economists such as Buchanan and Hayek in many ways do not represent the mainstream in economics.

This in turn sheds light on a central result of this chapter. While it is certainly difficult to find common normative standards, it does not seem to be much easier to achieve agreement on a comprehensive socio-economic theory. The disagreement on socio-economic facts will also be reflected in the decision of the RoCD.

Utilitarians:	Although thinkers such as John Stuart Mill and Jeremy Bentham are considered to be classical liberal thinkers, there is nothing within utilitarianism that requires utilitarians to adopt a classical liberal concept of the market. Therefore, utilitarians cannot be expected to vote unanimously for or against the approach.
Deliberative democrats:	Deliberative democrats share a strong belief that there are other means – mainly various deliberative mechanisms – that might be more appropriate to improve our current modus vivendi arrangements. Furthermore, deliberative democrats tend to be very skeptical of the social, environmental and also economical outcomes of the market order as envisioned by Buchanan and other liberal thinkers. From the perspective of the deliberative democrats, a move towards a classical liberal order seems unacceptable.
Realists:	There is good reason to believe that realists do not necessarily share a socio-economic theory. Thus, there would most likely be no unanimous vote within this group. Furthermore, realists would point out that a constitutional revolution that locks our current society in a classical liberal equilibrium seems utterly infeasible given the current socio-economic beliefs of both society and academia.
Egalitarians:	Egalitarians outrightly reject this proposal for two reasons. First off, egalitarians in general tend to have more faith that there are viable economic alternatives to the market system. Thus, they will naturally be very skeptical towards the socio-economic theories on which the argument of constitutional economics is based. Second, a classical liberal order will essentially perpetuate and enshrine inequality. For that reason alone, this proposal must fear an outright rejection by egalitarians. Our current democratic order with its plentiful possibilities of social tinkering has to look more appealing to egalitarians than CL.
Natural rights libertarians:	Defenders of natural rights, like Nozick, will not be satisfied with the rights violations that a constitutional revolution will most likely entail. In contrast, natural rights libertarians will surely agree to a move in the direction of CL.

In conclusion, I can state that, although the proposal of constitutional economics does have a number of attractive features from a theoretical point of view, it fails to convince – mainly because the RoCD sharply disagree on the underlying socio-economic theory on which the argument of constitutional liberalism builds.

Notes

1 Buchanan and Tullock (1999). For a concise introduction to constitutional economics, see Buchanan (1990). The main academic outlets of this research program are *Constitutional Political Economy* and *Public Choice,* both published by Springer. The core contributions of Buchanan to constitutional economics are Brennan and Buchanan (2000), Buchanan (2000) and Buchanan and Tullock (1999). It should further be noted that there is certain overlap in concepts and ideas between constitutional economics and German *Ordnungsökonomik* (order economics), *Ordoliberalismus* (order liberalism) and *Ordnungsethik* (order ethics). Important contemporary contributions include Wegner (2008), Homann (1988), Homann and Blome-Drees (1992), Goldschmidt and Zweynert (2013), Pies (1993), Lütge (2005), and Lütge (2015).
2 Lütge (2015, p. 27).
3 Meadowcroft (2013), Thornton and Thommesen (1987).
4 Homann (2002).
5 Buchanan (2000, pp. 110–111).
6 I will use the terms 'classical liberal economists' and 'constitutional economists' for the most part as synonyms. The positions of Buchanan, Hayek and Mises, with respects to the conundrum this essay attempts to answer, are very similar. I will thus at times treat their positions as interchangeable. This is not to deny the profound methodological gap that divides these thinkers. From a purely political point of view, though, they are in much greater agreement.
7 Buchanan (2000, p. 19).
8 I will work with this stipulative definition of a 'small state' throughout this chapter. Furthermore, I will treat the terms 'constitutional liberalism,' 'constitutionally restrained democracy' and 'small state' as synonyms.
9 Brennan (2012a).
10 Buchanan (1987, p. 246).
11 Buchanan (2000, p. 10). A zero-sum game is essentially a game in which one party gains at the expense of another party, while in a negative-sum game everybody loses in the long run.
12 Hayek (2012, p. 100).
13 I think this simple claim holds for many political economists in the tradition of classical liberalism. In Müller (2013), I attempted to show that at least Mises makes a similar argument.
14 Buchanan and Congleton (1998, p. 18).
15 The scope of this essay does not allow for a detailed economic discussion of why Buchanan thinks that a free market is more efficient in providing most goods. It is important to note that classical liberal thinkers do not think that a 'market failure' is a sufficient reason to outsource the production of a certain good to the government, since there is also 'political failure'. Based on their economical theory of political institutions, classical liberal theorists expect that most of the time, because of the incentive structures innate to the political process, it is rational – even in the case of expected market failure – to rely on markets rather than on government. Pennington, for instance, has recently argued that a small state does a better job than a welfare state when it comes to "poverty relief" and the supply of "public services" like health care, education and environmental protection; see Pennington (2011, chap. 6–8), Pennington (2010) and Pennington (2008). Furthermore, classical liberal thinkers argue that there should be

very few limits to "what can be bought and sold" (Brennan and Jaworski 2016). Markets for organs, sex or surrogate parents seem to them overall a better choice than the social results that stem from government interference.

16 For an introduction to modern public choice theory, on which much of the comparative 'market failure' versus political failure literature hinges, see Mueller (2003), Simmons and Mitchell (2011) and Tullock (1964). For more classical treatments of comparative institutional and political economy, see Mises (1944), Hayek (2007) and Hayek (2012).
17 The term 'reasonable' is here used as it has been throughout this entire essay.
18 Recasted from Ostrom (2005, p. 24).
19 Buchanan (2000, p. xvi). See also "[the] politico-legal order is a public good; disorder is a public bad" (Buchanan 2000, p. 11).
20 For reasons of brevity, I abstract from particular persons that have enough leverage to single handedly change the outcome of elections. For these people, it will, of course, be rational to be informed about politics.
21 Jason Brennan discusses these proposals in his *Ethics of Voting* (Brennan 2012b).
22 Mantzavinos (2001, chap. 7.4–8.1).
23 Caplan (2007, chap. 2).
24 Caplan (2007, p. 42).
25 Caplan (2007, p. 44).
26 Tetlock (2005, p. 63).
27 Tetlock (2005, p. 231).
28 Economists often rely on revealed preference theory. This theory basically states that it is only from the actions of individuals that we can infer what they truly want. It should be noted that seems to be a tension between the treatment of political preferences and revealed preference theory. Political economists in the classical liberal tradition, though, have always thought that choices are open for rational critique, since choice behavior reflects not only preferences, but also instrumental beliefs.
29 Hayek (2012, p. 95).
30 Friedman (2005, p. 48).
31 Huemer (2012, p. 12).
32 Buchanan (1986, p. 117).
33 Hayek (2012, 100–101).
34 Mises (1985, p. 55).
35 Buchanan (2000, p. 212).
36 Buchanan (2000, p. 213).
37 Brennan and Buchanan (2000, pp. 165–166).
38 Reisman (1990, p. 79).
39 Buchanan and Tullock (1999, p. 290).
40 For a very comprehensive and easily accessible overview, see Meadowcroft (2013, pp. 107–132).
41 Buchanan (2000, p. 210).
42 Hayek (2013, pp. 382–383).
43 Buchanan and Congleton (1998, p. 18).
44 Buchanan and Congleton (1998, p. 8).
45 Buchanan and Congleton (1998, p. 96).
46 Buchanan and Congleton (1998, p. 96).
47 Notice that anti-discrimination laws as they apply to race or gender are usually grounded in moral values like dignity or fundamental human rights.
48 Buchanan and Congleton (1998, p. 8).
49 Buchanan (2000, p. 213).
50 Shearmur (1996, p. 199).
51 Brennan and Buchanan (2000, p. xv).

5 Escaping modus vivendi

Summary

In the first part of this essay, I have looked at three important strands of political philosophy. Although these theories have very different origins and thus employ very different strategies to show us a way out of modus vivendi, they nevertheless share a fundamental premise: They all view reasonable disagreement as a problem that needs to be overcome. The three approaches that I have covered all admit the challenge presented by pluralism,[1] but they nevertheless hope that behind a veil of dissonance and disagreement lies some common ground that is accessible to all citizens. Interestingly enough, the political economist Paul Dragos Aligica recently came to a very similar conclusion. He writes that "moderates," like "John Rawls, James Buchanan and Jürgen Habermas," acknowledge the "profound challenge of diversity and pluralism," but nonetheless try to "build their approach on a common grounding principle [. . .] able to anchor in the last resort both social agents and the theory of social order."[2] The motivation behind the continuing search for consensus is plain enough: In absence of an agreement on fairness or a set of distinctive institutional brakes, democracy could easily devolve into a generalized prisoner's dilemma. As we have seen, such a dilemma will come about not only under a public with sordid attitudes, but might also develop under a society of rather well-meaning people who subscribe to plural theories of the good and of the right. Reasonable disagreement is thus not only an interesting problem from a purely academic point of view, but also poses an acute political problem.

Nicholas Rescher notes that in philosophy, throughout history, consensus was not only viewed as something desirable, "but as something whose eventual actualization is effectively assured by some principle deep-rooted in the nature of things as we humans confront them in this world."[3] Even though modern political philosophers have come to doubt that the nature of things ensures that consensus will be achieved in the end, they nevertheless hope that we can achieve a social consensus.[4] The hope behind the modern consensualist view is summed up nicely by Gaus:

> If we could only achieve "normalization," if only the problem of social evaluation could be reduced to the reasoning based on a single perspective, then we would have solved the problem of uncovering the social

rules (laws, basic structure, or whatever) that would promote the common good.[5]

To conclude: The first part of this essay reviewed three political theories, each relying on a different strategy to neutralize disagreement. Let me briefly summarize these strategies.

In Rawls's *A Theory of Justice* (TJ) we can distinguish two mechanisms to reduce diversity. The first mechanism is the original position. In the original position, as I have described earlier, our theories of the good as well as our socio-economic knowledge get standardized. The normalized agents behind the veil of ignorance then deliberate about principles of justice that suit them. The simulated discourse finally arrives at one specific solution. Since there is great controversy in the literature about the kind of principles that agents behind a veil would really agree on, the simulated discourse itself might be understood as a second mechanism of taming diversity. As I have discussed, the Rawls of TJ thinks that under favorable conditions a society could grow around principles of justice that stem from the abstraction theory. It might be noted in passing that, as Rawls himself notes, "a normalization of interests attributed to the parties to the contracts" is not in any way specific to his project, but "common to social contract doctrines."[6]

The second approach that I discussed was deliberative democracy. Deliberative democracy, in contrast to approaches in the contract tradition, attempts to reduce the set of reasonable disagreement through a process of deliberation. In the end, deliberative democrats hope to achieve consensus by deliberation. Since deliberative democracy is at least loosely tied to fallibilism, the process of deliberation and voting is best understood as an iterative political process that is open to feedback. The deliberative approach also aims at reducing both normative and instrumental diversity.

The third approach that I covered is constitutional economics. While constitutional economics does not necessarily promise to yield a fully justified solution, it at least promises to deliver a better modus vivendi. What is especially interesting is that constitutional economics tries to achieve this result by assuming away our instrumental diversity. If we could find agreement on socio-economic theory, the constitutional economist argues, we could already achieve a much more pleasant modus vivendi. Table 5.1 summarizes these results.

Table 5.1 Taming Diversity

	Evaluative Diversity	*Instrumental Diversity*
Rawls	Idealized away	Idealized away
Gutmann and Thompson	Procedural hedging	Procedural hedging
Buchanan	–	Idealized away

What becomes apparent in this summary is that evaluative as well as instrumental diversity are almost exclusively seen as inconveniences. Taming diversity and achieving consensus is seen as the only way out of modus vivendi politics. D'Agostino seems to have a very similar chart in mind when he comments: "In particular, neither Rawls nor most of his commentators have treated [. . .] pluralism as anything other than an inconvenience. Certainly, it has not generally been treated as, rather, one of the most glorious opportunities for humankind."[7]

Notes

1 Pluralism, as it is understood in this essay, refers to the social factum that reasonable people in modern societies disagree about conceptions of the good and the right as well as about important matters of fact with regard to politics. As I noted earlier, I stay agnostic towards questions such as the nature of value as discussed under the rubric of 'moral pluralism' in ethics.
2 Aligica (2014, p. 2).
3 Rescher (1993, p. 1).
4 Rescher (1993, p. 1).
5 Gaus (2011b, p. 72).
6 Rawls explains: "In Hobbes, it is our fundamental interests in self-preservation, conjugal affections, and 'riches and the means of commodious living'. In Locke it is lives, liberties, and estates" (Rawls 2007, p. 226).
7 D'Agostino (2004, p. 354).

Part II

How to make use of diversity?

6 Diversity

Nuisance or asset?

In the first part of this essay, I established that the leading second-order theories fail to convince the RoCD. This suggests that escaping our current modus vivendi by looking for a hidden consensus behind the curtain of reasonable disagreement might be a dead end. Since we are not able to neutralize diversity significantly by way of argument, this essay wants to propose a philosophical U-turn. Rather than asking *how can we hedge diversity?* this essay wants to change gears and ask *how can we make use of diversity?* Although diversity is seen mainly as an inconvenience in political philosophy, diversity also has many advantages.[1] Let me give a few examples.

Imagine that Benni wants to build a start-up. Benni is a creative guy but not very good with numbers or getting up early. If he wants to be successful, it is surely wise for him to team up with people who are more level-headed, people who have essential skills that he is lacking. The right mix of people and skills is essential for the success of Benni's start-up. But diversity is not only essential when it comes to solving problems; it is also essential for getting to know our own preferences. Consider Rea, who is a nerdy type and has not left her home much over the last few years, both physically and mentally. Imagine that one day, while browsing her favorite internet forum, she falls in love with Linnea, who is very different from herself, and they become lovers. Linnea soon introduces her to a host of foreign restaurants in the vicinity and takes her on vacations all over the world. After three years, they split up, but Rea is a different person by now.[2] She has uncovered parts of her personality that she was not even aware of. If Linnea had not introduced her to all those new worlds, Rea would have never known what she was missing. As a final case, let us consider diverse risk profiles. We will assume that everybody in a geographically excluded community has the same risk profile. In particular, let us assume that everybody is extremely risk-averse. In such a community, there will never be any progress – and slight changes in the environment might lead to the extinction of the community. The opposite case, of course, would be no better. If everybody in the small community wants to be an inventor, nobody will work the fields and the community will be in a similarly precarious position. Homogeneity of risk profiles thus, prima facie, seems to be detrimental to the success of the community.

A heterogeneous set of risk profiles, however, might allow the community to be robust in the face of a changing environment.

Let us now turn to a more philosophical topic: moral progress. Although the notion of moral progress is, for many reasons, analytically cumbersome, we can hardly do without it. Moral progress entails that we move from one set of rules to the next. The move from one to the next set of rules is usually a slow process that relies on somebody questioning or breaking the old rules while at the same time advocating new ones. "Moral innovation," as Gaus notes, "like cultural innovation in general, starts with trendsetters who act on their own evaluation of what is best."[3] Thus, diversity seems to be a necessary condition for progress in general and moral progress in particular. These cursory reflections might suffice to strengthen the intuition that evaluative as well instrumental diversity should not be viewed exclusively as regrettable inconveniences, but also as some kind of asset.

Although, as far as I know, there are no political philosophies that explicitly build on the idea of employing instrumental and evaluative diversity, philosophers have nonetheless thought about employing diversity for the benefit of society. These thoughts can be tentatively grouped into two paradigms: deliberative and polycentric.[4] The deliberative paradigm points to collective deliberation as a prime mechanism not only for reducing diversity, but also for reaping and communicating the potential gains of diversity. The polycentric paradigm, on the contrary, emphasizes evolutionary learning processes under appropriate rules as the central mechanism to create public gains of diversity. Let me add a few strokes to sharpen both profiles.

6.1 The deliberative paradigm

In a world of perfect rationality and full knowledge, deliberation would have no place. In the actual world, however, citizens possess only bits and pieces of knowledge, and reasoning is costly both in time and cognitive energy. In addition, people often hold false beliefs and are prone to make mistakes in reasoning. In such a world, collective deliberation is used to share knowledge and to critically examine arguments. The benefits of deliberation have been identified very early in the history of philosophy. Aristotle, for instance, observes:

> Each of them by himself may not be of a good quality; but when they all come together it is possible that they may surpass – collectively and as a body, although not individually – the quality of the few best, in much the same way that feasts to which many contribute may excel those provided at one person's expense.[5]

What Aristotle suggests here intuitively has a great pull. If people with diverse views come together to discuss and assemble the available knowledge, they might very well arrive at the single best solution that "excel[s]" and "surpass[es]" "the quality of the few best." The deliberative paradigm, furthermore, relies on the "unforced force of the better argument,"[6] both in arriving and in communicating the best solution. This approach seems to reflect our own experience. When facing big decisions, we usually consult with our friends or even talk to experts before we reach a final conclusion. By reviewing different perspectives and assembling different sets of information, we hope to arrive at the best possible solution.

6.2 The polycentric paradigm

What I call the 'polycentric paradigm' can perhaps be best illuminated against the backdrop of the deliberative paradigm. The polycentric approach in general is skeptical about the merits of deliberation regardless of whether deliberation is conducted individually or collectively. What the polycentric approach emphasizes is that deliberation will often fail because the knife of reason is not as sharp as we would hope. The polycentric approach is skeptical about deliberation both when it comes to mainly instrumental as well as to more evaluative tasks. Three statements from the philosopher and economist Hayek will allow us to get a better grip on this approach. In the first quote, Hayek emphasizes his skepticism about the chances for deliberating groups to divert to its best member without the opportunity for real-world experiments:

> The true basis of [the individualist's] argument is that nobody can know *who* knows best and that the *only* way by which we can find out is through a social process in which everybody is allowed to try and see what he can do.[7]

In the second statement, Hayek points to the problem that we often do not know in advance what we want. In this sense, we need real-world experiments to make up our mind in the first place:

> It is because every individual knows so little and [. . .] because we rarely know which of us knows best that we trust the independent and competitive efforts of many to induce the emergence of *what we shall want when we see it.*[8]

Hayek doubts that, at least when it comes to hard cases, we can establish ex ante what we want or who knows best. But Hayek is skeptical not only about the epistemic power of deliberation, but also about its ability to convey or diffuse knowledge. He writes:

> The successful combination of knowledge and aptitude is not selected by common deliberation [. . .] [on the contrary] it is the product of individuals imitating those who have been more successful and from their being guided by symbols, such as prices [. . .] or *expressions of moral or aesthetic esteem* [. . .] – in short, of their using the results *of the experience* of others.[9]

Instead of relying foremost on deliberation for spreading knowledge, the Hayekian approach emphasizes imitation and real-world experience as central mechanisms for diffusing knowledge. The polycentric paradigm basically states that the knife of reason will be blunt unless it is supplemented by real-world experiments. In this Hayekian view, real-world demonstrations are important (a) to reveal who knows best, (b) to reveal what we really want and (c) to diffuse knowledge of what works and who knows best.

The second part of this essay has two goals. The first one is to provide a better conceptual understanding of the gains of diversity (Chapter 7, Section 7.1). The second goal is to compare the deliberative (Chapter 7, Sections 7.2–7.4) and the polycentric approaches (Chapter 8) with regard to their respective ability of making use of diversity.

Notes

1 Ryan Muldoon's 2016 *Social Contract Theory for a Diverse World: Beyond Tolerance* is a notable exception to that trend in modern political philosophy.
2 It is important to note, though, that Rea did not change her preferences. In the words of Paul, she had an epistemic transformation, but not a *transformative experience* (Paul 2014, pp. 11–16). Compare also [1.2].
3 Gaus (2011c, p. 442).
4 I use 'paradigm' here in the sense of a Weberian 'ideal type'.
5 Aristotle (1998, 108, 253).
6 Habermas (1996, p. 306).
7 Hayek (1980, p. 15). Emphasis in original. "*Who*" refers to the interests of individuals in this essay, but it seems to make equal sense with regards to beliefs.
8 Hayek (2012, p. 27). Emphasis added.
9 Hayek (2012, p. 26). Emphasis added.

7 Deliberation and the gains of diversity

In Section 7.1, I will illuminate the connection between deliberation and diversity. The guiding question in this section will be how collective deliberation between people with different levels of knowledge might increase the group's ability to solve hard problems. After having gained a first conceptual foothold, I will analyze the limits of deliberation in Section 7.2. Finally, I will summarize the results of this chapter in Section 7.3.

7.1 Deliberation and diversity

In this essay, I have presented deliberative democracy as a theory that is primarily concerned with establishing procedures for hedging diversity in a morally appropriate fashion. However, some deliberative democrats defend the democratic process not only on moral, but also on epistemic grounds.[1] These philosophers claim that the deliberative process not only *accommodates diversity*, but also *makes good use of diversity*.[2]

In this section I want to get a better understanding of the relation between deliberation and the gains of diversity. I want to understand what it means to say that deliberation is "epistemically productive" as Elizabeth Anderson suggests.[3] To get a firmer grip of the benefits of deliberation, I want to distinguish three forms of deliberation that can make use of diversity: 'deliberation as teaching,' 'deliberation as piecing together a puzzle' and 'deliberation as creating synergy effects.' Let me discuss the three concepts in turn.

7.1.1 Deliberation as teaching: raising the bottom line

Deliberation can be used as a method to diffuse knowledge. Imagine a chess teacher is asking his or her class to solve a chess problem, such as finding a checkmate in three moves. Given the instructor knows the solution to the problem, deliberation will not add anything to the solution. The teacher might ask the students about the advantages of this or that move, but these deliberations have mostly an educational character. In discussing the problem, the students will suggest bad moves, propose tactical motives and strategies that do not lead to success and so on. In this exercise, the task of the instructor is to explain to the students either directly or maybe in a Socratic fashion why certain moves in that particular position are bad and why certain motives do not apply. The process of teaching involves therefore both explanations of why a certain move in a certain position is good, but also why certain alternative moves are bad. Thus raising the level of knowledge involves both criticizing faulty believes as well as teaching correct ones.

Deliberation as a particular form of diffusing knowledge is one important part of what I have in mind when I talk about 'public deliberation.' Public deliberation partly consists of experts sharing their knowledge with the public and explaining why certain policies are better than others.

7.1.2 Deliberation as piecing together a puzzle: hidden profiles

When thinking about public deliberation, however, we usually have quite another picture in mind. Deliberation is most commonly thought of as piecing together a puzzle. Every participant sees one part of the picture, but only by putting their different pieces together do they finally manage to see the big picture – or, as psychologists call it, the "hidden profile."[4] Thus, in order to solve a hidden-profile problem, deliberation mainly needs to aggregate all the knowledge that a given group of people already possesses. When we are thinking about the gains of public deliberation, or the gains of deliberating in small groups, we usually have a picture like this in mind. This model seems to be especially apt with regard to hard problems. Think about a hard problem such as the 2015 European refugee crisis. To come up with a solution or even just a reasonable action plan, we have to consider various dimensions of the problem. First, we have to get a deeper understanding of the reasons why people are seeking asylum. Gathering this knowledge will make it necessary to communicate with various specialists in area studies. We will soon notice that the people looking for asylum have very different social, economic and religious backgrounds. This opens up the question of what the internal relations between the various groups of refugees are. Moreover, the refugees will need to settle somewhere. Wherever they settle, they will have an impact on the local community and on the local economy. However, we also need to keep in mind the national political, social and economic impact of the various proposed solutions, and so on. The lesson here is simple: To solve hard problems, we need adequate knowledge. The knowledge to solve hard political problems is usually dispersed over many heads rather than concentrated in one. In these cases, inclusive deliberation with experts and stakeholders is one important method to aggregate the relevant knowledge.

7.1.3 Deliberation as creating synergy effects

As shown by Scott Page, combining diverse perspectives and heuristics often creates synergy effects.[5] This means that by adding one heuristic to another, we do not get two heuristics, but three. To give an example, imagine a bottle that is hard to open. Anna's heuristic is to just pull the cap of the bottle up, since she notices that it is somewhat loose. Gabriel's heuristic, however, is to turn and twist the cap of the bottle. Regrettably, neither of them, individually, are successful in opening the bottle. However, if they share their heuristics with each other, both now have three and not just two heuristics in their bag: pulling, turning and pulling while turning.

According to this view, deliberation not only allows us to unlock hidden profiles but also to create new reasons, perspectives or knowledge. Psychologists call this an "assembly bonus effect"[6] or, in short, an 'assembly bonus' or 'assembly effect.' "An assembly effect," according to Collins and Guetzkow, "occurs when the group is able to achieve collectively something which could not have been achieved by any member working alone or by a combination of individual efforts."[7] However, in the psychological literature, the 'assembly bonus effect' is sometimes used rather loosely to point to any gains of deliberation. In my discussion, I will use the term when I refer to synergy effects as outlined before.[8]

While synergy effects in my sense are hard to manage experimentally and thus under-studied, the meaning of synergy effects is in principle rather easy. Let us look at another example: Imagine that Anna and Gabriel are wandering around at a flea market and come across a blue folding bike. Both consider buying it. Anna is interested in the bike because of its blue color. Unfortunately, she does not notice that the bike actually is a folding bike. Before deliberation, Anna has thus one reason (r_1) to buy the bike. Gabriel also likes the color blue (r_1), in addition, he is a fan of folding bikes (r_2) and easily identifies the bike for what it is, a folding bike. Gabriel thus has two reasons to buy the bike. Sadly though, both Anna and Gabriel are rather hesitant when it comes to buying new things. So, they need to have at least three good reasons before they buy something. Now, imagine Gabriel shares with Anna that the bike is actually foldable. We can imagine that this new information sparks up a third reason for Anna to buy the bike. Having a foldable bike would allow them to take a bike to the next family vacation (r_3). Since this reason also applies to Gabriel, both now have three reasons and thus have a conclusive reason to buy the bike. What is important here is that the total set of reasons before deliberation was two, and after deliberation it is three. While in the hidden profile paradigm the number of reasons that are available to the group before and after deliberation is constant, in the case of synergy, it has actually increased as result of deliberation.

7.2 The limits of deliberation

There are undeniable potential gains to collectivizing deliberation. Certainly, many tasks can potentially gain from a diversity of minds and approaches. A marketing team might benefit from different insights about consumer behavior, and a difficult engineering problem might be best solved by a diverse team of engineers and scientists. Or think about social questions, for instance, whether organ trading should be allowed or outlawed. Surely, such a problem can best be solved by combining medical expertise about which organs can be transplanted with an economic rationale that explains the incentives of a market for organs and an ethical perspective that brings the appropriate ethical concerns to the table.

However, there are also certain limitations to deliberation. This is the topic of this section. In his seminal work, *Groupthink: psychological studies of policy decisions and fiascoes*, Yale psychologist Irving Janis tells a sad story about the small mining town of Pitcher in Oklahoma that disregarded the warnings of a local mining engineer. He writes:

> The local mining engineer had warned the inhabitants to leave at once because the town had been accidentally undermined and might cave in at any moment. At a Lion's Club meeting of leading citizens, the day after the warning was issued, the member joked about the warning and laughed uproariously when someone arrived wearing a parachute. What the club members were communicating to each other by their collective laughter was that 'sensible people like us know better than to take seriously those disaster warnings; we know it can't happen here, to our fine little town.' Within a few days, this collective complacency cost some of these men and their families their lives.[9]

The idea that a single expert is overruled by a group of stubborn deliberators should be all too familiar. However, even with no knuckleheads in the room, deliberation often fails. The banking crisis in 2007 is a good example for a situation in which the majority of experts failed to pay heed to the warnings of their epistemic peers. Stories of deliberating experts dismissing important evidence, dismissing the bearer of bad news or ridiculing groundbreaking research, are well known and build the foundation of countless novels and Hollywood movies.

You might wonder if we cannot do better than gather anecdotal evidence for the assertion that deliberating groups sometimes fail to gravitate to their internal expert. Thankfully, social psychologists have compiled a huge amount of experimental literature on this question. In particular, social psychologists concerned with problem-solving in small groups have put considerable effort into testing the 'truth wins' hypothesis.[10] The hypothesis basically states that a group of people should always be able to solve a problem if any one member can solve the problem by himself or herself. To test this hypothesis, psychologists usually rely on problem-solving tasks with a dichotomous answer that can be correct or incorrect.[11] An example for a problem-solving task is, for instance, the husbands-and-wives transfer problem. In this task, six couples are standing on the bank of a river and want to cross the river with a rowboat. The problem is this: The rowboat has only three seats, and none of the jealous husbands permits his wife to be in the company of another man unless he is also present. In addition, the group faces the problem that only the husbands can row.[12] The question that concerns us here is how good the 'truth wins' hypothesis fares in the laboratory. A large number of laboratory studies, interestingly enough, could not corroborate the 'truth wins' hypothesis. Mark Stasson and Scott Bradshaw provide a useful summary:

> Instead of finding an assembly bonus effect, many studies actually found an *assembly decrement*. The majority of these studies compared group performance on a single problem to members' pretest performance on the same problem and found that there were instances in which groups did not select the correct alternative even though one or more members bad been correct on the pretest.[13]

Surveying the literature, Cass Sunstein comes to a similar conclusion.

> There is no systematic evidence that deliberating groups will usually succeed in aggregating the information held by their members. With respect to questions with definite answers, deliberating groups tend to do about as well as or slightly better than their average members, but not as well as their best members.[14]

Sunstein's conclusion concurs with the results of several meta-studies in small-group research.[15] This, of course, opens up the question of why deliberating groups sometimes fail to unlock the gains of diversity. In the past forty years, a whole literature that attempts to carve out the inhibitors of deliberative success has emerged. In the first part of this section (7.2.1), I want to review some of the literature that deals with the shortcomings of actual deliberation under laboratory conditions. In the second part (7.2.2) I want to touch upon the problem that collective deliberation is constrained by transaction costs of deliberation. Finally, in the third part (7.2.3) I want to argue that the potential for deliberative success is not only limited by our psychological outfit and transaction costs, but more fundamentally by the boundedness of rationality itself.

7.2.1 *Psychological findings*

Before I begin to review the psychological findings with regard to the limits of deliberation, we first need to get a better understanding of the experiments on which these results are based. Garold Stasser and Beth Dietz-Uhler present a useful way of thinking about the tasks that social psychologists study in the laboratory. They distinguish tasks that can be exclusively executed by a team or by a single individual.[16] Think about soccer. This sport can only be played by teams, while a sport like bowling – throwing a bowling ball in the general direction of pins – is an individual task. In contrast, the studies that are of interest to us concern themselves with tasks that can be done by either an *individual or by a group of people*. Moreover, I am interested in experiments that focus on *cognitive* tasks as compared to *physical* tasks. A third distinction is the distinction between cooperative and competitive tasks. A classical cooperative task might be rowing a boat, while bargaining and negotiating are surely competitive tasks. Cooperative tasks are often positive-sum games like in the example of rowing. If two people row together, they might be reaching their common goal faster than if both would individually rowed their own canoes. Nevertheless, it is still possible that, with inexperienced rowers, an uncoordinated effort of rowing will lead the boat to steer left and right and thus cause the team to be slower collectively than they would have been individually. A competitive task, however, is, conceptually speaking, a zero-sum game. Whatever A gains in a bargain, B loses.[17] I am here primarily interested in cooperative ventures. The tasks that I am interested in are thus *cognitive, cooperative* tasks that can be conducted *either by individuals or teams.*

Again following Stasser and Dietz-Uhler, I want to make two important distinctions within these tasks. The first distinction is between *selection* and *rating*. An act of selection simply means to choose one or more options from a set of options. Such a task would be, for instance, to select two balls from a red urn. Rating refers to an act of evaluation. In an act of evaluation, we locate "a target along a continuum."[18] 'How much do you like this apple at a scale from one to ten?' might be an example. Another example would be locating different institutional systems on a scale from low justice to high justice. The second distinction is between *intellective* versus *judgmental* tasks. Following Patrick Laughlin and John Adamopoulos,[19] Stasser and Dietz-Uhler define an intellective task as one that has a "demonstrably correct answer."[20] Judgmental tasks, on the contrary, are tasks where no demonstrably correct answers exist. This distinction is, interestingly enough, not about truth but about cognition. Take for instance a simple math problem like finding the zero of this quadratic equation: $x^2 - 4 = 0$. The equation has two zero points for $x = 2$ and $x = -2$. While this answer is true, it might not be intelligible to a six-year-old who still struggles with more basic concepts like subtraction and summation. If a teacher tries to explain the answer to this problem, it might well be the case that the child will not understand the explanation. Demonstrability is thus not a binary concept – but there is a continuum between high and low intelligibility and, on the flip side, between low and high demonstrability. "One group's intellective task may" thus "be another group's judgmental task."[21]

We are now at the point where I can present cognitive, cooperative tasks in a simple matrix shown in Table 7.1.

Table 7.1 Schema for Categorizing Group Tasks[22]

		Response Format	
		Select	*Rate*
Demonstrability	*Judgmental*	Choice	Judgment
	Intellective	Problem-solving	Estimation

All four classes of collective cognitive tasks are of relevance to us in some part of the work. When we study collective-choice tasks, we are usually interested in how collective choice is influenced by different choice rules. Buchanan's discussion of majority rules falls into this category. Work that is concerned with collective judgment is usually concerned with questions of how collective deliberation affects or changes the collective judgment of a group. In the following sections, I will mainly be concerned with problem-solving tasks. Let me then begin to review some of the psychological findings with regard to the limits of deliberation.

The common knowledge bias

Intuitively, deliberation should be a prime means to diffuse and aggregate knowledge in order to create better problem-solutions. Psychologists have attempted to test whether deliberating groups are usually successful in diffusing and aggregating knowledge.

The results of these studies are quite sobering. Deliberating groups in general tend to mute unique information, while emphasizing common knowledge. Psychologists speak of a *common knowledge effect* if the "influence of a particular item of information is directly and positively related to the number of group members who have knowledge of that item before the group discussion and judgment."[23] Although the actual term was coined in 1993 by Daniel Gigone and Reid Hastie, the effect itself was first established in 1985 in a seminal paper by Garold Stasser and William Titus.[24] To get a grasp of the common knowledge effect, it is worth taking a look at these psychologists' initial experiment. Their experiment simulates a political caucus in which the participants *individually* had good reasons to perceive one candidate as favorable, but *collectively* did not. The simulation was something like this: Imagine you have four participants. Each one gets a sheet of information on two political candidates, Anna and Benni. Everybody in the group receives the same list with arguments about Anna. Anna's description contains four points in favor of her and four points against her. Benni's description is different. Everybody receives a description of four negative points and two positive points. The important thing is this: The negative points in Benni's description are the same in every list, while the positive points differ. This means that while everybody initially has two arguments for Benni and four against him, there exist eight arguments in favor of him and only two against him within the whole group. Consequently, in the beginning of the deliberation, everyone should be in favor of Anna, but after deliberation everybody should be in favor of Benni, since the balance of reasons clearly tilts in his favor. Yet Stasser and Titus's experiment with university students shows that participants often do not uncover the *hidden profile*. On the contrary, their result "suggests that group discussion tends to focus on information that members already share before discussion and information that supports, rather than opposes, the predominant sentiment within the group."[25] Gigone and Hastie confirm: "Cues have more impact on group choice when they are known by several group members before discussion than when they are known by a single group member, independent of their validity for the choice."[26] Stasser and Titus's initial paper has motivated many similar experiments. Lu and her coauthors summarize the last ten years of common knowledge effect research in a meta-study and find that "previous studies have consistently found that group members discuss disproportionately more common than unique information."[27] The coauthors further point out that although studies show that there are certain measures to ameliorate the common knowledge effect, "most studies find that a differential nevertheless remains."[28] Moreover, experiments show that "groups are less likely to repeat unshared information than shared information after it is first mentioned."[29] The common knowledge effect has also been shown to be robust under circumstances more akin to real-world scenarios.[30] Related results show that when a "shared task representation" exists within a group, "alternatives consistent with the representation will be easier to defend and thus more likely to end up as the group's collective choice."[31] Not surprisingly, Stasser, after many years of research, draws the conclusion that "if unique information surfaces at all, its impact is muted."[32]

The social comparison effect

While the *common knowledge effect* is about deliberators not picking up cues or evidence that were put on the table – figuratively speaking – *the social comparison effect* is about not putting cues or evidence on the table in the first place. The basic insight of studies of the social comparison effect is, basically, that people abhor playing the role of the sole dissenter. It is important to note that, while the common knowledge effect is associated with a distinct research field, studies on the social comparison effect are not.[33] I want to use the term here to denote the disposition of humans to conform to the majority opinion against better evidence. Hans Christian Andersen has enshrined this human weakness in literature with his story "The Emperor's New Clothes." Since anecdotal evidence and relying on the psychological insights of Danish poets is not good enough – at least not according to academic standards – social scientists from many fields have tried to reproduce the disposition of humans to conform or succumb to majority opinion even against superior evidence.

A well-known series of experiments that reproduced this psychological effect are the Asch conformity experiments.[34] In his experiments, Solomon Asch proved how susceptible the human psychology is to majority influence. Asch's experiment is pretty simple. Asch showed a group of students two cards. The first card had one line on it and the second card had three lines. The participants were then asked which line of the three lines matched the line of the first card in length. The interesting part in this experiment was that seven of the eight participants were confederates of Asch (i.e. actors). The confederates were told to answer 12 of 18 trials incorrectly. Every round Asch asked the participants to answer the question loudly so that every participant knew what everybody else was answering. The participants were seated in such a way that the only real participant was always the last to respond. The goal of the trial was to see whether the real participant would conform to the wrong answers of the confederates or stick to what he or she saw on the cards. Asch tested 123 real participants all in all and found that the real participants gave the wrong answer 36.8 percent of the time. A control group erred just 0.7 percent of the time.

An explanation for this behavior is surely that human beings in large wish to be perceived in a good light by their peers and thus dislike to take on the role of the contrarian. Sunstein comes to a similar conclusion: "People want to be perceived favorably by other group members, and also to perceive themselves favorably. Once they hear what others believe, they adjust their positions in the direction of the dominant position."[35]

Even though, ideally, a deliberative group would operate under the normative guidelines that Habermas has elaborated in his framework of an ideal speech situation,[36] real deliberative groups – be it in science, business or politics – are always embedded in a social context. Deliberations within a group are often dominated by a leading expert or a fashionable set of ideas. The individual with cognitively peripheral ideas thus not only needs to have considerable stamina to put forward her or his ideas, but also might reasonably fear consequent punishment. Punishment in this context must, of course, be understood rather broadly. In a business context, a superior might judge employees that do not support his or her ideas in business meetings as a possible threat and act accordingly when it comes to promotions. Similarly, exhibiting unorthodox views within scientific circles might harm our reputation and thus endanger our career. Surely, we would be mistaken to think that discourse in science is solely disinterested and only directed by the better argument. Max Planck, summarizing his career in his *Scientific Autobiography*, sadly remarked that "a new scientific truth does not triumph by convincing its opponents and making them see the light, but rather because its opponents eventually die, and a new generation grows up that is familiar with it."[37]

In some cases, the incentives of a collective group make it difficult for an individual to express her or his innovative ideas or tentative solutions. This may lead the individual to withhold any tentative problem-solutions from the public altogether or defend them only half-heartedly once they encounter opposition.

Deliberation inhibits creativity

In this section I want to look at how creative deliberative groups are in comparison to nominal groups. Nominal groups, as James Larson tells us, "are groups that comprise the same number of members as the interacting groups with which they are compared"[38]; the only difference is that the members of a nominal group are not interacting. If we compare the results of nominal groups to those of deliberative groups, we thus compare groups that interact with groups that do not. In general, we would expect that deliberative groups outperform nominal groups in tasks that require creativity. Deliberation, as I have outlined in Section 7.1, is associated with strong synergy effects; thinking together should, taking a cue from Page, allow deliberators to achieve *superadditivity* not only with respect to heuristics, but also when it comes to generating new ideas.

Interestingly enough, a host of experiments suggests that nominal groups often outperform deliberative groups when it comes to tasks that involve high amounts of creativity. The results of a "meta-analytic integration of previous research on productivity loss in brainstorming groups" show that, "generally, brainstorming groups are significantly less productive than nominal groups, in terms of both quantity and quality."[39] Furthermore, Larson writes that the central finding in the brainstorming literature is that "under most circumstances, groups demonstrated a very strong tendency to generate fewer ideas than an equivalent number of individuals working independently."[40]

This short overview suggests that letting people deliberate instead of polling them individually, followed by aggregating their answers, is not always a good idea. This is an interesting result, because deliberating presents an extra effort for everybody involved – we would thus in general assume that this extra effort should pay off in higher rates of creativity. This, as studies show, does not always hold. On the contrary, deliberation sometimes even leads to an 'assembly detriment.'

7.2.2 The problem of transaction costs

I want to leave the field of psychological research and turn to another factor that puts certain brakes on the epistemic capacity of deliberation: transaction costs. Imagine a group of fifty participants in which everybody has thirty minutes of speaking time. Such a group would need twenty-five hours just to let everybody speak. This numerical example reminds us that group deliberation processes are meaningful only with a relatively small number of participants for reasons of transaction costs. However, because group sizes need to be limited due to transaction costs, there is always a good chance that a particular group of deliberators does not include the particular agent with the best (tentative) solution. Although this point seems trivial, it is very important. In 1998, presumably all expert deliberation with regard to search engine optimization that took place in the boardrooms of many multi-million dollar companies, was far off target: The two people with the best tentative solution to the problem of search engine optimization were sitting in a garage in San Rafael.[41] Also, presumably until 2002, almost all expert deliberation taking place at Harvard, the Massachusetts Institute of Technology and Cambridge was off with regard to the *Poincaré conjecture*, while the individual with the best answer was in St. Petersburg living the life of an eremite. These somewhat flashy examples should not deceive us into thinking that it is just under special circumstances that an expert deliberation group does not include the best solver. *Indeed, it seems plausible to think that most expert deliberation groups do not include the best solver.* After all, every small group of experts in a particular deliberation group is somewhat randomly drawn from a very huge pool of all relevant experts. Thus, one big problem for deliberation groups is that they often cannot defer to the best solver, because the best solver simply is not a part of the group. Transaction costs thus severely limit the possibility of deliberation to make use of existing diversity.

7.2.3 Bounded rationality and the limits of deliberation

Up to this point, I have discussed the limits of deliberation from a psychological perspective and through the lens of transaction costs. In this section, I want to analyze the limits of deliberation from the perspective of bounded rationality. While there is no doubt that collectivizing inquiry can, both in principle and in practice, ameliorate some of the common weaknesses of individual inquiry, there are nevertheless certain limitations to individual inquiry that cannot be overcome. If we want to understand the limits of collective inquiry, it is thus advisable to understand the limits of individual inquiry first. For this reason, I want to discuss some aspects of human epistemic boundedness. What is commonly called 'bounded rationality' can be understood in at least two distinct ways. First of all, bounded rationality can be understood as an umbrella concept for a host of research that is concerned with locating failures with regard to norms of rationality. This concept is associated with the famous research of Daniel Kahneman and Amos Tversky in psychology and Richard Thaler in experimental economics.[42] Through the work of Sunstein and Thaler, the results have also found wide acknowledgement in political philosophy.[43] Bounded rationality, as "the discrepancy between human reasoning and the laws of probability or some form of optimization,"[44] however, is not what I am concerned with here. The reason for this is that these weaknesses of individual deliberation, like those I discussed in Section 7.2.1, can indeed be ameliorated by expert deliberation and certain deliberation techniques. Therefore, I am here concerned with a second, deeper understanding of bounded rationality that emphasizes that we are indeed

> in a wide variety of cases [precluded], from considering all the options and all the data not merely "practically," but, in fact, "in principle." [. . .] It is, rather, a fact about any being that is not infinite in her powers [and] it doesn't disappear simply by collectivizing enquiry.[45]

At this point, there is no full exposition of bounded rationality – neither of the first, nor of the second kind.[46] Evidently, spelling out an exposition of bounded rationality is very difficult. This also precludes me from delivering *en passant* an adequate account of bounded rationality. What I will provide instead is a short review of some elements of bounded rationality, which will be significant for a better appreciation of the subsequent argument in this section and the more general argument of this essay. I will briefly review the following five elements: inexhaustibility of description, fundamental uncertainty, reflexivity, deliberation about means, deliberation about ends and collective deliberation about tentative solutions.[47]

Inexhaustibility of description

As Rescher contends, "endlessly true remarks can be made about any real object."[48] Consider for instance all the true remarks that could be made about a specific pencil and its history. Let us for this purpose indulge for a moment in the self-narrated history of a very prominent pencil:

> My family tree begins with what in fact is a tree, a cedar of straight grain that grows in Northern California and Oregon. Now contemplate all the saws and trucks and rope and the countless other gear used in harvesting and carting the cedar logs to the railroad siding. Think of all the persons and the numberless skills that went into their fabrication: the mining of ore, the making of steel and its refinement into saws, axes, motors; the growing of hemp and bringing it through all the stages to heavy and strong rope; the logging camps with their beds and mess halls, the cookery and the raising of all the foods. [. . .] Consider the millwork in San Leandro. The cedar logs are cut into small, pencil-length slats less than one-fourth of an inch in thickness. These are kiln dried and then tinted for the same reason women put rouge on their faces.[49]

I will cut short the story here, before the pencil starts talking about the history of its graphite, which is "mined in Ceylon." What is important here is to point out that, until now, we have only learned about the production history of the pencil. But there are certainly many other dimensions of the pencil that we could talk about. We could talk about its shape, its weight, its use in arts and so on. The inexhaustibility of descriptions itself – as a philosophical concept – is grounded in the continuous growth of total knowledge itself. "New descriptive features ongoingly come into view with the progress of knowledge,"[50] thus the "realm of reality-appertaining fact inevitably outruns the reach of our descriptive information."[51] New descriptions can in turn lead to new perspectives, to new questions and – in the end – to new solutions. By collectivizing deliberation, we can surely consider a wider range of problem descriptions and solutions, but we certainly cannot consider every deliberation-relevant description of the problem and its solutions.

Fundamental uncertainty

Uncertainty must be distinguished from risk. A decision under risk takes place whenever "unambiguous probabilities"[52] can be assigned to all the possible outcomes of a decision. Hence the classic example of risk is roulette. If we cannot unambiguously assign probabilities to outcomes, or if we cannot even conceive of all possible outcomes, we are deciding under uncertainty.

Predictions and planning activities are especially open to uncertainty because, in the real world, we can seldom assign unambiguous probabilities, nor can we usually even conceive of all the possible outcomes. There are at least two major reasons why planning activities are riddled with uncertainty. One is reflexivity, which I will talk about in the following section, and the other is radical novelty. Radical novelty can be understood as unimaginable or unimagined future states or events.

> If [we] are planning now, at t_0, a course of action that we will take over some future period t_1–t_2, then, unavoidably, our understanding of the environment and opportunities for action during t_1–t_2 will be limited to what, at t_0, we can predict and/or imagine. But there are very good inductive grounds for believing that, on certain matters, our understanding at t_0 of planning-relevant environment and opportunities during t_1–t_2 will often be extremely poor.[53]

An example from the military might be suitable to further illuminate the point. Many defense departments in the 1990s ordered military equipment and invested in military research with cold war military scenarios in mind. The development of technology often takes many decades. Consequently, much of the military investments made in the 1980s and 1990s were instantly ineffective when, after 9/11, it became clear that the new battles would mainly take place in deserts and urban terrain.

Reflexivity

Another reason why planning for the future is often plagued by uncertainty is reflexivity. Reflexivity pertains if the explanations, predictions or actions of an observer about a certain system change the system itself. To give a simple example, if social scientists predict that over the next twenty years there will be a huge increase in obesity, it might very well be the case that that very prediction might induce politicians to issue policies to combat obesity. Another example for reflexivity is the self-fulfilling prophecy. Whereas in the first false, a self-fulfilling prophecy causes real-world changes that render the very prediction true.

Deliberation about means

What deliberation can achieve depends decidedly on the subject matter of the debate. The philosopher of science Larry Laudan distinguishes three stages of inquiry: the "context of discovery," the "context of pursuit" and "the context of ultimate justification."[54] He explains:

> For one thing, these three contexts mark the temporal, if not the logical, history of a concept. It is first discovered; if found worthy of pursuit, it is entertained; if further evaluation shows it to be worthy of belief, it is accepted.[55]

In principle, deliberation can be applied to every stage of inquiry. We can use deliberation to come up with new ideas,[56] we can discuss which ideas we want to pursue and we can deliberate about the worthiness of a solution, given some epistemic evaluation criteria.

The crucial point is this: Many hotly disputed questions in political philosophy, applied ethics and political theory are actually questions of implementation.[57] What we are doing in these discussions, at least to some extent, is essentially coming up with tentative solutions and debating about what tentative solution we want to pursue. In Laudan's schema we are thus moving back and forth between the "context of discovery" and "the context of pursuit." When we are deliberating about these problems we are thus not in a "context of justification," which includes, among other things, epistemic concepts like "evaluation, test, defense, success, truth, and confirmation."[58] Furthermore, what follows is that the solutions we will come up with, individually or collectively, will always be open for contention.[59] This is the case because the very knowledge we would need to have to be able to judge the tentative solution with a high degree of certainty is exactly *what we are missing in the context of pursuit*. Even if one of the tentative solutions X in deliberation is true (viewed from a god-like perspective), the advocates of X at the stage of deliberation do not usually have the means to demonstrate that X.[60]

This result then suggests that, on epistemic grounds, we should not have very high expectations of what collectivizing deliberation can achieve in the contexts of discovery and pursuit.[61]

Deliberation about ends

When it comes to the means-ends distinction, bounded rationality talk usually focuses on the means aspect. What I want to focus on in this section is the other part of the equation: the ends.[62] When it comes to hard problems, we are often not quite sure about what we want, or, to put it in the terms of the economist: our trade-off rate. This applies to individual decisions and (maybe even more so) to collective decisions. Let me first give a simple example. Consider that you really like white chocolate and you have four new brands of white chocolate. For every chocolate brand, you have a detailed list of the ingredients. In addition, you can examine the bar of chocolate with your eyes; you can also break the chocolate bar into small pieces, take in its scent and get a feel for its texture and density. Given that information, you have to rank the chocolate brands according to their expected tastiness. After this, you can eat the chocolate bars and thus test your preference ordering. It is plausible to think that, if we were to conduct such a test, many people would need to correct their initial orderings. The reason for that is that there seems to be a gap between the expectation and the actual tasting experience.

This seems to be true not only for actual taste experiences, but for a wide range of circumstances. The expectations derived from descriptions of a holiday differ from the actual holiday experience; the expectations derived from descriptions of a new mobile phone differ from the actual experience with the actual phone; and so on. This basic notion of the unavoidable gap between mere expectations and real experiences can be applied to any context of relevance in political theory. If we contemplate different social states, for example, we might infer that the more distant a social state is from the current status quo, the harder it is to foresee all the relevant facts and thus to evaluate the social state correctly. This is essentially affirmed by psychologists:

> By virtue of their novelty, information relevant to the key attributes of highly original new ideas will not be readily accessible. People, as a result, will tend not to apply this information in evaluation and decision-making. This point is of some importance because accurate assessment of relevant attributes is required for appropriate evaluation of new ideas, and these attributes will be less accessible for highly original new ideas than less original new ideas.[63]

I would like to generalize the point in the following manner: when it comes to hard problems and a set of solutions to the problem, we can only have expectations or hypotheses about how we would like the actual outcomes. This means that the ranking of possible worlds at the stage of deliberation and at the stage after deliberation might be very different when we experience the different worlds.

Collective deliberation about tentative solutions

In this section, I want to inquire under which general conditions a tentative solution – which ex post will turn out to be true (TS_t) – will be selected by a deliberating group. I should first emphasize that a tentative solution, which will ex post be corroborated, does not usually have any properties that allow deliberators to identify them ex ante without a doubt. Maybe there are properties that allow us to sort out some tentative solutions, but this is again a very difficult question. It is common knowledge that, historically, even tentative solutions or working hypotheses that seemed to be very implausible (or were even thought to have been falsified), turned out to be right. Furthermore, since the deliberators within the group do not know which tentative solution is the right one, they also lack the reasons that establish or back up truth claims as well as the pull that accompanies the reasons that establish or corroborate truth. To give a quick example: If we want to know whether medicine X cures disease Y, the best way to find out is to conduct clinical double-blind tests. If the test confirms that X cures Y in 85 percent of the cases, we have gained some piece of information. Consequently, if someone were to ask us why we believe that X cures Y, we can state our theory, but, in addition, we can also state our test results. Since diverse theories tend to predict many results in the result space, empirical evidence is often the best way to convince somebody of a particular solution. Unfortunately, the one reason that potentially should win over the majority (having the empirical evidence) is missing in the repertoire of the TS_t advocate.

Nonetheless, maybe we can say something about the circumstances under which deliberation tends to defer to TS_t. I think it is obvious that, generally, a group of reasonable deliberators will choose to pursue TS_t if it initially has a strong majority. I thus will be mainly concerned here with a more specific question, namely: Under which circumstances will a deliberative group *pick the best tentative solution, in the case the tentative solution is initially a minority position within the group?*

To get a better understanding of the question, I propose the following thought experiment: Let us imagine that we have ten experts deliberating about the best answer to solve X. Of the ten experts, eight share a tentative solution. Their perspective thus can be called *central*.[64] We can think of them as representing the mainstream or a current paradigm. The remaining two experts hold two different tentative solutions. The tentative solutions are thus in a sense *peripheral*. We thus have in total three tentative solutions. Let us further assume that the best tentative solution is a peripheral solution. The question is then: Under which circumstance will the majority converge to the minority position?

Rationality demands a tipping scale of reasons

Let us begin with a simple observation: Peripheral tentative solutions in general have to fight an uphill battle in which they need to present sufficient reasons, so that the scale of reasons (from the point of view of the majority), tips in the direction of the peripheral view. If the peripheral view cannot deliver these reasons, the majority will simply stick to the default option. According to the standards of rationality, we should – after sufficient deliberation – choose the option with the better reasons in favor of it. A group decision of deliberators that would not conform to this minimal standard of rationality would be to some extent unintelligible. Imagine a situation in which a group of experts, who are invested in their own methods of conceiving and solving problems, would throw their tool set overboard and accept another (foreign) perspective, even though they think their own tool set better. I think that if we encountered such a case, we would surely look for external reasons (i.e. threats or bribes) that would explain the seemingly irrational behavior of those experts. A minimal requirement of rationality thus demands that TS_t does not only need to be plausible, but also must give sufficient reason, so that the scale of reasons tilts in the direction of TS_t (from the perspective of the majority).[65] But maybe I can say a little more about the material circumstances under which the scale of reasons tips in the direction of the minority.

In general, it is surely right to think that groups will consider and recognize the reasons in favor of a peripheral tentative solution, if these reasons are in some sense highly salient. If salience and opaqueness are the corresponding endpoints of a scale, I can state the following: The more cognitive or inferential steps it takes for the majority to grasp the reasons in favor of a peripheral tentative solution, the more opaque are the reasons of the solution. The more opaque the given reason is, the more implausible it will seem to be for a particular deliberator. Opaqueness and salience are thus distance measures with regard to cognitive models. Opaqueness and salience furthermore are not the same as plausibility and implausibility, but instead predictors for the plausibility of a reason. The more opaque the tentative solution is, the more important it will be for the inquirers to share a relevant *system of inference*.[66] A system of inference eases the process of taking inferential steps to see the reasons for a given peripheral tentative solution. Furthermore, the system must be relevant to the problem: If the deliberators are concerned with an economic problem, nothing is to be gained by them sharing certain models in astrophysics (understood as a system of inference).

A few comments seem in place here. The term 'system of inference' should be understood very broadly. A system of inference includes rules of inference as known from classical logic, but it also includes (among other systems) scientific models, religious belief systems, a register of authorities and the senses. Let us give an example to clarify what I mean by a system of inference.

Consider this case of a laymen's deliberation: Gabriel, who defends a peripheral tentative solution, tells the other deliberators that Simon – an expert who is cherished by the whole group – agrees with his solution. This induces the group to believe Gabriel's tentative solution. Here is another example: A group of neoclassical economists is deliberating about a certain political measure. If Gabriel, who defends a peripheral tentative solution, can show the majority that his solution strictly follows from the shared neoclassical model of economics, he surely has a better chance of convincing his peers. A shared inferential system thus is a tool to provide other members of the group with standing reasons for accepting some other, not yet shared, reason.

In my broad definition of a system of inference, the senses themselves in some cases can also induce a change of beliefs in a group. Imagine that an expert group of deliberators wants to create a new ice cream flavor that maximizes profit. Six of ten deliberators think we should create a new variety of chocolate ice cream, because most consumers like chocolate. Three other deliberators think we should create a new sherbet without refined sugar, because health is an ever-more important issue with consumers. One of the deliberators, call her Rea, suggests that we should create an ice cream with big chunks of cookie dough in it. This last proposal strikes everybody as quite peripheral. At first glance, none of the other nine experts can see any merit in the cookie dough solution. Some of the deliberators find the idea inherently disgusting, others just point out that there is no empirical evidence in favor of the cookie dough thesis. Luckily, when it comes to ice cream, there exists an inferential system that makes the opaque merits of the solution instantly visible: giving samples. Let us assume, the experts taste the new variety and judge that the ice cream tastes unbelievably good. Thus Rea managed to make the merits of her tentative solution visible. Note though, that Rea's tentative solution is now only seen as *more plausible* by the deliberators. Rea has not shown that her ice cream will maximize profit for the ice cream company.[67]

I can thus summarize: In order to convince a majority of a peripheral TS_{t}, we need to present sufficient reason, so that the scale of reasons from the perspective of the majority tips over in its advantage. Under two conditions, a peripheral TS_t has a chance to win the uphill battle. A majority will sometimes defer to the peripheral tentative solution if the reasons for the peripheral TS_t are (a) highly salient or (b) if there is a relevant system of inference that eases the process of taking inferential steps to seeing the merits of a given peripheral TS_t. On the flip side, if (a) the reasons in favor of the peripheral TS_t are very opaque to the majority of deliberators and if (b) the majority and the holder of the peripheral TS_t do not share a relevant system of interferences, there is little chance that the majority will defer to the peripheral TS_t.

7.3 Conclusion: the conservative bias of deliberation

Our results suggest that Aristotle's confidence in expert deliberation is somewhat misplaced. As we have seen, transaction costs as well as our psychological and epistemic outfit put certain brakes and limits on what we should expect from deliberation.

In this section, I want to conclude by arguing that the findings of Section 7.2 suggest that deliberation tends to exhibit a *conservative bias*. Conservatism is partly about disregarding novel ideas and solutions, while emphasizing beliefs, institutions and values that are already established. Furthermore, to say that a deliberative result is conservative means that the result of deliberation is in line with the beliefs of the majority of deliberators before they entered the debate. Thus, we would expect that if nine Keynesians and one Hayekian macro-economist talk about the best way of a recovery for the economy, the final statement of the debate will be Keynesian in spirit. Along the same line, we would expect that if one Keynesian and nine Hayekian macro-economists were discussing the best way for an economic recovery, the final statement of the debate would be Hayekian in spirit. Regardless of the content, both results would be conservative. The term 'conservative' here thus decidedly does not refer to the content of the deliberation.[68] In order to argue that deliberation tends to have a strong conservative bias, I will summarize the results of Section 7.2:

- Deliberation empirically tends to emphasize what is shared at the expense of the novel and unshared (7.2.1).
- Innovative solutions that initially have few supporters within the group of deliberators usually will not be chosen or even be seriously considered (7.2.1).
- People hate to be the sole dissenter and thus often do not share knowledge or reasons that might threaten their status within the group (7.2.1).
- There is evidence that deliberation inhibits creativity (7.2.1).
- Deliberation as mechanism for aggregating knowledge is very expensive with regard to transaction costs. This means that very innovative solutions will often not even be represented in the debate due to transaction costs (7.2.2).

- The very nature of the political problems that we are interested in often precludes even well-meaning experts from recognizing ex ante which solution will ex post turn out best; under uncertainty, the majority opinion ex ante tends to prevail (7.2.3).

In conclusion, I can thus state that deliberation does not seem to be particularly well-suited to dealing with novelty or with innovative solutions. This in turn sheds doubt on the thesis that the deliberative approach is especially well-suited to enable society to gain from diversity.

Notes

1 List and Goodin (2001).
2 Anderson (2006), Landemore and Page (2015).
3 Anderson (2006, p. 9).
4 Stasser and Titus (2003).
5 Page (2007b)
6 Collins and Guetzkow (1964, p. 58).
7 Collins and Guetzkow (1964, p. 58).
8 It should be noted that my use of the concept of synergy is also different from Larson's definition of synergy as outlined in Larson (2010, pp. 6–7).
9 Janis (1982, p. 3).
10 Laughlin and Adamopoulos (1980).
11 For a good introduction into the methodology of these tests, see Larson (2010, chap. 4).
12 Larson (2010, pp. 122–124).
13 Stasson and Bradshaw (1995, p. 297). Emphasis added.
14 Sunstein (2006, p. 194).
15 Hill (1982), Larson (2010), Lu *et al.* (2011) and Stasser and Dietz-Uhler (2001).
16 Stasser and Dietz-Uhler (2001, pp. 31–34).
17 This is a of course a rather restricted sense of competition.
18 Stasser and Dietz-Uhler (2001, p. 32).
19 Laughlin and Adamopoulos (1980), see also Laughlin and Ellis (1986).
20 Stasser and Dietz-Uhler (2001, p. 33).
21 Adapted from Stasser and Dietz-Uhler (2001, p. 33).
22 Source: Stasser and Dietz-Uhler (2001, p. 34).
23 Gigone and Hastie (1993, p. 960).
24 Stasser and Titus (1985).
25 Stasser and Titus (1997, p. 81).
26 Gigone and Hastie (1997, p. 139).
27 Lu *et al.* (2011, p. 55).
28 Lu *et al.* (2011, p. 55).
29 Stasser (1999, pp. 49–50).
30 Stasser *et al.* (2012).
31 Tindale *et al.* (2001, p. 13).
32 Stasser (1999, p. 49).
33 The term seems to be at least originally inspired by Festinger (1954). In contrast, I draw on a much simpler concept by D'Agostino (2010).
34 Cf. Asch (1952), Asch (1951).
35 Sunstein (2006, p. 194).
36 Habermas (1990, pp. 43).

37 Quoted from Kuhn (2012, p. 150).
38 Larson (2010, p. 13).
39 Mullen *et al.* (1991, p. 3). See also Brown (2001, p. 176).
40 Larson (2010, p. 117).
41 Google (2014).
42 Kahnemann and Thaler (1991), Kahneman and Tversky (1979), Tversky and Kahneman (1981).
43 Thaler and Sunstein (2010), Thaler and Sunstein (2003).
44 Gigerenzer and Selten (2001, p. 6).
45 D'Agostino (2010, p. 20).
46 Grüne-Yanoff (2007).
47 A deeper and more thorough exposition of bounded rationality can be found in: D'Agostino (2010, chap. 3).
48 Rescher (1998, p. 31).
49 Read (1999).
50 Rescher (1998, p. 32).
51 Rescher presents a much more formal argument than I do here.
52 Binmore (2009, p. 35).
53 D'Agostino (2010, p. 23).
54 Laudan (1980, p. 174).
55 Laudan (1980, p. 174).
56 As I have discussed earlier, experimental evidence puts a huge question mark behind collective deliberation in coming up with new ideas.
57 Compare the discussion about deep and shallow pluralism in Chapter 1, Section 1.2.
58 Kordig (1978, p. 110).
59 An interesting point, which I cannot pursue further is, in how far error is necessary to finding new and creative solutions:

> One of these models holds that error is an inherent aspect of creative thought, potentially a beneficial aspect, as people capitalize on error, to take advantage of serendipitous juxtapositions and use these juxtapositions as a basis for the progressive refinement of new ideas.
>
> (Mumford *et al.* 2006, p. 76).

60 Interestingly enough, even after we have tested a tentative solution, what we can say about the solution is just that (given we share evaluative standards) the new situation after implementing X is better than the original situation. What we have not shown is that X performs a better job than the competing tentative solutions that we have not yet tried out.
61 Constraining the generation of tentative solutions with too heavy a justificatory burden would surely hamper scientific progress. Popper confirms this when he writes:

> the initial stage, the act of conceiving or inventing a theory, seems [...] neither to call for logical analysis nor to be susceptible of it [...] there is no such thing as the logical method of having new ideas or a logical reconstruction of this process.

Having somewhat looser constraints for coming up with ideas is important since "innovative reasoning frequently is inconsistent with established principles and constraints."
62 I already discussed this in great detail in Chapter 1, Section 1.2. Therefore, I will be brief here.
63 Licuanan *et al.* (2007, p. 4).
64 The distinction between central and peripheral solutions is inspired by a similar distinction by Kameda *et al.* (1997).
65 An interesting question is of course the case in which the weights of opposing reasons cancel each other out. This question, although interesting, is not important for our endeavor and would lead us too far astray. For a good discussion of the problem of indeterminacy, see Gaus (2011c, chap. 16).

66 This exposition is influenced by Stasser and Dietz-Uhler (2001, p. 33).
67 It could very well be the case that the taste of the experts is not representative. It might also be the case that it is very expensive to produce that ice cream, and the price increase is higher than the marginal increase in taste from the consumer's perspective.
68 Of course, in many cases, the conservative solution will indeed be the best solution judged from a god's eye view.

8 Polycentric paradigm

In this chapter, I will pursue two goals. First, I want to give a general outline of polycentrism in Section 8.1. Although many philosophers and social scientists in the last sixty years have touched upon this idea, there are very few general statements of polycentrism. Second, I want to argue that 'polycentric search' outperforms 'expert deliberation' when it comes to hard problems. The argument proceeds in two steps. In Section 8.2, I will argue that that the two epistemically most productive institutions – 'the market' and 'organized science' – can legitimately be viewed as instances of polycentrism. In Section 8.3, I want to explain why polycentric systems outperform 'expert deliberation' when it comes to hard problems. In short, I will make the argument that polycentric search outperforms expert deliberation, because it is able to neutralize the inhibitors of collective deliberation outlined in Chapter 7 and thus take full advantage of the possible gains of diversity.

8.1 Polycentric search

The term 'polycentricity' was first introduced by Michael Polanyi in his *Logic of Liberty* (1951). Here, Polanyi makes the argument that, for epistemic reasons, the sciences as well as economic systems should be organized in a polycentric instead of a monocentric manner. He writes:

> My argument for freedom in science bears a close resemblance to the classical doctrine of economic individualism. The scientists of the world are viewed as a team setting out to explore the existing openings for discovery and it is claimed that their efforts will be efficiently co-ordinated if – and only if – each is left to his own inclinations. This statement is very similar to Adam Smith's claim with regard to a team of business men, drawing on the same market of productive resources for the purpose of satisfying different parts of the same system of demand.[1]

Polanyi further explains that "these two systems of maximized utility are indeed based on similar principles; and more than that: they are only two examples of a whole set of parallel cases."[2] While Polanyi sees many other social institutions apart from the market and organized science[3] as polycentric, he expands only on one other case, which is the common law.[4] Although Polanyi's concept of 'polycentricity' never experienced a breakthrough in its own right, it still influenced the studies of a surprisingly diverse field. His concept diffused to law studies[5] and the philosophy of science; its biggest impact, however, was on governance studies[6] and political economy[7]. There are also interesting controversies about how Polanyi's interlinked ideas of "polycentricity," "personal knowledge" and "spontaneous order" influenced Hayek's concept of spontaneous order and Thomas Kuhn's philosophy of science.[8]

The concept of polycentrism that I will employ here is influenced by Polanyi, but essentially builds on the work of Aligica and Vlad Tarko.[9] The reason for this is that Polanyi's concept of polycentricity was interlinked with his own contentious philosophy of science and in many ways remained sketchy. The outline presented by the social scientists Aligica and Tarko, on the contrary, while inspired by Polanyi, is very accessible. Let me spend a few more words on the term 'polycentricity' itself. In Polanyi's original statement, polycentricity is a description of a certain kind of interaction or relation between a multitude of decision centers, or knots.[10] Yet, Aligica and Tarko mostly use the term to talk about *the institutions* that facilitate the interaction of multiple decision centers. To avoid this ambiguity, I will speak of 'polycentric systems' or 'polycentrism' when referring to the institutional framework and 'evolutionary competition' when addressing the processes between various decision centers. In the conceptual analysis by Aligica and Tarko, polycentric systems have three basic features:

1 An overarching system of rules.
2 A multiplicity of decision centers.
3 An evolutionary competition between the decision centers.

Let me discuss each point briefly, before I go into an in-depth analysis of polycentrism and its constitutive parts (see Sections 8.1.1). A necessary component of polycentric systems is that they provide an "overarching system of rules"[11] and an "institutional and cultural framework"[12] or constitution. This condition differentiates polycentric systems from anarchic ones. While an anarchistic system has many decision centers, it lacks an overarching regulatory framework. Furthermore, polycentric systems feature a multiplicity of decision centers. A system has a multiplicity of decision centers, if diverse players are free "to implement their different methods"[13] and if there exist different decision centers at every point in time. Freedom in this context means that they are permitted, given certain restraints, to actively "exercise their different opinions."[14] The third condition is that the rules of the game generate an "evolutionary competition between the different decision centers' ideas, methods and ways [. . .] of doing things."[15] Before analyzing the constitutive parts of polycentric systems in more detail, I first want to briefly say something about the connection between diversity and polycentricity and expand on the definition of polycentricity by Aligica and Tarko.

8.1.1 Polycentrism and diversity

The second part of this essay essentially asks how we – as a society – can make use of our instrumental and evaluative diversity, our diverse 'hunches,' perspectives and heuristics. Polycentric systems can be understood as social technologies for *exploiting* and *dealing with* diversity. In Sections 8.2 and 8.3, I will discuss in detail how polycentric systems are able to make use of diversity. Right now, I want to come back to the epistemic premises on which the polycentric approach rests. As I stated in Chapter 6, the polycentric approach rests on the premise that in the face of hard problems, the knife of reason is usually too blunt to tell us unambiguously where we should look for solutions. Will we find those precious islands of knowledge by sailing to the south or rather to the north? Very often, there is just no way to know for sure. Different explorers have to rely on their 'hunches,' and sometimes the most unlikely candidate will return home with the biggest bounty. This problem obviously pertains in science, in the market and every other area where we are confronted with hard problems. That is why the polycentric paradigm is premised on the idea that, when it comes to hard problems, real-world experiments are usually indispensable in order to (a) *find out what works and who knows best,* (b) *reveal what we really want* and (c) *diffuse knowledge about what works and who knows best.* A polycentric system can thus be understood as an *institutional framework that facilitates a regulated process of experimental*[16] *exploration of a certain search space to create knowledge.* This process of experimental exploration itself is then fueled by our instrumental and evaluative diversity. Let us now turn to a more detailed analysis of the constitutive parts of a polycentric system.

A regulatory framework for competition

In principle, a polycentric system's *regulatory framework* could be forged by a diverse set of regulatory agencies or social processes. In this essay, I am concerned with the rules of the game of a nation state. For that reason, I will here focus on the government of a nation state and its responsibility to regulate polycentric systems. The regulatory framework of a polycentric system has several distinct tasks. I want to deal primarily with two: regulating the *scope* of exploration and the *frequency* with which a search space is being explored.

In modern democracies, the constitution regulates which issues can be decided at the legislative level. The decisions at the legislative level in turn influence and affect what is done at the operational level. The regulatory framework of a certain polycentric system should be understood as the cumulative result of the constitutional, legislative and informal rules that affect the day-to-day decisions within a certain search space. The regulatory framework basically defines the boundaries – or the *scope* – of the search space. In regulating the boundaries, the framework prescribes which hypotheses can and which cannot be tested. An example might be illuminating: If we are strolling through the streets of Berlin, New York or Tokyo, we will notice that there is no great diversity in the design of new cars – especially in comparison with the designs of earlier decades. The reason behind the diminishing diversity of car designs is the increase of directives and regulations. Every new rule and regulation in effect curbs the total design space of cars. The existing regulations for car designs encompass rules for the "location and identification of controls and displays," "occupant protection in interior impact" and rules about what materials can be used in the interior of the car.[17] The design space is further diminished by regulations about the "permissible sound levels and the exhaust system of motor vehicles."[18] There are also rules that prescribe how many headlights a car is allowed to have, rules about how far headlights need to be apart from each other and so on.[19] Since modern car producers usually want to sell their cars in many markets around the world, the actual design space for cars is limited by the combination of directives and regulations from the European Union, United States of America, Japan and many other countries. Every new regulation curbs the design space and thus limits the possibilities of car designs.

The regulatory framework of a polycentric system defines and limits its search space. But the rules of the game not only determine the scope of the search space, but they also influence the frequency of searches. The regulatory framework can steer the frequency of search with a wide array of tools. One way of steering the frequency of search is limiting or promoting the entry to a particular search space. For instance, if the governments of modern nation states did not promote scientific research, the search spaces of physics, metaethics or classical Chinese poetry would not be as thoroughly explored as they currently are. Depending on its goals, a framework can either promote the frequency of search by incentivizing entry or limit the frequency of search by making entry and search more costly.

To get a better grasp of the responsibilities of the government within the polycentric paradigm, Polanyi's distinction between supervision and planning is quite helpful. "Planning by definition," writes Polanyi specialist Mark T. Mitchell "entails a central authority that initiates and directs the actions of all practitioners in a vertical command structure."[20] The job of the government in a polycentric system, on the contrary, is 'supervision.' Polanyi explains:

> Supervision presupposes human activities which are initiated from a great multitude of centres, and it aims at regulating these manifold impulses in conformity with their inherent purpose. It achieves this by making generally available social machinery and other regulated opportunities for independent action, and by letting all the individual agents interact through a medium of freely circulating ideas and information.[21]

In polycentric systems, the job of the government then, is to supervise the search by a multiplicity of diverse agents, as well as to set appropriate boundaries and incentives to explore the search space. I want to touch upon another important point here. As I have mentioned, it is the government's task to regulate the entrance to a certain search space. In many countries, for instance, a special license to distill whisky is needed to explore the search space for new bourbons. On one hand, this might well limit the frequency in which this particular search space will be explored. On the other hand, such a regulation might enhance food security for consumers. A related issue is this: Since every search space would presumably benefit from more inquirers, but inquirers are scarce, there is a trade-off concerning the innovation rate within different polycentric systems. By setting incentives, one way or another, governments necessarily influence the innovation rate across search spaces.[22] The regulatory framework of a polycentric system is thus necessarily involved in managing value trade-offs. I will come back to that point on several occasions.

Many entrepreneurs – a multitude of decision centers

In a polycentric system, diverse decision centers are allowed and sometimes even encouraged to pursue their own ideas, tentative solutions and projects. These decision centers, or entrepreneurial agents, might be individuals, teams of experts, companies, communities or – as we will learn later – cities. Which project or tentative hypothesis an entrepreneurial agent deems worthy of pursuit is a complex function of her or his values, beliefs, ideals and her or his risk profile. Diversity in values, ideals, risk profiles or trade-off rates leads entrepreneurial agents to set out in different directions and explore different parts of the search space. Allowing diverse entrepreneurial agents to pursue their different projects within a suitable regulatory framework enables society to discover valleys and mountains that would have never been discovered if people had homogeneous values, ideals or trade-off rates. Entrepreneurial walks through the search space have certain features of a public good. This becomes clear when we look at unsuccessful innovators. Take a scientist who has pledged her life to a heterodox idea, but still, after many years of continuous effort, has nothing to show for it. If she records her work, the community of scientists will learn more about some uncharted territory of the landscape, but the one who had to pay the highest price for this unsuccessful endeavor was the particular scientist. This is also true for the marketplace, where entrepreneurs on a daily basis try to push for innovations knowing that most of the innovative attempts will not succeed. If an entrepreneur with an innovative idea of how to cater vegetarian products to the wider population opens a restaurant with his own money, but needs to close shop after a year, everybody in the vicinity knows that there is actually not enough demand for a vegetarian restaurant, but the entrepreneur was the one who paid for that new piece of knowledge.[23]

Diversity in values and ideals, in summary, becomes an asset in polycentric systems, since it naturally leads to a more comprehensive exploration of the search space. Furthermore, diversity in values ensures that entrepreneurs will search different parts of the search space, which, on a social level, facilitates a better spreading of risks.

An artificial process of evolutionary competition

Polycentric systems – in contrast to processes of natural selection – have an inherently teleological property. I can define a polycentric system, in slight deviation from my earlier statement, as 'an institutional framework that sets up an artificial process of evolutionary competition to explore a certain search space in order to further a bundle of goals.' At this point, I want to illuminate what I mean by an 'artificial process' of evolutionary competition. To get a better understanding, it is useful to distinguish between 'artificial' or 'purposeful' on the one hand and 'natural' or 'blind' on the other hand. The best example for natural or blind evolution is biological evolution. The selection pressures that animals face in nature are not put in place purposefully; nature rather selects blindly. Take a population of rabbits for instance. At t_1 the rabbits are subjected to many centuries of harsh winters; later, at t_2, the same population is confronted with a huge increase in fast-running carnivores. If we look at the population of rabbits in t_3 and compare it to t_1, we may discover that the rabbits have genetically adapted to the new environment. By the same logic, the rabbit population would have most likely shown a set of different traits if they had been subjected to other kinds of selection pressures. Natural selection is thus in a sense random. This blind selection can be contrasted with 'artificial' or 'purposeful selection' that can be created through human institutions. In *The Variation of Animals and Plants Under Domestication,* Charles Darwin writes:

> Although man does not cause variability and cannot even prevent, he can select, preserve and accumulate the variation given to him by the hand of nature almost in any way in which he chooses. [. . .] Man may select and preserve each successive variation, with the distinct intention of improving and altering a breed, in accordance with a preconceived idea.[24]

Pets are typically not selected for by blind evolution, but by purposeful selection. For example, we tend to select dogs not according to their likely fitness in rough winter nights, but to a whole other set of criteria, such as looks, kindness towards children and so on. The same goes for our foods. Fruits, for instance, are often artificially selected for sweetness. In addition to distinguishing natural from artificial selection, we can also distinguish between natural and artificial variation. While it might not have been possible in Darwin's time to create artificial diversity (or variety), human beings nowadays can influence the rate of variation in different systems.

Let us apply these insights to polycentric systems. I have defined a polycentric system as an institutional framework that sets up and facilitates an 'artificial process of evolutionary competition.' We can now appreciate that the term 'evolutionary competition' in this statement refers to a process that can encompass both *artificial variation* and *artificial selection*. In the marketplace, governments often provide special funds for start-ups and thereby increase the diversification of supply in a specific market. At the time, what gets produced depends on an artificial selection criterion: 'consumer's preferences.' In Hobbes's state of nature, on the contrary, what is produced is not a function of consumer preference, but a function of a host of very different variables. In Hobbes's state of nature, life is nasty, brutish and short. Under those conditions, people will limit their productive activities in general to what they themselves can consume and carry with them.

Let us now turn to another but related discussion: the relation between artificial evolution and spontaneous order. The evolutionary process within a polycentric system can be understood as a spontaneous order. A spontaneous order can be differentiated from a planned order by the intention of the agents. In a spontaneous order, the problem on a macro-level – which as Chrysostomos Mantzavinos notes, can be characterized as such only by an external observer – is solved as a side effect of agents solving their own problems.[25] In a planned order, on the contrary, the problem on the macro-level must first be recognized as such and then be solved by a conscious effort of the agents. Since 'spontaneous order' is strongly associated with Hayek, a comment seems to be necessary. Although Hayek sometimes seems to have a very encompassing concept of spontaneous order, he clearly distinguishes the rules of the game and its product (the spontaneous order):

> While the rules on which a spontaneous order rests, may also be of spontaneous origin, this need not always be the case [...] and it is at least conceivable that the formation of a spontaneous order relies entirely on rules that were deliberately made. The spontaneous character of the resulting order must therefore be distinguished from the spontaneous origin of the rules on which it rests, and it is possible that an order which would still have to be described as spontaneous rests on rules which are entirely the result of deliberate design.[26]

What is interesting is that, in Hayek as well as in Polanyi, there seem to be at least two kinds of spontaneous orders. In the first kind, the rules of the game are itself subject to evolution as opposed to planning. Morality, the crafts, language and many more, seem to fall into this category, according to both philosophers.[27] The second kind, however, seems to be very similar to the concept we are currently exploring.[28]

Let us now turn to another question. Throughout this chapter, I have depicted evolutionary competition as a search process. In this section, I want to evaluate evolutionary competition from an epistemic point of view. In particular, I want to inquire whether a polycentric system will always, or at least with some certainty, find the global optimum in a given search space. There are at least three important aspects to the question. First, it is usually not possible to tell – for real-world applications – whether we have indeed found a global optimum, because identifying a global optimum would presuppose a god's-eye view. Hayek interestingly enough has understood this point very early:

> When, however, we do not know in advance the facts we wish to discover with the help of competition, we are also unable to determine how

> effectively competition leads to the discovery of all the relevant circumstances that could have been discovered.[29]

Hayek continues:

> The curious fact that the merits of competition cannot be empirically verified in precisely those cases in which it is of interest is also shared by the discovery procedures of science in general. The advantages of established scientific procedures cannot themselves be scientifically demonstrated.[30]

A second aspect is the following. Even if in a certain search space, there is a search strategy that would find the global optimum eventually, it might be the case that the selection mechanism of a particular polycentric system terminates the search before its time. We can imagine that such a preemptive selection is common in the marketplace, where start-ups often have only very limited time spans to prove themselves before they run out of money. Luigi Marengo makes the same point, when he writes:

> It is remarkable that correct [. . .] strategies might not always prevail when nested in competitive environments characterized by some form of selection. In fact, while they are able always to locate the global optimum with certainty, the time required might be so long that they are actually eliminated by the selection mechanism.[31]

Marengo has also pointed out a third important aspect: Even if the selection mechanism works perfectly and does not prematurely terminate the search, it might very well be the case that the generative mechanisms of a polycentric system would not produce the best solution in the first place.

> In problems whose solutions involves the exploration of high-dimensional spaces, agents endowed with limited computational capabilities and with a limited knowledge of the interdependencies can explore only a subset, possibly very small, of solutions. Even if we assume that the selection mechanism which selects among alternative solutions works perfectly [. . .], the outcome of selection is bound by the set of solutions produced by the generative mechanism. It may well be the case that optimal or even 'good' solutions will never be generated at all, and thus that they will never be selected by any selection mechanism whatsoever.[32]

8.2 Two polycentric systems: market and science

In the previous sections, I stated that scholars who worked on the concept of polycentricity have long argued that organized science and the market system can be understood as instantiations of polycentrism. In this section, I want to make the case that organized science and the market can be legitimately viewed as polycentric systems.

8.2.1 The market

In order to make the case that the market can be legitimately viewed as a polycentric system, I need to confirm that our current market order features the three components of a polycentric order. In this section, I am thus concerned with interpreting the market order in polycentric terms.

In all modern nation states, competition between different agents in the market is restrained by a *regulatory framework* of some sort. This regulatory framework "has the task to maintain the proper functioning of the competitive pro[c]ess, i.e., to safeguard competition against restraints and the use of 'unfair means'."[33] Ideally, this framework ensures "that the only road to business success is through the narrow gate of better performance in service of the consumer."[34] An important part of such a framework is usually an anti-trust agency. The responsibility of this agency is to sustain competition and fend off tendencies towards monopoly or oligopoly. Think about the following case: The three biggest suppliers of food threaten a supermarket chain that they will not supply their goods if the supermarket chain continues to rent shelf space to their new competitor. If the conglomerate were successful, their evolutionary survival would result from their threat potential and not from their ability to satisfy consumer demand. Although there are some doubts about the persistence of such power asymmetries in free markets, similar scenarios are at least imaginable. The regulatory framework of the market, as it is understood here, encompasses a whole range of policy measures to ensure competition and prevent collusion. Such measures include special funds for start-ups, special training for entrepreneurs and tax exemptions for small businesses.

Let us now turn to the second condition. If competition is ensured, the market features a multitude of entrepreneurs. Given a suitable regulatory framework, entrepreneurs can make a profit only by solving the problems of consumers. "Entrepreneurs," as Mantzavinos explains, "participating in the exchange process [. . .] face a constant flow of new problems deriving ultimately from the volatility and peculiarity of consumers' wants."[35] The entrepreneurs' main goal is to satisfy the desires of consumers better than the competition. To achieve this goal, entrepreneurs need to continually search the product space for better solutions. Since entrepreneurs work under uncertainty, they can never be sure whether a new line of products will find consumer approval. From this vantage point,

> the supply of products is best understood as the testing of certain types of hypotheses: how effective is the bundle of parameters such as price, quality, service and so on in solving the problems of consumers, that is, satisfying their wants?[36]

Consequently, in buying and in abstaining from buying, the consumers reveal their wants, and the entrepreneurs' hypotheses are corroborated or falsified. In the continual process of hypothesis creation and feedback, the 'search space of consumer wants' is explored. Of course, this search space should not be understood as constant or invariable. Preferences change over time, and so does the geography of the search space.

The marketplace is intimately connected with the idea of competition. Competition can be qualified as a process

> during which [. . .] knowledge about possibilities of substitution (i.e., opportunity cost) is discovered and disseminated, control of the use of property is exerted through actual and potential substitution of partners (and objects) of exchange, and incentives to reassess the individual structure of property rights are signaled in coded form through the pecuniary external effects of transactions.[37]

While there is no doubt that the market process is competitive, we might still wonder if market competition can be legitimately qualified as 'evolutionary.' Conceptually, evolution has three important features: variation, selection, and the survival and growth of the selected. I have already mentioned that entrepreneurs – backed up by the regulatory framework of the polycentric system – create variation. The selection environment of the market has two important features: the rules of the game and the consumers. The rules of the game prescribe which kinds of hypotheses or experiments can be undertaken and by whom. In Germany, for instance, only people with specific certificates are allowed to experiment with brewing beer. At the same time, the rules of the game prohibit what substances can be used to enhance the beverage. A marijuana beer – while is might be successful – is not in the set of beers that can be tested under current market conditions. While the rules of the game mainly prohibit the testing of hypotheses, aggregated consumer demand decides which lines of products survive. We can further distinguish between products that just survive in a niche and lines of products that expand. The owners of small, local bakeries are often satisfied with bare survival and have no interest in or possibility of expanding their businesses, while other businesses will expand their production as demand increases. Since the production capacity of a society and the aggregated consumer budget is (at least in the short run) constant, increase in one line of production implies that there is a decrease in another line of production. Entrepreneurs who face a substantial decrease in demand need to adapt by imitating more successful entrepreneurs or by innovating their products. The competition in the market is thus driven by "innovation and imitation."[38]

Let me comment briefly on another feature of the market system. In the beginning, I stated that all polycentric systems are in some sense teleological. The question then is, what is the goal of the market – understood as a polycentric system? The goal of the market process is to discover what people want and how to produce the goods that people want most efficiently. In "The Use of Knowledge in Society" and "Competition as a Discovery Procedure" Hayek points to two distinct mechanisms that explain how the market achieves both goals at the same time. The first mechanism that he points to is the *price mechanism*. This mechanism mainly facilitates the adaption of society to a changing environment. To put it in Hayek's own words, the price mechanism facilitates the "continuous adjustment of activities to unavoidable small changes,"[39] and a continuous adaption is essential "simply to maintain the previously attained level [of production]."[40] The second epistemic mechanism of a free society is *free competition,* which is understood as a discovery process. Free competition facilitates the continuous search for new and better ways of production.

In summary, I conclude that the market order – as it exists in most modern societies – can legitimately be viewed as an instance of polycentrism, since it features the three constitutive parts of a polycentric order.

8.2.2 Science

Sometimes scientific progress is understood as a 'natural' outcome of disinterested scientists pursuing truth. Science in this view is a natural phenomenon within society that is disconnected from the institutional framework. Popper reminds us that John Stuart Mill and Auguste Comte held such a view of scientific progress. Comte, summarizes Popper, "believes that the law of progress is deducible from a tendency in human individuals which impels them to perfect their nature more and more."[41] The philosopher of science further tells us that "in all this, Mill follows him completely, trying to reduce his law of progress to what he calls the 'progressiveness of the human mind' whose first 'impelling force . . . is the desire of increased material comforts'."[42] Thus, according to Popper's reading, both thinkers hold that scientific progress is unconditional and law-like. If Comte and Mill are right, then scientific progress is not a result of a clever institutional mechanism but simply of the human desire for progress. This understanding of scientific progress can easily be put to the test. The epistemic hypothesis underlying the polycentric approach is that scientific progress is essentially a function of the rules of the game. We can simply ask whether scientific progress could be arrested by "closing down or controlling laboratories for research, by suppressing and controlling scientific periodicals and other means of discussion, [. . .] by suppressing Universities and other schools, by suppressing books, the printing press, writing, and, in the end, speaking."[43] The answer to that question seems unambiguous. Without these institutions, scientific progress is hardly imaginable. Popper agrees: "This immediately leads to the realization that a psychological propensity alone cannot be sufficient to explain progress."[44] The idea that scientific progress is to a large degree a function of the formal and informal rules of the game or, as Popper put it, "progress depends very largely on political factors,"[45] thus seems very plausible.

While for a present reader, Popper's ideas might have the ring of typical philosophical thought experiments, it might be of interest to note that, at the time Popper was writing, the Soviet Union was actually experimenting with an alternative approach to scientific progress. Polanyi not only describes those alternatives of scientific organization under the rubric of "planned science,"[46] but also calls to attention that after the Second World War there was a movement in Britain for the planning of science. This movement pushed the idea that "all scientific work must be integrated under the guidance of planning boards on the model of those established in wartime"[47] to promote the welfare of society.[48] But let us not digress too much. Up to this point, I have established that scientific progress depends at least in part on a suitable institutional environment. Now I want to make the case that organized science, as it pertains in modern nation states, can legitimately be viewed as a polycentric system.[49]

The first question is whether or not we can identify an artificial overarching system of rules that creates and sustains a multiplicity of decision centers and facilitates an evolutionary process. I want to follow D'Agostino here, who thinks that current rules of the scientific game ought to be – and actually are[50] – instituted in a way as to preserve and perpetuate what he calls, with reference to Kuhn, "the essential tension."[51] The essential tension in a field of research is given if there is a balanced distribution between scientific conservatives, who "ensure that the founding concepts or approaches of the community are [. . .] stretched to their limits,"[52] and scientific mavericks. Following D'Agostino in part, here I want to identify five essential institutional means that allow the regulatory framework of science to coordinate research:

1 Intellectual freedom.
2 Novelty premiums.
3 Asset ownership.
4 Induced diversity.
5 Negative rules.

It should be noted that these elements are of course not exhaustive, but are only the most obvious tools that are used by politics to create a polycentric system of scientific inquiry. Let me quickly review these elements. Securing 'intellectual freedom' entails that the state tries to establish an order of scientific inquiry in which everybody can voice their opinion without fearing "the consequences of their expressed opinions on their material well-being."[53] The state not only needs to establish the right of free speech, but also needs to make sure that dissenters do not have to fear voicing unorthodox opinions. Other than that, the state also implements intellectual freedom through "systems of tenure"[54] and "principles of intellectual freedom"[55] that protect academics from some of the adverse consequences of group think. D'Agostino also points to informal implementations of the same ideas in the practice of anonymous refereeing so as to protect referees from payback. A second feature of the order of scientific inquiry is the 'novelty premium.' The regulatory framework incentivizes scientists to come up with new methods, experiments and research programs. The incentive system is ideally set up in a way such that breakthroughs give the researcher a higher chance of getting tenure at an elite university or of collecting grants.[56] A third feature, which is closely related to novelty premiums, is asset ownership. The overarching rules of the game in many fields of research give scientists the opportunity to patent their ideas. Scientists thus have another incentive to resist the 'social comparison effect.' In addition, some states strictly punish any form of plagiarism – which further encourages scientists to put their minds to new problems. A fourth element is certainly the artificial induction of diversity. Many states have started to grant special privileges to female researchers, in hope of reaching a more balanced distribution between female and male researchers. In addition, governments attempt to encourage the international exchange of scientists by offering grants for setting up conferences and inviting foreign researchers. Also, the state often tries to diversify the social backgrounds of scientists by encouraging students from all strata of society to pursue an education that would allow them to participate in science. 'Negative rules,' which prohibit certain kinds of inquiries and experiments, can be viewed as the fifth element. In some polycentric systems of science, for example, experimenting with embryos is prohibited; in other orders experiments with animals are strongly restricted. Polycentric systems of scientific research might in turn sometimes prohibit certain fields of enquiry entirely.

Let us now turn to the second building block of polycentric systems. The multiplicity of decision centers is discussed under a multitude of rubrics in the philosophy of science. Stuart Kauffman writes: "[We] call it by a variety of names, from federalism to profit centers to restructuring to checks and balances to political action committees."[57] D'Agostino calls it the "'federal model' of collective enquiry."[58] Since scientists essentially work under uncertainty, it is just not clear which research program will succeed and which will not. Under uncertainty, it seems reasonable to let different agents follow their own hunches and tentative solutions. D'Agostino makes a related point:

> As Kuhn says [. . .] 'individual variability in the application of shared values may serve functions essential to' rational enquiry. In particular, individual variability in (constructively) partitioning and exploring the multi-dimensional problem spaces by which rational enquiry is typically characterized offer a better response to boundedness and complexity than does a simple division of that problem space. *We need both division and diversity to pursue enquiry in complex situations.*[59]

This is an important point for us, since the diversity of epistemic standards – through the competition of multiple decision centers in organized science – is transformed from a problem into an asset. Popper seems to agree:

> Science, and more especially scientific progress, are the results not of isolated efforts but of the *free competition of thought*. For science needs ever more competition between hypotheses and ever more rigorous tests. And

> the competing hypotheses need personal representation, as it were: they need advocates, they need a jury, and even a public. This personal representation must be institutionally organized if we wish to ensure that it works. And these institutions have to be paid for, and protected by law.[60]

Lakatos also emphasizes the necessity of competition:

> The history of science has been and should be a history of competing research programmes (or, if you wish, 'paradigms'), but it has not been and must not become a succession of periods of normal science: the sooner competition starts, the better for progress.[61]

The question then becomes what competition is about, and between which decision centers we would expect competition to take place. Since science operates under conditions of scarcity, there is not enough money or human resources to investigate every topic in every discipline. This means that various scientists are in competition for the funding of their research. This funding might be for experiments, technology or staff. In addition, there is at any given time a limited number of graduate students – and graduate students need to decide in which direction they want to set sails. Scientific paradigms can survive only if enough graduate students in every generation decide to invest their careers in a given research program. If there are not enough graduate students who judge that a certain research program has sufficient potential, it will slowly die. But there is, of course, not only recognition to be gained from graduate students, but more importantly by the respective scientific field. To gain the respect of renowned peers, it is important in most fields to publish in particular journals. These journals artificially restrict the amount of papers accepted for publishing, so as to effectively signal distinction. This competition takes place within a given field, but certainly also across different fields of enquiry. We may ask what the evolutionary process operates on. It surely works on paradigms or research programs, but it also works on the evaluative standards of science and their relative weights as well. Mantzavinos writes:

> During an evolutionary process of trial and error, explanatory activities are undertaken according to the prevailing rules of the game, and a permanent flow of explanations is produced, tested, and retained or discarded. Novelty is a permanent feature of this process since new ways of representing the phenomena constantly emerge new ways of testing are being constantly designed, and new means of criticism are constantly invented.[62]

The goal of this type of competitive evolution, which is steered by the polycentric organization of science, is, furthermore, "to identify an approach which is best, or at least to winnow out the better from the worse strategies for enquiry."[63]

In summary, I can conclude that organized science – as it exists in most modern societies – can be legitimately viewed as an instance of polycentrism, since it features the three constituting parts of a polycentric order.

8.3 How polycentrism solves the problems of expert deliberation

In Chapter 7, Section 7.2, I argued that deliberation suffers from a conservative bias for three main reasons: epistemic problems associated with bounded rationality (7.2.3), psychological biases (7.2.1) and transaction costs (7.2.2). In this section, I want to argue that polycentric systems outperform expert deliberation, in part because they can neutralize the inhibitors of collective deliberation outlined in Chapter 7 and thus take full advantage of the possible gains of diversity.

8.3.1 Hidden champions and sequential persuasion: ameliorating the problem of bounded rationality

In Chapter 7, Section 7.2.3, I showed that when it comes to *hard problems*, in many instances, bounded rationality prevents even very good deliberators from knowing with certainty *what they really want* and *what works*. In this section, I want to argue that polycentric systems ameliorate the outlined problems by allowing for *sequential persuasion*. In the process of sequential persuasion, the layers of uncertainty wrapped around an innovation are peeled away as the innovation gradually diffuses through society.

I want to illustrate the concept of sequential persuasion with a simple model. In the model, the innovator Inger wants to convince a group of people of a certain innovative product. In the first case, she presents her innovative product to a panel of deliberators, and in the second case, she develops her product in a polycentric system. Both forums are composed of three persons: Gabriel, Benni and Philipp. Gabriel is willing to buy a product that is 'highly innovative' (r_1). Benni considers buying a product if it is highly innovative (r_1) and has 'an enduring entertainment value' (r_2). Philipp, in turn, is interested only in products that fulfill the conditions r_1, r_2 and an additional condition r_3: the product must be 'beneficial in everyday working life.'

Now let us compare the two environments: the deliberative scenario and the polycentric system. In the first scenario, Inger submits her innovative product to the deliberative panel. All three participants immediately recognize that the product is indeed very innovative. Everybody in the group thus sees one reason to buy the product. While Gabriel is willing to buy the product, Benni and Philipp are uncertain whether the innovative product truly has an 'enduring entertainment value' (r_2) or whether it will be useful in the workplace (r_3). Since the deliberative panel must decide unanimously for or against the product, the panel abstains from buying the product. Let us now consider the persuasion process in the market. Suppose Inger in t_1 produced an innovative product P and sold it to Gabriel. Gabriel now uses the innovation mainly for entertainment purposes. Since Gabriel in t_2 is having fun with P, Benni is convinced that P actually has an enduring entertainment value. He now possesses the reasons r_1, r_2 and buys P, too. Benni, in contrast to Gabriel, uses P not only privately, but also professionally to solve a problem for which P was not originally intended. Philipp has indeed heard of P in t_1 and t_2, but previously perceived P as a toy for geeks. The use of P in the office leads Philipp to conclude that, contrary to what he used to believe, P actually has a practical value and indeed reduces the everyday workload. Since Philipp therefore has the reason r_3, he will at last join the group and buy the product as well.

The point of this first model is this: By allowing some people who are willing to take risks to test an innovation at their own costs, *the layers of uncertainty are removed not only for the early adopter, but also for the people around him.*

With regard to P, the problem was essentially that Benni and Philipp initially did not see the possible applications of it and thus misjudged its utility. They simply did not see all the reasons that applied to them.

Let me put the core idea that motivates the example a bit more formally. Rational deliberation consists of two parts. The rationality requirement demands that a deliberator aggregates, critically examines and systematizes the available evidence in the process of forming an opinion. The second part of the rationality requirement demands that the deliberator chooses the alternative from the set of alternatives that is best backed up by evidence.

Definition: rational deliberation

- Rational deliberation aims at aggregating and systematizing the available evidence for the purposes of choice. The rationality requirement, inter alia, requires that deliberators choose the alternative from the set of alternatives that is best backed up by the available evidence.

What is important for our purpose is that the definition of rational deliberation helps us to spell out the exact conditions under which rational deliberation will pick out the objectively best alternative of an option set. Rational deliberation will always pick out the objectively best alternative in a given choice set, if the objectively best alternative is the one that is best backed up by the evidence.

Let us call an alternative that is both best backed up by the available evidence and from an objective point of view the best option a *salient champion.*

Definition: salient champion

- A proposal is a salient champion if and only if it is the best proposal within a choice set *and* it is the proposal that is best corroborated by the available evidence.

What becomes immediately evident is that choosing in accordance with the demands of rational deliberation cannot ensure that we pick out the best solution in a given choice set. Sometimes the option that is best backed up by the evidence and the option that is best from an objective point of view do not coincide. Occasionally it is the case that even if we flawlessly aggregate and critically examine the evidence, the processed evidence will fail to point us to the best solution. In such cases, a choice set features what I want to call a 'hidden champion.'

Definition: hidden champion

- A proposal is a hidden champion if and only if it is the best proposal within a choice set, but there is at least one proposal in the choice set that is better corroborated by the available evidence.

It follows then that a choice set features a hidden champion if and only if the evidence is tilted against the best solution. Now, the notion of rational deliberation as well as the notion of a hidden champions presupposes something like an evidential standard. An evidential standard among other things determines what counts as evidence and how to weigh different kinds of evidence. I will assume here without further discussion that for the purpose of political reasoning various reasonable evidential standards exist.

What is important for my purposes is the following: Let us assume that there are three proposals A, B and C, where A is the best proposal from an objective point of view. Moreover, assume that there are two persons, Inger and Gabriel, who share a certain preference order, meaning they are aiming for the same goal. Unfortunately, however, they cannot agree on the best means for the goal, because they base their evaluation of what constitutes the best means on different evidential standards. If Inger and Gabriel are asked to evaluate the same three options for producing a desired result, given the same batch of evidence, both thus come up with a different ranking of the proposals.

Assume Inger produces the ranking A > C > B, while Gabriel evaluates the options on the basis of his evidential standard and comes up with the ranking C > B > A. They each have come up with different rankings after evaluating the set of proposals according to their own evidential standards. What bears emphasizing here is that the same proposal A is a salient champion given Inger's evidential standard, but a hidden champion given Gabriel's evidential standard.

Inger and Gabriel are thus faced with a shallow disagreement. The question then is, how can they resolve their dispute? Perhaps the most important thing to note is that this disagreement cannot be resolved by *more* deliberation. The deliberators already have critically reviewed the available evidence and brought their beliefs into reflective equilibrium.

The only way, I submit, to resolve this shallow disagreement is creating additional evidence. The only way that Inger can rationally convince Gabriel that A is the best proposal is by producing additional evidence in favor of it.

To see the importance of hidden champions more generally, assume that the majority of society shares Gabriel's perspective. Thus the majority shares his evidential standard and also his goals. For the sake of the argument, assume further that, if adopted, the proposal A would lead to a huge welfare increase. (The nature of the proposal does not need to concern us. It could be a scientific, political or business proposal.)

To unlock the hidden champion, the advocate of the hidden champion needs to be able to produce sufficient evidence to rationally convince the majority. However, whether Inger is permitted to generate the evidence in question depends on the institutional surroundings. What is specific about polycentric systems vis-à-vis institutions across domains that rely heavily on centralized, collective deliberation and decision-making is that advocates of hidden champions are in a much better position to create the sets of evidence that are needed to rationally convince the majority. What makes the market society and modern scientific systems so productive, in my view, has to do with the polycentric structure of these systems. What distinguishes polycentric and monocentric systems is that in a polycentric system there are by definition a multiplicity of decision centers, each with a huge degree of independence to put their own plans into practice. Moreover, in the case of the market and modern science, the rules of the polycentric structure not only *permit* but *incentivize* advocates of peripheral ideas, to create the evidence that is needed to unlock hidden champions.

I have said multiple times now that the advocate of the hidden champion needs to be able to produce additional evidence. However, this should be understood as a shorthand. In some cases, the advocate will need to produce the evidence by herself or himself, but – as becomes evident from our earlier example – sometimes the production of evidence is part of a social process. In our earlier example, for instance, it was not Inger that produced the evidence to convince Benni and Philipp; Gabriel in using P convinced Benni, and Benni in using P convinced Philipp.

Moreover, research on innovation diffusion shows that – the issue talk about hidden champions and sequential persuasion is not just a philosophical fancy. In his seminal work *Diffusion of Innovations*, Everett Rogers shows that innovations are typically adopted with a time lag between different social groups.[64] In the first phase, only so-called *innovators* are interested in a new product. Innovators, following Rogers, are risk takers and usually have an above-average budget. If innovators show interest in a certain innovation, this prompts early adopters to familiarize themselves with the innovation as well. Early adopters are also more willing to take risks, and furthermore are well connected and often take the role of opinion leaders in a given society. The early adopters are thus the group that introduces the product to a wider audience. The diffusion process speeds up from there and reaches the early and late majority. At the end of this process of diffusion there are the laggards. The process of innovation diffusion is nicely captured in Figure 8.1.

The process of deciding for or against a certain innovation from the perspective of the individual "is essentially an information-seeking and information-processing activity in which the individual is motivated to reduce uncertainty about the advantages and disadvantages of the innovation."[65] In order to reduce

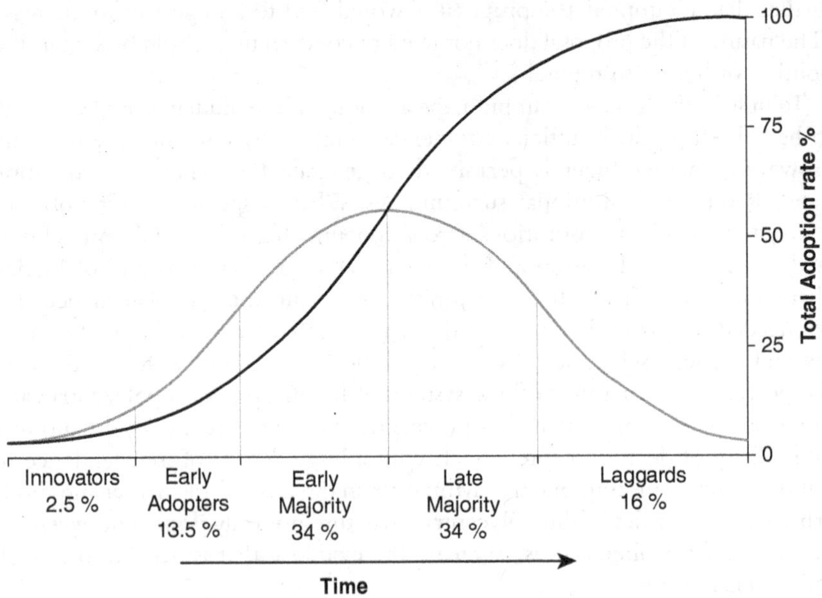

Figure 8.1 The S-Curve of Adoption[66]

uncertainty, the individuals will listen to opinion leaders and friends, and will try to experience an innovation firsthand. Rogers writes:

> For most individuals, one means of coping with the inherent uncertainty about an innovation's consequences is to try out the new idea on a partial basis. In fact, most individuals will not adopt an innovation without trying it first on a probationary basis to determine its usefulness in their own situation. This small-scale trial is often part of the decision to adopt, and is important as a means to decrease the perceived uncertainty of the innovation for the adopter.[67]

Thus the degree to which an innovation is observable, trialable and its effects are demonstrable, strongly influences the rate of its adoption and diffusion.[68] The more an innovation diffuses through society, the easier it gets for individuals to talk to people who have actually experienced a certain innovation or get a firsthand experience themselves. Rogers agrees:

> results of various diffusion investigations show that most individuals do not evaluate an innovation on the basis of scientific studies of its consequences [. . .]. Instead, most people depend mainly upon a subjective evaluation of an innovation that is conveyed to them from other individuals like themselves who have previously adopted the innovation.[69]

It should be further noted that observability and trialability is not only an important aspect when it comes to innovations in the marketplace, but also with respect to social innovations.

> Change agents often seek to speed up the innovation-process for individuals by sponsoring demonstrations of a new idea in a social system, and there is evidence that this demonstration strategy can be quite effective, especially if the demonstrator is an opinion leader.[70]

In general, demonstration projects seem to be a prime means for testing new social technologies and persuading a skeptical majority. Earlier, I outlined that Hayek is skeptical towards the capabilities of deliberation to find out who knows best.

> The successful combination of knowledge and aptitude is not selected by common deliberation [. . .] [on the contrary] it is the product of individuals imitating those who have been more successful and from their being guided by symbols, such as prices [. . .] or *expressions of moral or aesthetic esteem* [. . .] – in short, of their using the results *of the experience* of others.[71]

In the endnote of this paragraph, Hayek cites the following passage by W. A. Lewis to corroborate his thoughts:

> These innovators are always in a minority. New ideas are first put into practice by one or two or very few persons, whether they be new ideas in technology, or new forms of organization, new commodities, or other novelties. These ideas may be accepted rapidly by the rest of the population. More probably they are received with skepticism and unbelief, and make their way only very slowly at first if at all. After a while the new ideas are seen to be successful, and are then accepted by increasing numbers.[72]

Lewis, in 1955, thus essentially described the same diffusion process that Rogers popularized some decades later. This should not come as a surprise, though, since a host of disciplines – including public health, sociology, anthropology and communication studies – have uncovered the principles of innovation diffusion quasi simultaneously.[73] Rogers writes: "Despite the distinctiveness of these approaches to diffusion research, each 'invisible college' uncovered remarkably similar findings; for example, that the diffusion of an innovation followed an s-shaped curve over time."[74]

Let me summarize the argument. I have argued that due to bounded rationality, rational deliberation will often produce shallow disagreements, especially when evaluating innovative proposals. Shallow disagreements are particularly troubling in cases in which the majority gets it wrong, when the majority after evaluating the available evidence backs – what is from an objective point – the wrong proposal or idea. In cases like this, the majority perspective features what I have called a 'hidden champion.'

I have argued that unlocking hidden champions is particularly important and that often the only way to do this is to permit the advocates of the hidden champions to produce additional evidence. To put it differently: To unlock hidden champions, innovators need space to demonstrate the value of their ideas, and to generate the evidence that is necessary to convince the 'lukewarm supporters' and eventually the skeptics. Polycentric systems are particularly well-suited to ameliorate the issue of hidden champions, because polycentric systems are built not only around the idea of giving individuals the freedom to speak in favor of their ideas, but also around the idea of granting to the agents enough space for developing and demonstrating their ideas. As an innovation gradually diffuses through society, the layers of uncertainty wrapped around a hidden champion, get slowly removed.

8.3.2 Motivational

In the last section I dealt with the question of how polycentric systems ameliorate the epistemic problems of expert deliberation. In this section I want to talk about how polycentric systems ameliorate the 'common knowledge bias' and in particular the 'social comparison effect' (discussed in Chapter 7, Section 7.2.1). Individuals, as I pointed out earlier, usually hate to be sole dissenters and advertise ideas that are unpopular in their community. Polycentric systems essentially ameliorate this problem by incentivizing dissent. In polycentric systems like the marketplace and science, we have an additional reason to communicate our knowledge or to follow our peripheral ideas against the ridicule or resistance of our epistemic peers. This communication can take different forms. If Philipp is convinced that people will buy personal computers, even if all the experts in the world are betting against him, he has the opportunity to start a company – and in the case of success – make huge profits. The same goes for science: If Philipp is convinced that a certain strand of research will achieve unprecedented results – and he succeeds – he will be published in top journals and might be awarded a high-paying position in academia. Polycentric systems thus pay a 'novelty premium' to people who successfully push peripheral ideas.

8.3.3 Failure to include the best member

Since deliberative groups are, for reasons of transaction costs, most of the time rather small, there is always a good chance that a particular group of deliberators does not include the agent with the best solution. The failure to include the best member is a big problem for all groups of experts and boards of directors in companies. Hayek himself pointed to this problem and its polycentric solution:

> As far as the management decisions of a genuine economy or of any other organization are concerned, it is only the knowledge of the organizers or managers alone that can have any impact. [. . .] Contrast this with the two advantages of a spontaneous market order or catallaxy: it can use the knowledge of all participants.[75]

As I pointed out earlier, deliberative groups have very clear limits when it comes to including diversity. Deliberative groups are not well-suited to gain from a huge number of slightly diverse cognitive models or from a small number of very diverse cognitive models. Polycentric orders, on the contrary, have prima facie no such limitation. An increase in cognitive models should be positively correlated with the epistemic goals of a polycentric system. To make this point more salient, compare two cases. In one case, there is an expert panel deciding how to go about a specific problem. In the other case, there is a polycentric system consisting of many decision clusters, each deciding on its own how to go about that very same problem. At a certain cutoff point, it makes no sense to add additional experts to the panel. The marginal contribution of one expert or another hundred experts to the panel will be zero if not negative. Meaningful deliberation – in the modes discussed earlier – is just not possible above a certain threshold. However, a polycentric order in principle can accommodate an unlimited number of experts, each trying on their own or in cooperation with others to solve a specific problem. Think about the recent expansion of the international market and of the scientific community due to the progress of globalization.

However, this is not to say that the law of diminishing returns does not apply to polycentric systems. Every society is at any point of its existence confronted with a multitude of problems and thus has to decide how to distribute its limited resources, both in terms of money and brainpower, to the various problems it sees itself confronted with. Thus even though a polycentric system in principle can accommodate an indefinite amount of decision centers, this does not mean that it should. Nevertheless, it is important to note that polycentric systems seem to have a clear advantage in epistemic terms over systems based on inclusive deliberation, when society is in the fortunate position that it can put the heads of a great multitude of problem-solvers to work.

8.3.4 Summary

In Chapter 7 (Section 7.2), I concluded that expert deliberation seems not to be particularly well-suited in dealing with novelty or innovative solutions for three reasons: the epistemic problems associated with bounded rationality (7.2.3), the psychological biases (7.2.1) and the problem of transaction costs (7.2.2). In this section, I outlined how polycentric systems ameliorate all three of the problems and thus overcome the 'conservative bias of deliberation.' The results of this chapter suggest that polycentric systems outperform expert deliberation, because they are better fitted to secure the gains of diversity.

Notes

1 Polanyi (1998, p. 189).
2 Polanyi (1998, p. 189). Polanyi also deems literature, the various arts, the crafts, medicine, agriculture and various technical services as instances of polycentric systems. See Polanyi (1998, p. 202.).

3 I use the term 'organized science' to denote the 'scientific game' that results from institutions that protect free speech, incentivize novel research and so forth. I will have to say more on this in Section 8.2.2.
4 Polanyi (1998, p. 189).
5 Fuller (1995), King (2012).
6 Ostrom (2005).
7 Aligica and Tarko (2012), Aligica and Boettke (2009) and Ostrom (1997).
8 Jacobs (2000), Jacobs (2000) and Bladel (2005).
9 Aligica (2014), Aligica and Tarko (2012).
10 Polanyi (1998, p. 208).
11 Aligica and Tarko (2012, p. 18).
12 Aligica and Tarko (2012, p. 18).
13 Aligica and Tarko (2012, p. 18).
14 Aligica and Tarko (2012, p. 18).
15 Aligica and Tarko (2012, p. 18).
16 I understand the term 'experiment' in a Popperian sense: An experiment is "a means of acquiring knowledge, by comparing the results obtained with the results expected" Popper (2002b, p. 78). Italics deleted.
17 IXDA (2005).
18 European Commission (2015).
19 European Commission (2015).
20 Mitchell (2006, p. 45).
21 Polanyi (1997, p. 127).
22 Compare Kitcher's discussion of 'well-ordered science' (2001, chap. 10).
23 This is of course an oversimplification. In the actual market environment it is often not clear why a specific entrepreneurial activity failed.
24 Darwin (2010, pp. 3–4).
25 Mantzavinos (2001, p. 92).
26 Hayek (2013, p. 44).
27 Buchanan for instance notes that "evolution may produce *social dilemma* as readily as social paradise" Buchanan (2000, p. 211). Emphasis added.
28 It would surely be interesting to discuss how this concept relates to "invisible hand" explanations (e.g. Nozick (1994)). But that would lead us too far astray at this point.
29 Hayek (2002, p. 10).
30 Hayek (2002, p. 10).
31 Marengo (2000, pp. 779–780).
32 Marengo (2000, p. 760).
33 Vanberg and Kerber (1994, p. 210).
34 Vanberg and Kerber (1994, p. 210).
35 Mantzavinos (2001, p. 195).
36 Mantzavinos (2001, p. 194).
37 Streit (1992, p. 265).
38 Mantzavinos (2001, p. 196).
39 Hayek (2002, p. 18).
40 Hayek (2002, p. 18).
41 Popper (2002b, p. 141).
42 Popper (2002b, p. 141).
43 Popper (2002b, pp. 142–143).
44 Popper (2002b, p. 142). Italics deleted.
45 Popper (2002b, pp. 142–143).
46 Polanyi (1998, pp. 72).
47 Polanyi (1998, p. 106).

48 Of course, suppressing free research and scientific publications, as in the case of the Soviet Union, is qualitatively different from centrally planning science, as was proposed in Britain (Polanyi 1998, p. 106).

49 Lütge works on a similar project, but on a more fundamental level, when he connects Buchanan's research program to a naturalized philosophy of science. See Lütge (2003), Lütge (2004) and Lütge (2001).

50 "We have, I think, reason to believe that some such balance of these forces pro and con has been achieved, institutionally and culturally, in some of our most familiar institutions, including jurisprudence, science, and the learned professions more generally" D'Agostino (2010, p. 161).

51 D'Agostino (2010).

52 D'Agostino (2010, p. 12).

53 D'Agostino (2010, p. 67).

54 D'Agostino (2010, p. 68).

55 D'Agostino (2010, p. 68).

56 Organized science in modern societies is thus set up in order to achieve long-term scientific progress. Historically, this has not always been the case – quite to the contrary, throughout history scientific enquiry has often been discouraged instead of incentivized.

57 Kauffman (1992).

58 D'Agostino (2010, p. 150).

59 D'Agostino (2010, pp. 133–134). Italics in original.

60 Popper (2002b, p. 143). Italics in the original.

61 Lakatos (1980, p. 69). Italics deleted.

62 Mantzavinos (2013, pp. 619–620).

63 Bergh and Höijer (2008a, p. 137).

64 According to Backer, *The Diffusion of Innovations* is one of the books most often cited in the social sciences (Backer 2005, p. 288).

65 Rogers (1983, p. 172).

66 Adapted from: https://commons.wikimedia.org/wiki/File:Diffusion_of_ideas.svg

67 Rogers (1983, p. 172).

68 Rogers (2003, chap. 6).

69 Rogers (1983, p. 18).

70 Rogers (1983, p. 172).

71 Hayek (2012, p. 26). Emphasis added.

72 Hayek (2012, p. 371).

73 Rogers (1983, chap. 2).

74 Rogers (1983, p. 38).

75 Hayek (2002, p. 14).

Part III

Polycentric democracy

9 A polycentric political order

> One must learn by doing the thing, for though you think you know it – you have no certainty, until you try.
>
> – Sophocles, 400 B.C.[1]

In the last chapters, I argued that polycentric systems are for different reasons especially well-suited to let society gain from a diversity of instrumental beliefs, preferences and risk profiles. In this chapter I want to apply the idea of polycentrism to the realm of politics. In Section 9.1, I want to start out by giving a rough outline of polycentric democracy. My goal is primarily to give you an intuitive grasp of the idea and sketch the likely outcomes of such a political order. In Section 9.2, I will get a bit more technical and discuss the constituting parts of political polycentric systems. In Section 9.3, I will close out by debating various options for implementing polycentric democracy.

9.1 An outline of polycentric democracy

I will give a rather technical argument in favor of polycentric democracy in Chapter 10. In this section, the primary aim is only to convey the more general idea of polycentric democracy.

Following Aligica, I define a political polycentric system – or for short, a polycentric polity – as

> an institutional arrangement involving a multiplicity of decision centers acting independently but under the constraints of an overarching set of norms and rules that restrict externalities and create the conditions for an emergent outcome to occur at the level of the entire system via a bottom-up competitive process.[2]

A polycentric democracy, accordingly, is a polycentric system in which competition between multiple decision centers is regulated by a framework for institutional competition that is itself democratically legitimized and supervised. I can state the following.

	Definition
Polycentric Democracy:	An institutional arrangement involving a multiplicity of decision centers acting independently but under the constraints of a democratically supervised and legitimized framework for institutional competition that restricts externalities.

As Aligica and Tarko have shown, there are different institutional implementations for political polycentric systems.[3] For now, I want to postpone the question of what kind of institutional implementation might be most adequate from the perspective of the RoCD. I will come back to that question in Section 9.3. What is important is this: In polycentric systems there are a multitude of decision centers that have a high degree of autonomy. These decision centers are usually states within a federal order, free cities – cities with a high degree of municipal autonomy – or special experimental zones. For lack of a better name, let us call these decision centers 'polities.' Simplifying, I can state that in a polycentric democracy each polity will endeavor to achieve the best 'living conditions' for its citizens.[4] *Well-regulated* competition between polities achieves three outcomes that could be interesting from a diverse set of normative perspectives.

	Outcomes
Polycentric Democracy:	• *Discovering new heights.* Since competition is a discovery process, a political polycentric system should constantly find new and better 'ways of living together' or simply better 'modus vivendi arrangements.' • *Reducing shallow disagreement.* Much disagreement in political philosophy is most likely due to our disagreement on non-normative facts. In a polycentric system, a lot more socio-economic claims can be tested than in our current democratic systems; this should reduce disagreement. • *Defusing deep disagreement.* It is highly likely that at least some of our reasonable political disagreements are best explained by fundamental disagreements about the right and the good. In a polycentric system, people who reasonably disagree are allowed to enter into polities with more like-minded people. Thus, tensions in society could be reduced.

It should be noted that the outlined outcomes are achieved as a result of allowing diverse polities to follow their own evaluative and instrumental standards. Polycentric democracy, to put it differently, achieves these outcomes by an invisible hand process, a process of artificial variation and selection (see Chapter 8). Let me then briefly comment on the individual outcomes and how they connect with different threads of my discussion.[5]

Discovering new heights

In Chapters 7–8, I discussed the limitations of individual and collective deliberation in detail. Simply put, for epistemic and psychological reasons, deliberation is not as good as one would hope in evaluating highly innovative ideas or solutions. Even if deliberators are experts in their respective fields and work under the best possible incentives, they often fail to appreciate the worth of an innovation. The creativity researcher Brian Licuanan and his colleagues provide three telling examples:

- When J. K. Rowling wrote her first book in the *Harry Potter* series, it was rejected by a long list of publishers who saw little appeal, and little originality, in the idea of a school for wizards.
- When executives at International Business Machines (IBM) were presented with the first personal computers, they viewed personal computers as toys having no real implications for IBM's key product at the time – mainframe computers.
- When the US military was first presented with the Wright brothers' flying machine, it failed to anticipate the marked impact airplanes would have on our world.[6]

If experts are bad at evaluating even these relatively easy cases, we might legitimately question how good political philosophers, political scientists, economists or intellectuals in general are in evaluating innovations in their respective fields.

Focusing here on political philosophy, it is surely not wrong to say that political philosophers are, in a specific sense, entrepreneurs. Although most philosophers are preoccupied with rather abstract conceptual or normative questions, they often hint at the institutional changes that their favorite principles would entail. The moral philosopher Huemer for instance wants to convince us that an anarcho-capitalistic order is in everybody's best interest.[7] Rawls, on the contrary, favors a kind of democratic socialism, while Hayek wants to persuade us of the advantages of a small state.[8] But we do not need to look only at proposals that aim to shift the social reality in an encompassing way. We can also look at proposals that constrain themselves to very limited changes of the social world. Take Philippe Van Parijs's defense of a basic income.[9] When political philosophers propose such institutional changes for which there is no precedent, a reader needs to evaluate what this "perturbed social world"[10] would look like.

Such an evaluation usually involves very complex normative and descriptive questions.[11] Predicting the equilibrium for which the perturbed world would settle is very hard – or even outright impossible when all unintended consequences and unforeseeable side effects are included.

It might very well be that some of these proposals for changing our institutional setup would create large social benefits. The crucial point is simply that, without letting philosophers (or more likely political entrepreneurs who build on their ideas) experiment with their ideas on a small scale, there is just no way to know *what works, who knows best* and even – as I showed in Chapter 8 – *what we really want*. Furthermore and equally important, there is usually no way of convincing the whole of society without having demonstration projects first, as my results in Chapter 8, Section 8.3.1 suggest. I will discuss these points in some detail in Chapter 10, Sections 10.3 and 10.4.

Reducing shallow disagreement

The experimental exploration of the institutional search space creates knowledge about what works (new heights), but also about what doesn't work. Exploring the search space should thus in the long run reduce shallow disagreement. The reduction of shallow disagreement should itself be viewed as a social process. A recent experiment published in *Science* is very illuminating to understand how social learning processes – that are not primarily based on deliberation – function.[12]

In the experiment, the participants could choose in every round between two institutional setups for a public goods game: a sanctioning community and a sanction-free community. In the first round of the game, only one third of the participants chose the sanctioning community, presumably because the participants judged 'punishment' as a moral bad. During the game, however, the problem of free riding became more and more salient as the sanction-free community was not able to sustain cooperation. In consequence, more and more participants migrated to sanctioning institutions. At the end of the game, almost every participant had migrated to the sanctioning community that in the beginning seemed so unpromising. In a follow-up paper Gürerk used the same experimental setup, but provided the subjects with the results of the first study. As a result of providing subjects with "a social history," as Gürerk dubs it, participant's initial acceptance of the sanctioning community was much higher and "full participation" in the punishment institution was achieved earlier.[13] Again, the interesting point of this paper is that, initially, the institution that performed well in increasing contributions to the public good and thus in yielding long-term payoffs was neglected by the majority. Institutional competition by providing exit and entry on the one hand and information about alternative coordinating mechanisms on the other facilitated a social learning process and thus made up for the initial lack of foresight on the individual level.[14]

Defusing deep disagreement

It is plausible to assume that if we knew all the relevant facts about psychology, economics, sociology and so forth, the set of disagreement between reasonable people would shrink dramatically. However, it is also plausible to assume that the set of disagreement would not be empty. There is good reason to believe that some disagreement will always remain about ethical principles themselves, their application and their respective trade-off rates. Polycentric democracy has the advantage that, in letting different polities follow their own evaluative standards, it also succeeds in defusing disagreement on a macro-level. Defusing 'deep disagreement' is again a side effect of letting polities discover new 'ways of living' – a side effect, though, which is essential for the evaluation of polycentric democracy as a whole. I will develop the idea of defusing deep disagreement in Chapter 10, Section 10.3.2.[15]

9.2 The building blocks of polycentric democracy

In the last section, I tried to convey a rough understanding of polycentric democracy. Painting with the big brush, I outlined some of the institutional features of polycentric democracy as well as some of its normatively interesting goals. In this section, I want to zoom in and discuss polycentric democracy in more detail. Polycentric systems, as noted, have three defining features: a regulatory framework, multiple decision centers and an emerging evolutionary competition. Next, I will translate the concept of polycentrism to the political realm.[16]

9.2.1 The regulatory framework

One of the three constituting parts of a polycentric polity is a framework for regulating the competition between polities. To make sense of the relationship between this regulative framework and the individual polities, Buchanan's conceptual distinction between the "protective" and "productive state"[17] is a good stepping stone. According to Buchanan, the protective state can be understood as the "'law' broadly interpreted," while the productive state is associated with "legislation."[18] The protective state's main function is to enforce the law and to adjudicate conflicts between individuals. The protective state thus includes institutions like the police, the military, a supreme court, the criminal justice system and so forth. The productive state, on the contrary, is "that agency through which individuals provide themselves with 'public goods'."[19] The distinction between the productive and protective state is accentuated if we apply it, as Buchanan did himself, to a polycentric polity. In Buchanan's own outline of a classical liberal federalism, "the central or federal government is constitutionally restricted to the exercise of [. . .] protective state functions, while all other functions are carried out by separated state or provincial units."[20] In this interpretation of a polycentric polity, the polities essentially provide different 'public goods' and compete for individuals and capital, while the central government enforces and adapts the rules for competition.

I think that the distinction between the protective and the productive state is conceptually very potent. For the goals of this work, however, I need to expand the notion of the 'productive state.' The productive state in Buchanan's work is mainly responsible for producing standard 'public goods' like roads, libraries, lighthouses, public education and so forth. While Buchanan's classical liberal account of the productive state allows different polities to experiment with different school systems and different tax rates, there seem to be clear boundaries. As Buchanan's outline of the productive state is predominantly concerned with overcoming market failures, it seems unlikely that his system would also allow for socialist, strongly communitarian or paternalistic polities. In Buchanan's federalism, people, for example, are forced to participate in the 'free market' and respond to economic incentives. This forces the farmer and watchmaker to keep track of recent trends in consumer behavior and adapt to the most efficient modes of production. It is surely the case that many people would prefer to live in a society in which economic and the social life is more predictable, even though this entails monetary opportunity costs. In Buchanan's system this is not possible. Communities are not allowed to impose tariffs on certain products or ban certain products (e.g. electronics) altogether. The principle of free trade outlaws such 'ways of living.' If we want to get an overlapping consensus between the RoCD, we cannot exclude these and other important proposals for peacefully living together.

We can conclude that the polities in a polycentric democracy need to have more freedom to manage their affairs than in Buchanan's proposal to secure an overlapping consensus for polycentric democracy. How much freedom the polities have, however, needs to be decided by a bargaining process between the diverse factions of a polycentric democracy. In Chapter 10, I will come back to normative aspects of this question (see Section 10.6); for now, I will be concerned with institutional aspects of the regulatory framework. If we understand the protective state as the 'law' or the constitution of a national state, the framework that regulates competition between polities is a part of the constitution of the national state.

The political scientist Jenna Bednar recently wrote that "constitutional design needs to leave illusions of precision behind because the components of a constitutional system are inevitably flawed."[21] What is true for constitutions in general is also true for a framework that regulates competition between polycentric polities. Working out a detailed regulatory framework – or even a set of principles – for regulating a polycentric system would be too tall an order for this essay, and presumably for every single scholar, since the interplay between questions of law, economics and ethics is indeed intricate. I thus need to confine myself to a few very general considerations about the tasks of a regulatory framework for competition between polities. I want to comment here on four important tasks:

1 Defining the scope of the search space.
2 Regulating the frequency of searches.
3 Defining rules for exit and entry.
4 Regulating + institutional competition.

The framework for institutional competition defines the boundaries of the scope of the search space; it thus constrains the set of possible polity experiments. To put the same thought in a more spirited way, I might also say: The framework for institutional defines the rules under which the polycentric competition searches for 'realistic utopias.'

In a polycentric democracy, it is the job of the central government to define the boundaries of the search space. As I will later explain in more nuance, to ask for a detailed plan for how to regulate the search space would be to misunderstand the normative goals of the present approach. In practice, the boundaries of the search space will be defined through an ongoing bargaining process of the political parties. The parties to the bargain, however, must be aware that the narrower they define the search space, the more likely it becomes that society misses out on a realistic utopia or better ways to organize important subsystems of society. For instance, if every polity needs to respect a right to private property, this means that polities will hardly be able to test out versions of democratic socialism or versions of a property-owning democracy. Thus, if we define the search space too narrow, we might miss out on the best of all worlds. To put it differently, if we define the search space too narrow, we prohibit the proponents of ex ante unconvincing institutional proposals, the very chance to produce the evidence that is needed to persuade the rest of us.

At the same time, even though we do not have a good grasp on what the best political arrangement looks like (if there is one), we can certainly agree on a certain set of rights that every such political arrangement needs to respect. For instance, it is hardly imaginable that we would want to tolerate institutional experiments that allow for child abuse or instances of clear exploitation (i.e. slavery). A modern polycentric system furthermore would certainly prescribe certain minimum requirements regarding social security, health care and public education.

Moreover, the regulatory framework can at least indirectly steer the frequency of new political experiments, and thus the frequency and thoroughness in which the institutional search space gets traversed. The framework for institutional competition can do this mainly by setting incentives and disincentives. The central government could for instance incentivize existing regions or cities to file for more political autonomy, and incentivize the founding of new special economic zones, charter cities and so forth. It also could incentivize existing cities to come up and experiment with different social security models and so on. As a rule, the easier it gets for polities to experiment with new legislation, the more policy experiments a polycentric polity will feature. By the same token, if a regulatory framework makes it very expensive for political units to experiment with polices, interesting policy experiments will be less frequent.

A central task of the regulatory framework is to establish rules that regulate the entry and exit of new polities within the boundaries of the polycentric system. There must be rules that regulate under which conditions a new polity can be established – and, accordingly, there must be rules in case a polity wants to dissolve. By defining the rules that regulate the entry of new polities, the framework indirectly steers the frequency of searches. Furthermore, the framework also needs to define rules for entry and exit of individuals and capital. The reason for this can be illuminated by a simple example: Gabriel has always lived in 'Libertopia.' Now he is sixty-five and thinks about his retirement. Unfortunately, he has not saved a single dollar in his whole life. It seems intuitively plausible that if Gabriel decides to move to a 'Rawlsian polity', he cannot expect to receive the same pension as the citizens of the 'Rawlsian polity.' The prudent citizens in the Rawlsian polity after all have contributed to the pension scheme for a long time. Although setting adequate rules for entry and exit of individuals is surely difficult, the experience of the European Union shows that it is possible.[22]

Regulating competition between different polities is one of the central tasks for any framework. One of the central advantages of a polycentric polity is epistemic in nature. If people decide to adopt a polycentric democracy, one of the reasons for that decision is surely that such a system is reasonably good at using diversity to 'find new heights.' Unfortunately, there are two ways for a polity to create better living circumstances for its citizens. On the one hand, it might create better institutions and thus increase the efficiency of its services. On the other hand, a polity might also try to enhance its services by shifting its burdens to other polities, for instance, by imposing externalities on them.[23] The economist Viktor Vanberg points to the same problem: "Governments may, of course, respond to the noted competitive pressure in different ways, not all of which may work out to the mutual benefit of their citizens, and some of which may impose costs on citizens in other jurisdictions."[24]

If polities are allowed to 'privatize' the gains of their policies and socialize the costs by burden-shifting, it is hard for the citizens of a polycentric system to get a clear picture of the advantages and disadvantages of a certain polity. Furthermore, the behavior of such a polity might simply be judged as unfair. The regulatory framework thus needs to fend off negative externalities for epistemic as well as for normative reasons – or, to put it in more economical terms: "To adequately constrain governments' choice of strategies in their competition with each other is, in the first instance, the task of national constitutions."[25] When it comes to institutional competition, one common worry is that competition between polities necessarily erodes the welfare state against the will of the overwhelming majority. This is an especially important matter and I will discuss it in detail in Chapter 10, Section 10.6.2.

9.2.2 Multiplicity of decision centers

In a polycentric democracy, there are a multitude of polities at any time. These polities might be categorized with respect to their degree of innovativeness or originality, judged from the status quo. Since most people are relatively risk-averse, it is safe to assume that most polities will be very similar to what we know. Some polities might essentially just attempt small changes to our existing institutional fabric. Polities might for instance experiment with the following:

- Different collective choice rules.
- Different modes of redistribution.
- Different degrees of paternalism.
- Different modes of production.

Furthermore, there might also be very innovative polities that experiment with more radical changes in organizing social life. Some polities might put an emphasis on ecology as in the Green City or the Garden City movements. Other polities might emphasize technological progress. There also might be very radical experiments as, for instance, various implementation attempts of Rawlsian, libertarian or anarchist ideals. If the regulatory framework for competition will be interpreted rather libertarian, we might imagine even more radical experiments. Nozick paints a picture of such an everything-goes institutional competition:

> Visionaries and crackpots, maniacs and saints, monks and libertines, capitalists and communists and participatory democrats, proponents of phalanxes (Fourier), palaces of labor (Flora Tristan), villages of unity and cooperation (Owen), mutualist communities (Proudhon), time stores (Josiah Warren), Bruderhof, kibbutzim, kundalini yoga ashrams, and so forth, may all have their try at building their vision and setting an alluring example.[26]

Yet, it seems rather unlikely that a polycentric democracy – given the diversity of its factions – would arrive at such a libertarian interpretation of the regulatory framework. Furthermore, I should note that there are certain gains from scale. A polity cannot have a variety of restaurants, consumer goods, music halls, theaters, malls and so forth, if the total population is just around 10,000. Polities that feature the variety of products that most people in modern societies do not want to miss out need to be of a certain size. As the polity gets bigger, it will presumably also become more heterogeneous. Given that most people do not want to miss the advantages that come with population size, I assume that the most attractive polities will be based on new and more effective mechanisms for mediating the disagreement that comes with heterogeneity.

Applying our discussion of innovation diffusion, it seems plausible that, at least initially, most people would stick to the institutions that they know and trust. The majority of people will abstain from joining more innovative polities and will only join as the effects and the utility of a new institutional innovation have been clearly shown. Presumably, the adoption of innovative institutions will be along the lines that I described earlier (see Chapter 8, Section 8.3.1). Nozick seems to agree: "Not everyone will be joining special experimental communities, and many who abstain at first will join the communities later, after it is clear how they actually are working out."[27] A multitude of polities gives citizens the chance not only to live in the society they initially think would be best for them, but also the opportunity to get a better understanding of what they really want. Although it might be "humiliating to human pride,"[28] advancing human institutions might be most efficiently done by trial-and-error, by stumbling onto a new set of institutions that initially might be unpersuasive for most, but will gain approval once they are in action.

9.2.3 Evolutionary competition

In this section, I want to talk a little bit more about the process of well-regulated artificial evolutionary competition between polities and the results such processes will likely yield. In a polycentric system, the polities compete for citizens and capital. It is important to point out, though, that evolutionary competition is not akin to sports tournaments, since sports tournaments are zero-sum-games. In evolutionary competition, on the other hand, 'survival' may count as winning. Applied to the evolutionary competition between polities this means that polities do not need to maximize their citizenry or their income (qua attracting capital). A polity just needs to reach a certain threshold that allows it to function properly. We can observe very similar processes in the market: Out of all very successful restaurant owners, only some feel the need to expand their business while others simply don't. Furthermore, since different people might look for different kinds of polities, polities might face direct and indirect competition. It is imaginable that different polities will try to compete for more or less Rawlsian minded citizens. I call these more like-minded polities 'polity-families.' These havens for Rawlsians thus directly compete with each other for citizens and only indirectly, say, with anarcho-capitalistic polities. This means that the pressure to innovate and to adapt to new successful innovations will surely be greater within a certain polity-family than between different polity-families. Nevertheless, there surely would also be competition for citizens between different polity-families. Related to that, I would also expect collective learning across the boundaries of family-polities. If a certain libertarian polity develops an interesting drug policy that shows great results across the board, there seems to be very little reason why a conservative Burkean society might not be interested in copying this policy. I will later talk in more depth about the goals that a polycentric democracy aims to achieve by permitting a multitude of diverse political units to exist and compete in one nation.[29] For now, a short list of the aimed-for goals suffices. First of all, by giving each reasonable political faction the opportunity to live according to political rules that track their preferred principles more closely, a polycentric democracy *defuses deep and shallow disagreement*. Giving (deeply) diverse views room for testing their ideas should considerably relax the tensions of society and thus lead to more harmony within society. Moreover, as a consequence of giving reasonable factions the opportunity to live more closely to their preferred principles, a polycentric polity tends to reduce shallow instrumental and evaluative disagreement. Permitting a multitude of political units to coexist under one framework should also have an indirect effect on rationalizing the public discourse. Political scientists argue that the mere option of foot voting gives voters additional reason to get informed.[30] Moreover, the mere existence of a variety of feasible political units is supposed to decrease the costs for voters to get informed. In addition, decreasing the size of political units is linked to ameliorating the ever-present issue of principal–agent problems in politics.[31]

9.3 Implementation of political polycentrism

In the introduction to this chapter, I said that the ideal of polycentric democracy could be implemented in various ways. In this section, I want to discuss several options for implementation. At the same time, I want to mention a few political approaches that seem to fall under the rubric without making the cut. In addition, I want to defend the implementation of political polycentrism that I deem most suitable given the normative questions that this essay grapples with.

Let me start with a few introductory remarks to give some context to the questions in this section. In the history of political philosophy, the idea of institutional competition is not foreign. Philosophers, especially in the Enlightenment, commented regularly on the benefits of peaceful institutional competition, such as the competition between neighboring nation states or cities. Immanuel Kant, for example, writes in his *Idea for a Universal History with a Cosmopolitan Purpose* (1784):

> The mutual relationships between states are already so sophisticated that none of them can neglect its internal culture without losing power and influence in relation to the others. Thus the purpose of nature is at least fairly well safeguarded (if not actually furthered) even by the ambitious schemes of the various states. Furthermore, civil freedom can no longer be so easily infringed without disadvantage to all trades and industries, and especially to commerce, in the event of which the state's power in its external relations will also decline. [. . .] If the citizen is deterred from seeking his personal welfare in any way he chooses which is consistent with the freedom of others, the vitality of business in general and hence also the strength of the whole are held in check. For this reason, restrictions placed upon personal activities are increasingly relaxed, and general freedom of religion is granted. And thus, although folly and caprice creep in at times, enlightenment gradually arises.[32]

Kant views institutional competition here as a tool that not only checks authority, but also ensures the progress of enlightenment itself.[33] Hume also revered institutional competition for its ability to check power as well as to improve a polities' culture in general:

> Nothing is more favourable to the rise of politeness and learning, than a number of neighbouring and independent states, connected together by commerce and policy. The emulation, which naturally arises among those neighbouring states, is an obvious source of improvement. But what I would chiefly insist on is the stop which such limited territories give both to power and to authority.[34]

Johann Wolfgang von Goethe makes much the same point in his conversations with Johann Peter Eckermann, when he cites the multitude of free cities, dukedoms and jurisdiction – in one word: territorial fragmentation – as a major source of Germany's cultural opulence.

> Whence is Germany great, but by the admirable culture of the people, which equally pervades all parts of the kingdom? But does not this proceed from the various seats of government, and do not these foster and support it? Suppose, for centuries past, we had had in Germany only the two capitals, Vienna and Berlin, or only one of these, I should like to see how it would have fared with German culture, or even with that generally diffused opulence which goes hand in hand with culture.[35]

It is curious that although many great philosophers have commented on various advantages of institutional competition, they have never spent much effort on generalizing the advantages of institutional competition.[36] This is even more curious since, as Hume recognizes, philosophy itself was conceived in the highly decentralized and fertile environment of ancient Greece. He writes:

> Greece was a cluster of little principalities which soon became republics [. . .]. Each city produced its several artists and philosophers who refused to yield the preference to those of the neighbouring republics; their contention and debates sharpened the wits of men; [. . .] and the sciences, not being dwarfed by the restraint of authority, were enabled to make such considerable shoots[,] as are[,] even at this time[,] the objects of our admiration.[37]

The relative neglect of institutional competition by political philosophers leads to the problem that at the very outset there is only a handful of proposals for implementing a polycentric polity. Let us then review the available options. If we want to define what counts as a polycentric polity, we first need a yardstick or a criterion. Our most basic definition of polycentrism states that polycentric systems have three constitutive parts: a constitution, a multitude of decision centers and evolutionary competition between these decision centers. According to these standards, there is only one real-world example that prima facie qualifies as a polycentric polity: the federation. Bednar writes that a federation needs to meet three structural criteria: First, there must be a "geopolitical division."[38] This mean that the "territory is divided into mutually exclusive states,"[39] provinces, regions and so forth. Second the component states or jurisdictions need to have a certain level of "independence."[40] A federation consists therefore of a centralized government and a set of partially self-governing jurisdictions. The power distribution between the central government and the component jurisdictions in a federation can be very diverse. Furthermore – on a vertical level – the autonomy that jurisdictions in a federation enjoy do not need to be symmetrical. This means that in principle there can be regions within a federal state that have different degrees of autonomy. The third constitutive part of a federation, according to Bednar, is "direct government,"[41] in the sense that each citizen in a federation is directly "governed by at least two authorities."[42]

Other than federalism in its various forms, there are a few political approaches that resemble a polycentric polity, but do not qualify. As I mentioned earlier, anarchic conceptions of the social order do not qualify. Although, theoretically and in practice, anarchism features a multitude of decision centers and sometimes also something akin to competition between decision centers, a crucial part is missing, namely an encompassing framework that regulates the competition between polities and the scope of the anarchic experiments. For the same reason, a world of independent nations and city-states, according to our definition, does not qualify as an instance of polycentrism.

Besides the real-world political instantiations of polycentrism, there are also two theoretical concepts that pro tanto qualify: First, there is Chandran Kukathas's "liberal archipelago." In Kukathas's concept, minority groups should have the right to live according to their own values. If somebody is dissatisfied with the rules of his or her "archipelago" (or association), he or she is free to exit. His concept then puts huge emphasis on freedom of association and the right to exit.[43] To my knowledge, Kukathas, though, does not offer a detailed institutional discussion of how such a liberal archipelago can be implemented. Nozick's concept of the minimal state as a meta-utopia is another theoretical contribution that pro tanto qualifies as a polycentric polity. Nozick does not flesh out his concept in detail either, but rather provides a sketch of such a polycentric society. In his view the minimal state provides a framework in which groups of like-minded people may form communities to live according to their tastes, moral standards and beliefs. Comparing both approaches, it seems clear that the scope of experimentation in Kukathas's framework is even greater than in Nozick's, since it allows for infringing on negative rights.[44]

There is also a third concept that seems to qualify: Bruno Frey's FOCJ-approach. Frey envisions a state in which the productive function of the government is carried out by *functional, overlapping* and *competing jurisdictions*.[45] Every single jurisdiction in Frey's approach is specialized in providing a single public good (schooling, security, public health etc.). The extent of the respective jurisdiction is relative to "geography of problems"[46] and not a rudiment of historical power struggles. The problem with the FOCJ-approach seems to be that it is – like Buchanan's concept of federalism – too narrow. It is concerned only with the efficient production of public goods that the market does not sufficiently provide. It does not allow for a lot of the experiments that are dear to many and possibly interesting for all. Large-scale experiments with, for instance, democratic socialism, deliberative democracy, or with anarcho-capitalism have no room in Frey's concept. In this sense, it does not fulfill the criterion of a multitude of heterogeneous decision centers.[47] This is in my opinion also a problem with much of the recent literature about polycentricity. In this literature, the idea of polycentricity is coupled intimately – although most of the time implicitly – with the idea of subsidiarity.[48] Although much of this literature is quite theoretical and does not flesh out alternative institutional systems, it is nevertheless apparent that the impetus of this literature is that social problems ought to be solved on the local level, wherever possible. However, this approach, like Frey's, seems to block the door for any political idea that is married to ideas of moderate or radical central planning.

We now have a rough overview of different options for implementing the ideal of polycentric democracy. As it turns out, theory and practice converge on a single broad model for implementing the ideal of polycentrism: federalism. In the next step, I want to pick out the federal model that seems to be most suitable with regard to the objective of this essay. The goal of this essay is to sketch a political concept that is, from the perspective of the RoCD, at least a Pareto improvement over our current democratic modus vivendi arrangements. If the polycentric democracy approach wants to stand a chance of convincing the RoCD, it must fulfill two conditions: First, it needs to be reasonably feasible, stable and weakly or strongly justified. Second, it must allow us to collectively gain from evaluative and instrumental diversity. The first condition derives from my earlier discussions of what counts as 'escaping modus vivendi' (see Chapter 1). The second condition, however, derives from my decision in Chapter 6 to look for a political philosophy (or political concept) that thrives on diversity.

Let me first turn to the real-world instantiations of federalism. Although they fulfill the feasibility constraint, even at first glance, they do not seem to fulfill the second constraint. There is no existing federal system – at least none that I am aware of – that allows for radical new experiments. It is close to unthinkable that a state or province of a federal state like Germany or the United States of America would, in the foreseeable future, radically change its institutional outfit. To my knowledge, in the last century there are no instances in which a province in an existing federation has attempted a radical experiment such as implementing a property-owning democracy or a libertarian minimal state. This might be explained by pointing to three features of real-world federations. First, there is no fluctuation (exit and entry) in the number of polities in existing federal states. The number of polities is usually constant or increases slightly as new territories are accepted (as in the case of the European Union). The institutions of existing federations are simply not designed to give entrepreneurially spirited people the opportunity to experiment with new institutional rules. Second, federal states usually consist of polities that are themselves marked by profound internal disagreement. Thus, the same political deadlocks that occur on the national level also occur on the state level. As I pointed out earlier (see Chapter 7, Section 7.2), it is almost impossible to simultaneously convince a large number of people of an innovative idea. New ideas have in general a very hard time being adopted, if there is no opportunity to demonstrate their utility in a process of sequential persuasion. This means that it is very unlikely that any polity will, under normal circumstances, agree to a drastic change of rules – and thus the existing heterogeneity of existing polities effectively prevents polities from experimenting with new forms of organizing social life. The third point harks back to the first one: Not only are existing federations not designed to allow – let alone incentivize – institutional experiments, but also their constitutional outfit often effectively prohibits polities from conducting even relatively small experiments. We can draw two lessons from this. First, existing federations do not experiment with different forms of living. Second, the first result suggests that real-world federations do not qualify as instances of polycentrism in the first place, since they are effectively preventing the implementation of new institutional experiments and thus fail to meet the second criterion of polycentrism. Remember that a system has a multiplicity of decision centers if diverse players are free "to implement their different methods" and there exist different decision centers at every point in time. Freedom in this context means that they are, given certain restraints, permitted to actively "exercise their different opinions."[49]

Since the real world offers no convincing examples for implementing a polycentric polity, I will need to shift my attention to theoretical conceptions. Let us consider Kukathas's and Nozick's approaches. Even without going into a detailed discussion, there seems little hope that one of the frameworks can (institutionally) ground any proposal that passes the RoCD Test. Both approaches require that existing central governments forfeit their powers in favor of the component polities. That entails that the central government is deprived of all instruments to prevent moral horrors within the component polities. Furthermore, the libertarian interpretation of federalism might lead to a radical erosion of the welfare state and thus threaten what some of the RoCD understand as important advances of the modern state. In addition, an unmitigated institutional competition between polities might lead to a race to the bottom and thus not only pose an additional threat to the 'advancements' of the welfare state, but also actually leave everyone worse off. It should be further noted that radical changes in the institutional structure – such as they are proposed by Kukathas and Nozick – always involve incalculable risks. For that reason, realists, as well as huge parts of society, should be expected to strongly oppose such kinds of utopian social engineering.[50] It is then evident that an overwhelming majority of the RoCD would strongly oppose a move towards such an interpretation of federalism. Most of the RoCD, it must be assumed, strongly prefer our current modus vivendi to a polycentric democracy that builds on Nozick's or Kukathas's institutional framework. In addition, under scrutiny, it becomes doubtful whether, in the institutional conception of both philosophers, the central government has sufficient rights to work out an appropriate framework for the competition between polities. This raises the question of whether both systems can appropriately be understood as polycentric systems in the first place.

This leaves us with the awkward result that neither the real-world examples nor the theoretical concepts for implementing a polycentric democracy seem appealing. Above that, a closer examination of both existing and ideal versions of federalism, reveals that it is doubtful whether these approaches should be viewed as instances of polycentrism in the first place.

9.3.1 The Free-City Approach

Since none of the available approaches fits our endeavor, I want to propose a somewhat new approach for implementing the ideal of a polycentric polity: the Free-City Approach. The idea is very simple. Instead of reforming the whole political structure of existing nation states, the approach suggests adding free cities and a regulatory framework for institutional competition to a given nation state. Free cities can be added to any given nation state regardless of its internal structure. Adding free cities can be done in at least two ways: First, the national government can assign greater municipal authority to a selected set of existing cities. Second, free cities can be created simply by founding new cities on stretches of uninhabited land within the borders of a sovereign nation state. While the first option is certainly viable, the existing heterogeneity within most cities would certainly prohibit radical political experiments. The second approach, on the contrary, would prima facie allow more radical or outside-the-box experiments.

Let me try to get a little more traction on the second idea. The economist Paul Romer has recently put forward the concept of charter cities. Charter cities, explains the philosopher Christopher Freiman,

> resemble special economic zones; that is, small regions that experiment with economic rules that differ from those governing their larger 'host' countries. Yet, unlike a special economic zone, a charter city would also experiment with its own legal and political rules.[51]

The concept of charter cities was initially developed by Romer as means to spur economic growth in third world countries. The driving idea was that many third world countries suffer from political deadlock that does not allow them to undertake necessary reforms. While these countries may not be able to reform their whole country, they very well might rent out certain regions in the hope that foreign investors will essentially create a new Hong Kong or Shenzhen on their own soil. In the original idea outlined by Romer, a host nation rents out land and supplies residents, while a third party country, "a guarantor nation[,] implements and enforces the city's charter."[52]

Coming back to our discussion, it is easily observed that in a polycentric polity there is no need for a foreign 'guarantor.' Furthermore, while charter cities are initially tools to create free-market havens within sometimes highly corrupt third world countries to spur economic growth, charter cities in a polycentric polity can be employed to create any kind of institutional experiment that is in line with the framework for political competition and the constitution of the nation state.

Romer sketched four principles that every charter city should abide by:

1 They must be built on a tract of uninhabited land suitable for a multi-million-person scale city.
2 The city's charter specifies in advance the institutional rules governing the city.
3 All residents enjoy complete freedom of entry and exit.
4 All institutional rules apply equally to all residents.[53]

Although we can certainly discuss the details of these principles, they give a rough anchoring point for further discussions about charter cities.[54] Let me now outline several reasons why the Free-City Approach seems to be especially suitable for implementing the ideal of polycentric democracy:

- The Free-Cities Approach seems to be the only way in which we could realistically experiment with new forms of living. Thus, it is also the only form that would allow us to make real progress when it comes to discovering new heights, reducing shallow disagreement and defusing deep disagreement.
- Many people in principle are in favor of innovative projects as long as they and their interests are not in any way directly affected. This general attitude has crystallized in the so-called Not In My Backyard principle. One of the salient features of local experimentation vis-à-vis policy experimentation in a unitary centralized state is that the experiments affect fewer people, and thus agreements on the desirability of certain experiment are easier to come by.
- Furthermore, the very idea of free cities has deep roots at least in the history of Europe. The political scientist and historian Francis Fukuyama, for instance, ascribes a major role in ending the institution of serfdom to the existence of free cities in Europe:

  The existence of free cities [. . .] made serfdom increasingly difficult to maintain; they were like an internal frontier to which serfs could escape to win their freedom (hence the medieval saying, "*Stadtluft macht frei*" – city air makes you free).[55]

- Moreover, great cities have not only been prime locations for moral innovation in the past; in a world in which the power of the nation state is decreasing, cities are again becoming more and more interested in establishing their own brand and developing their own culture.[56]
- Transaction costs, as I pointed out elsewhere,[57] are comparatively small in cities. This is especially important when it comes to collective action problems[58] like the implementation and enforcement of social moral rules.
- In a sense, the real problem of modern life is how to create better modus vivendi arrangements.[59] Cities, contrary to communities as envisioned by Nozick, can be prime motors in creating better institutional compromises.
- One reason to defend a polycentric approach is that it helps both expert and public debates to become more rational. Experiments in free cities are highly salient and thus might naturally be in the attention of the public.
- Establishing ground rules for introducing charter cities seems a much easier administrative task than reforming the laws of entire countries so as to fulfill, for instance, the principle of subsidiarity.
- One of the prime arguments against utopian planning is that it might lead to moral horrors. Changing the constitution of a whole country in order to fit the principle of individual sovereignty seems very risky, since such a huge change would surely have many unintended consequences – and at least would open much room for many small-scale moral horrors.

9.3.2 Summary

In Section 9.1, I tried to convey a rough idea of polycentric democracy. In Section 9.2, I discussed the constituting parts of polycentric polities in general. The last section of this chapter featured a discussion about the various implementation options for the ideal of polycentric democracy. I argued that, given the normative goals of this essay, the available options for implementing political polycentrism are not satisfactory. Building on this result, I outlined a more suitable alternative for implementing political polycentrism: *the Free-City Approach*. The approach suggests that modern democracies can be transformed into polycentric democracies by simply granting a set of existing cities greater municipal autonomy and adding charter cities to the existing institutional structure. Consequently, when defending polycentric democracy in the next chapter, I will have in mind a political institutional system that realizes the ideal of polycentrism by granting some cities more municipal autonomy and by promoting charter cities.

Notes

1 Sophocles (2007, p. 191).
2 Aligica and Tarko (2013, p. 727).
3 Aligica and Tarko (2012).

4 It is actually not necessary that all polities search for better 'ways of living' or more efficient ways of producing a given set of public goods. People may also value stability and predictability very highly. Indeed, in Section 9.3 I will suggest an implementation strategy for polycentric democracy that pays particular respect to people's interest in stability and predictability.
5 The normative status of the outcomes is difficult to ascertain, since different RoCD will evaluate these outcomes differently. One person might, for instance, value solving disagreement (and thus an increase in rationality) in and of itself. Another might value a reduction of disagreement for purely instrumental reasons. Here I am solely interested in a descriptive account of the effects of polycentric democracy.
6 Licuanan *et al.* (2007, p. 1).
7 Huemer (2013).
8 Hayek (2012).
9 Parijs (1991).
10 Rawls (2007, p. 500).
11 Müller (2014).
12 Gürerk *et al.* (2006).
13 Gürerk (2013).
14 I will come back to this discussion in Chapter 10 (Sections 10.3 and 10.4).
15 It should be noted that even polities which follow very different normative ideals could fertilize each other through various channels (socially, economically, institutionally, etc.).
16 Polycentric democracy is one instantiation of political polycentrism. The discussion in this section, though, should apply not only to polycentric democracy, but also to political polycentrism in general.
17 Buchanan (2000, p. 88).
18 Buchanan (2000, p. 89).
19 Buchanan (2000, p. 89).
20 Buchanan (1996, p. 261). A few essential public goods like the military and federal courts, however, are also provided by the protective state.
21 Bednar (2009, pp. 214–215).
22 I will come back to this topic in Chapter 10 [Section 10.6].
23 Bednar (2009, p. 9, also compare chap. 3).
24 Vanberg (2008, p. 126).
25 Vanberg and Kerber (1994, p. 216).
26 Nozick (1999, p. 316).
27 Nozick (1999, p. 312).
28 Hayek (2012, p. 27).
29 I will discuss these points in detail in Chapter 10.
30 Somin (2011).
31 Vaubel (2008).
32 Kant (1991, pp. 50–51).
33 Even though political philosophers have commented on different aspects of institutional competition, the single most important feature of institutional competition – from the viewpoint of philosophy – was always its ability to check power. I will later discuss the benefits of institutional competition in checking authority in some detail (see Chapter 10, Section 10.3).
34 Hume (2006, p. 120). Emphasis in the original.
35 Eckermann (2001, p. 351).
36 Vaubel (2008) presents a good first overview about 'institutional competition' in traditional political philosophy.
37 Hume (2006, pp. 121–122).
38 Bednar (2009, p. 18).
39 Bednar (2009, p. 18).

40 Bednar (2009, p. 18).
41 Bednar (2009, p. 18).
42 Bednar (2009, p. 19).
43 Kukathas (2007).
44 I will discuss both approaches in contrast to my own approach in more detail later (in Chapter 10, Section 10.6). For the moment, sketching their approaches in this fashion suffices for the goals of this chapter.
45 Frey (2005).
46 Frey (2005, p. 547).
47 Aligica and Boettke (2009), Aligica and Tarko (2012), Aligica (2014), Aligica and Boettke (2011a), Aligica and Boettke (2011b), McGinnis (1999), Ostrom (2005), Ostrom (1991), Ostrom (1997).
48 At times, though, also explicitly, Aligica and Tarko (2012, p. 256).
49 Aligica and Tarko (2012, p. 18).
50 Popper (2002b, pp. 61–64).
51 Freiman (2013, p. 40). See also Moberg (2014).
52 Freiman (2013, p. 43). See also Müller (2016).
53 Freiman (2013, p. 43).
54 Charter cities in my framework, for instance, do not need to be that big.
55 Fukuyama (2012, p. 376).
56 Bell and De-Shalit (2011).
57 Müller (2014).
58 Eichenberger and Funk (2011).
59 Buchthal (2013, p. 44).

10 The argument for polycentric democracy

The central goal of this essay is to find a more satisfying response to the problem of modus vivendi. In Chapters 9 and 10 I develop a new answer to this age-old problem. Whereas in Chapter 9 I spell out the institutional prerequisites of a polycentric democracy, I provide a normative argument in favor of polycentric democracy in Chapter 10. The final chapter proceeds in line with the presentation of the first three second-order theories in the first part of this essay. In Section 10.1 I give a description of the moral shortcomings of the modus vivendi from the perspective of the RoCD. In Sections 10.2–10.4 I present two arguments in favor of polycentric democracy. The first argument makes the case that a polycentric democracy, through various mechanisms, improves public discourse and reduces subjugation (Section 10.3). The second argument makes the case that if considerably more just ways of living together are possible, polycentric democracy presents society's best chance of discovering them (Section10.4). In the last two sections I cover the stability and feasibility (10.5) and some of the most pressing worries about polycentric democracy (10.6).

10.1 Interpreting modus vivendi

In this section, I want to get a better understanding of what is wrong with the current modus vivendi. As I have already stated in the beginning of this essay, detecting a normative problem always presupposes some kind of normative standard. For instance, Gabriel will view 'war' as a problem if he sees human suffering as something to be avoided. Yet, for Tsunetomo Yamamoto, who famously crafted the *Hagakure*, the Japanese warrior bible, a human life might not count as much.[1] To give another example, Mia will judge income inequality as a social problem only if she values income equality in the first place.[2] Therefore, a libertarian and an egalitarian will surely disagree about the features of modus vivendi that they find unjustified and subjugating.[3] From this it seems to follow that if the RoCD do not share a normative perspective, they will also not share a joint problem description.

This raises the question of whether we need a 'shared' problem description to sketch a solution to modus vivendi. I think not: Finding a 'shared problem description' is not necessary for finding a 'shared' solution, that is, a solution that every RoCD prefers to our current modus vivendi. To see this, remember that every free exchange presupposes that two persons have 'different problems.' If Gabriel has a banana and craves a sandwich, while Mia has a sandwich and craves a banana, both have different problems; they both see their own status quo as wanting for different reasons. However, although they have different problems, a simple barter will solve both their problems. Thus, there might be a solution to modus vivendi, although members of our RoCD do not share a problem description.

With these caveats in place, I will nevertheless attempt to give a shared account of the moral deficiency of modus vivendi. I want to identify properties of the current modus vivendi that all RoCD from their own perspectives deem morally problematic. Since the RoCD have very diverse perspectives, the problem description needs to be abstract. The problem description, I propose, centers around two notions. The first one I call 'the problem of subjugation.' The second one I will address as the problem of 'road-blocking utopia.' The problem description, I should emphasize, relates to our current modus vivendi in particular.

10.1.1 The problem of subjugation

As I have outlined in the beginning, a modus vivendi arrangement can be viewed as its total set of laws and regulations. From the perspective of a participant, say Benni, this set of laws can be partitioned in justified and unjustified laws. Justified laws are the laws that an agent has sufficient moral reasons to honor and uphold. Unjustified laws, on the flip side, are laws that an agent has no conclusive moral reasons to honor, but might still comply with.

Now, modern modus vivendi arrangements exist because we disagree about the core notions of morality, like justice, political authority, freedom and legitimacy. Since even well-meaning and informed deliberators (like the RoCD) disagree about these notions, we also find ourselves in disagreement about what counts as just, legitimate or justifiable. This is of course not only a philosophical problem, but also a real-world issue. It is reasonable to assume that large parts of the societies living under modus vivendi arrangements view parts of the legislation they are living under as unjustified. As democrats, citizens in the modus vivendi are not only the subject of law, but also in the driver's seat when it comes to legislation. Since we disagree about the basic notions of morality, we evidently do not only disagree about the justification for our current legislation, but also about what legislation and what obligations we are justified to impose on others, in case the elections give our faction the de jure right to rule. A social democrat, for example, might think that he or she is fully justified to burden a liberal with a high tax rate. A liberal might in turn see the adoption of LGBT-friendly legislation as fully justified, even if conservatives strongly disagree. Citizens thus settle for particular modus vivendi bargains "not because the outcome is one that they accept as 'just,' but because, for instance, what they take to be their vital interests are sufficiently protected and they are not prepared to devote further resources to political struggle."[4] Since this is the case, it is understandable that the attitude of citizens in striking bargains might best qualified with adjectives like "'grudging,' 'wary' and 'reluctant'."[5] Disagreement about what counts as justified in the political process crystallizes as subjugating legislation. While everyone, or at least every faction, has different reasons for judging one set of laws as justified and another one as unjustified, all parties, of course, would like to live under conditions that are less unjustified from their point of view. There is thus good reason to believe that any institutional modus vivendi arrangement that reduces subjugation will be judged favorably. Of course, reducing subjugation is not an easy task, because what one person judges as a reduction of subjugation another might see as an increase in subjugation. Since this is the case, it might be advisable to look at least in part to the roots of subjugation.

Subjugating legislation, as I stated earlier, is to a very large degree a result of disagreement. If disagreement leads to subjugation, then reducing disagreement should ceteris paribus lead to less subjugation. Let me illuminate what I have in mind here. Imagine two buckets. In the first bucket, we put all the legislation we have collectively consented to, and in the second bucket, we put all the legislation we are, collectively, disagreeing about. It is clear, then, that only the second bucket causes subjugation. Further, reducing disagreement means that we simply reduce the number of laws in the second bucket. This brings us back to the question of how we can reduce disagreement in the political arena. Undoubtedly, at least some of our disagreement in the realm of politics is due to what I have called lazy and shallow disagreement. It is of course, as mentioned earlier, very hard to assess what parts of our disagreements are caused by shallow and what parts are caused by deep disagreement. Although I cannot say much about this, analytically speaking, I might at least distinguish the cases in which Gabriel is subjugated because of lazy or shallow disagreement, and thus *by accident*, from those cases where Gabriel is subjugated because of deep disagreement. Let me give you a simple two-person model to illuminate what I have in mind here.

1 Deep disagreement

i Benni has imposed rule Y and rightly judges that Y is morally mandated.[6] Gabriel, on the other hand, sees no moral reason to honor Y. Gabriel consequently feels rightly subjugated.

2 Lazy and shallow disagreement

Disagreement on the basis of wrong instrumental beliefs:

ii Benni has imposed X_0 to further Y, but X_0 is not an appropriate means to further Y. Gabriel wants to further Y, too. Gabriel rightly proposed X_1 to further Y. Gabriel thus rightly judges that he has no reason to honor X_0 and feels rightly subjugated.

iii Benni has imposed X_1 to further Y, where X_1 is the appropriate means to further Y. Gabriel wants to further Y, too. Gabriel wrongly proposed X_0 to further Y. Gabriel thus wrongly judges that he has no reason to honor X_0 and feels wrongly subjugated.

Disagreement on the basis of an incorrect evaluative assessment:

iv Benni has imposed Y, but Benni wrongly judges that Y is morally mandated.[7] Gabriel sees no moral reason to honor Y, and consequently feels rightly subjugated.

v Benni has imposed Y, and Benni rightly judges that Y is morally mandated. Gabriel wrongly judges that he has no moral reason to honor Y, and consequently feels wrongly subjugated.

After dotting the i's and crossing the t's, I count four possible instances of subjugation by mistake and one case in which subjugation is based on deep disagreement. The set of disagreement and perceived subjugation could thus be reduced from five cases to only one, if Benni and Gabriel could get their facts and evaluations straight. If the five instances of subjugation are evenly distributed, then it would be four times more likely that a member of a modus vivendi is subjugated by accident, rather than because of deep disagreement. Unfortunately though, we do not know the true distribution. If we are attentive, we might note that there is also something like shallow agreement: that is, two persons agreeing, for instance, on moral principles, even though both persons – if they were better informed – would not agree. Thus we might object that, at least in principle, epistemic progress might shatter shallow agreements at the same rate as it resolves shallow disagreements.[8] If that were true, we might worry that epistemic progress will not necessarily lead to more agreement and thus less subjugation. My response to that is that it is plausible that there is shallow agreement about norms and even shallow agreement on instrumental questions. For instance, two people might wrongly believe (and thus agree) that X_1 is the best means to achieve Y, but in reality X_0 is the best means to achieve Y. However, the important thing to note is this: Although more (or full) information in evaluative tasks, in principle, can lead to more disagreement (say if value pluralism understood as ontological account is true), having full information with regard to instrumental beliefs cannot lead to an increase of disagreement. The reason is simply that there is a single truth about which means ($X_0 \ldots X_n$) is the best means to achieve Y. In instrumental tasks, full information leads from shallow agreement about the wrong means to warranted agreement about the right means. Thus even if we grant that epistemic progress shatters shallow moral agreements at the same rate as it resolves shallow moral disagreements, epistemic progress should on balance reduce subjugation.

In summary: It should be in the common interest of the RoCD to reduce cases of 'mistaken' subjugation. Reducing shallow disagreements requires epistemic progress. However, since the RoCD will put different weight on reducing mistaken subjugation, all we can conclude is this: Reducing mistaken subjugation is a goal that all members of the RoCD share. Thus if two arrangements are similar across all relevant moral dimensions, except in their capacity to reduce shallow disagreements, the RoCD would chose the one that is better at reducing shallow disagreement and thus mistaken subjugation.

10.1.2 The problem of institutionally road-blocking utopia

Modus vivendi arrangements do not spark enthusiasm. The reasons for this, I speculate, are twofold. First, modus vivendi arrangements are a second-best for all parties involved. While it is nice to live in peace and it is surely better than living in Hobbes's state of nature, living under a modus vivendi arrangement is burdensome in the ways outlined in the last section and the early parts of this essay. The second reason why living under such arrangements sparks no enthusiasm is that our modus vivendi arrangements do not even hold the promise that this will ever change.[9] Modus vivendi is not about solving our conflicts, but about reconciling them. The institutions of our current modus vivendi arrangements thus can be viewed as a "constitutional settlement"[10] that cements the status quo.

Given our lazy, shallow and deep disagreements, convincing one half of the population is a very difficult task, and persuading three fourths of them – as is usually necessary for changing modus vivendi arrangements – is nearly impossible. This, I venture, is affirmed by our experience as citizens. Our current modus vivendi arrangements are slow to adapt and the slightest improvements in the arrangements are cumbersome. Plans for reform usually get watered down to an extent that they are hardly recognizable. In modus vivendi arrangements, politics is thus rightly viewed as a muddy process that does not inspire much hope for change. What I want to emphasize here is that the bleak political reality stands in stark contrast to the common hope to live in a truly just society – a society in which the rules of the games are an expression of justice. In short, we might say that our current political arrangements are institutionally road-blocking every attempt to escape modus vivendi. Therefore, a political arrangement that allows for substantial progress has a good chance to be viewed favorably from the perspective of the RoCD.

10.2 Solving modus vivendi

In the history of political philosophy as well as in the history of political economics, we can find a number of arguments for a more decentralized political order. In this section, I want to organize the arguments developed in this essay and some of the classical arguments in order to make a powerful case for a polycentric democracy.

The goal of this section, however, is not only to make a case for polycentric democracy, but also to defend a more specific claim: *the Domination Claim*. The claim can be stated in the following manner:

Domination Claim: $\text{RoCD}_i\text{: Pol}_i > \text{PD} \geq \text{D}_{MV}$

The first part of this claim reads: For every RoCD, it is true that they prefer their own politico-philosophical conception to that of polycentric democracy.

This means that each representative, if she or he could choose to live in one of the two institutional sets, she or he would choose the institutional set that she or he initially put forward in the discussion (see Chapter 1). I will not discuss the first part of this claim ($RoCD_i$: $Pol_i > PD$) in detail, but rather assume its truth. In the following sections, I want to focus rather on the second part of the Domination Claim: $RoCD_i$: $PD \geq D_{MV.}$ This means that every representative would choose polycentric democracy over our current, rather centralized democratic modus vivendi arrangements, or would be neutral between both options.

In this section, I want to present two arguments to support this claim. Before I go into the arguments, let me briefly illuminate some of the normative implications of the Domination Claim. First, it seems clear that if the claim could be substantiated, I would have found a political system that Pareto dominates our current democratic modus vivendi. Unfortunately, even if this were the case, this would not imply that a polycentric democracy is justified from the perspective of the RoCD. That a political system A is better than a political system B from everybody's perspective is not a sufficient condition for A being intersubjectively justified.[11] Nonetheless, I will be content to defend the claim that *polycentric democracy is simply a better modus vivendi arrangement.*[12] Logically, it is of course conceivable that the polycentric system might be not only Pareto superior to our current modus vivendi arrangements, but also justified from the viewpoint of the RoCD. I must confess, though, that I do not think that any political order will be justified from the view of the RoCD. Making the case that a polycentric democracy Pareto dominates the existing modus vivendi democracies is in itself a tall order – and maybe the most we can hope for, anyway.

I now turn to the argument that substantiates the Domination Claim. The Domination Claim itself rests on two pillars: the Amelioration Argument and the Unblocking Utopia Argument. In these two claims, I will organize the arguments for a political polycentric system developed in this essay as well as those found in the history of political philosophy and economics. The two arguments that I will develop in the coming sections can be summarized in this fashion.

1 **The Amelioration Argument**: Polycentric democracy ameliorates the problem of subjugation by improving public discourse, mitigating the democratic principal–agent problem and defusing deep disagreement.
2 **The Unblocking Utopia Argument:** Social innovators need space to demonstrate the value of their ideas, to generate the evidence that is necessary to convince 'lukewarm supporters' and eventually skeptics. By giving every reasonable political doctrine space to generate additional and maybe decisive evidence for its own principles, a polycentric democracy will discover better institutional solutions and maybe even 'utopia' if it exists.

The first claim is original foremost in organizing classic arguments for polycentrism and institutional competition – some of which I have already briefly outlined in Chapter 9, Section 9.2.3. The second claim has a better claim of being an original contribution to the discussions of polycentrism. It should be further noted that the claims are internally connected in many ways so that some redundancy is inevitable.

For reasons of humility, I will not put my own approach through the RoCD Test. Every reader of this essay, I assume, is a representative of a certain comprehensive doctrine and thus might judge for himself or herself whether the Domination Claim might succeed.

10.3 The Amelioration Argument

As outlined earlier, the set of modus vivendi rules can be partitioned into justified and unjustified rules. In this section I set out to show how a political polycentric system ameliorates and eradicates what makes a modus vivendi burdensome: subjugating rules.

10.3.1 Improving public discourse

The quality of political discourse depends on at least two variables: an epistemic and a motivational variable. To work properly, our discourse about institutions needs to rely on proper knowledge as well as agents that are motivated to argue based on the best knowledge available. In the first part of this section, I argue that polycentric democracy improves the public discourse because it creates bodies of knowledge that will allow us to settle many important debates. In the second part, I argue that polycentric democracy creates additional reasons for the public to concern themselves with political questions and that this should enhance the quality of discourse. Finally, in the third part, I argue that institutional competition makes it easier for the public to evaluate the performance of their own governing body. Enhancing the discourse in these ways should decrease shallow as well as lazy disagreements and thus the set of laws that are deemed unjustified.

Rationalizing discourse

Many debates in political philosophy, in applied ethics and in the social sciences more generally, are marked by reasonable disagreement because we essentially lack the data to resolve the conflict. This point has been made by many philosophers as well as social scientists with diverse political ties. Helene Landemore writes:

> A lot of apparent 'value pluralism' – for example, the disagreement between Democrats and Republicans over the legitimate size of government – can arguably be explained by a disagreement about facts, including complicated facts such as causal relationships between big government and efficient spending in a given social and economic context.[13]

As Landemore hints at, this is surely not only true for the legitimate size of governments, but also for a lot of other issues that are hotly debated in public: for instance, drug policy, school policy, environmental policy, social security questions, basic income and health care reform. The crucial point here is this: People having more or less the same values might still disagree on the best way to achieve any of these goals. Such purely instrumental disagreements can be as fierce as disagreements about ends. A polycentric system gives its citizens and polities more freedom to experiment with policy alternatives. Granting polities more leeway in experimenting with policies will essentially solve many policy questions that set reasonable people apart. It should be noted that even in a polycentric society there are of course certain limits to experiments, which will be reflected in the data sets[14] – but it is, of course, better to have more data than less. We also prefer a medicine that is reasonably well tested to a medicine that is not tested at all.

It should be further noted that more data might also solve debates between philosophical rivals that from the outside seem irresolvable. Take for instance the debate between classical liberals like Hayek and egalitarian liberals like Rawls. Both thinkers point to very different political institutional sets. Rawls, as I pointed out earlier, thinks that the two principles of justice will most likely be best satisfied by the institutions of a property-owning democracy or the institutions associated with democratic socialism. Yet, it might very well turn out that – empirically – the two principles of justice will be best fulfilled by a classical liberal institutional set. Daniel Kofman agrees:

> Depending on how the characterization of economic, social, and psychological "reality" unravels, a standard egalitarian apprehension is that the [difference principle] could turn Rawls-the-would-be-egalitarian into a von Hayek or Milton Friedman in egalitarian clothing.[15]

It might be less known that even an ardent warrior for classical liberalism, such as Mises, thought that what sets liberals and socialists apart is not normative theory, but disagreement about socio-economic facts:.

> Liberalism is distinguished from socialism, which likewise professes to strive for the good of all, not by the goal at which it aims, but by the means that it chooses to attain that goal.[16]

Although it is surely true that much of our moral disagreement – especially in political philosophy – is based on our disagreement about facts and socio-economic theories, it is also true that sometimes our disagreement is purely normative. But normative disagreement can be shallow as well.

In his famous essay *Facts and Principles*, Gerald A. Cohen writes that "justice is not the only value that calls for (appropriately balanced) implementation: other principles, sometimes competing with justice, must also be variously pursued and honored."[17] These other values certainly include freedom, equality, security and a certain degree of economic prosperity. Other than that, we might wonder whether values such as creativity or a vibrant social life might be also values that we would look for in a society. It is certainly not uncommon that relatively poor people choose cities that have a vibrant culture and deep horizontal and vertical diversity over cities that might feature more equality, harmony and welfare.

In Chapter 1, Section 1.2, I introduced and discussed the notion of shallow disagreement. In our discussion, we came across the case of Mia, who is an ardent egalitarian and finds herself, after a long political struggle, in an egalitarian utopia. As I argued in the beginning of this essay, it is at least conceivable that Mia, after living in this community for a certain time, might judge that she was actually mistaken about her preference for egalitarianism. Perhaps she might find herself in agreement with Nietzsche's ideal of perfectionism that puts heavy emphasis on the value of individual struggle. Of course this blade cuts both ways: It might very well be the case that Murray, who has been an ardent libertarian since he read Ayn Rand at the age of fifteen, might find his expectations disappointed when he has the chance to live in the equivalent of Galt's Gulch. Maybe he will discover that a totally unregulated society is cognitively way too burdensome for the individual, and he will discover that social regulations simplify life to a degree that benefits everyone.

A small two-person model illuminates the best case of harmonization through epistemic progress. We have two agents, Gabriel and Benni. For both, we see the ordinal ordering of three social worlds X,Y and Z. Gabriel and Benni think that all these worlds are pro tanto better than the modus vivendi democracy in which they currently live. In the beginning, their preference ordering signifies strong political disagreement over hypothetical social worlds.

- Gabriel: $S_x > S_y > S_z$
- Benni: $S_z > S_y > S_x$

Let us now imagine that Gabriel and Benni, who are political opponents in our current world, live in a polycentric democracy. Imagine further that many citizens agree with Benni and believe that S_z might be the best conceivable and feasible social world. Consequently, they open up a charter city (see Chapter 9, Section 9.3) and try to put their ideal into practice. Unfortunately, while testing S_z, they find out that the innovative economic theory on which S_z is based turns out to be incorrect. The result of their trial is thus that S_z fails to produce the expected living standards. Everybody agrees after testing S_z that S_z is not an improvement over D_{MV}. Consequently, they erase S_z from the set of prima facie feasible improvements of D_{MV}.

Harmonization through epistemic progress

- Shallow disagreement based on wrong beliefs:
  - Gabriel: $S_x > S_y > S_z$
  - Benni: $S_z > S_y > S_x$

to:

- Gabriel: $S_x > S_y > \not{S}_*$
- Benni: $\not{S}_* > S_y > S_x$

Let us further imagine that the polycentric system tests both of the remaining options (S_y and S_x). There certainly might be a case where Benni basically sees his predictions substantiated through the experiment, while Gabriel – after experiencing both worlds – concludes that his hypothesis about his normative ordering was falsified. He still thinks that both S_y and S_x are better than D_{MV}, but he reverses his ordering.

- Shallow disagreement based on (empirically) wrong preferences:
  - Gabriel: $S_x > S_y$

A posteriori:

- Gabriel: $S_y > S_x$

In this admittedly schematic case, we turned strong disagreement between our agents Gabriel in Benni into harmony.

- Resulting harmony:
  - Gabriel: $\mathbf{S_y > S_x}$
  - Benni: $\mathbf{S_y > S_x}$

Although I have presented only a model, we should recognize that in history there are institutional sets that at some time were deemed to be superior to D_{MV}. Fascism and socialism come to mind. Both were falsified not (mainly) by intellectual debates, but by violent political experiments.

I can conclude then that a polycentric system tends to eradicate shallow instrumental and evaluative disagreement and in that should enhance the quality of political debates between reasonable people.

Motivating public discourse

The quality of political discourse depends on sufficient knowledge being available to citizens, and citizens being motivated to acquire the relevant knowledge for the purpose of public debates. While academic discourse has some strong internal reasons and external incentives to base arguments on the best available knowledge, this is hardly true for public discourse. One of the central problems of public discourse, as I discussed in Chapter 4 (see Section 4.1.2), is that the public usually has only marginal incentives to invest much time in their voting decision. Schumpeter writes:

> The typical citizen drops down to a lower level of mental performance as soon as he enters the political field. He argues and analyzes in a way which he would readily recognize as infantile within the sphere of his real

> interests. He becomes a primitive again. His thinking becomes associative and affective.[18]

Why is it the case that people – as countless studies confirm[19] – are usually not well informed about politics? Or to put it in comparative terms: Why is it the case that the typical individual will usually spend more time becoming informed about what mobile phone to buy than about which politician to vote for? The reason for that has something to do with the fact that purchase decisions are individual decisive, while voting decisions are not. If Benni spends more time becoming informed about various mobile phones, he will increase the chance to end up with a mobile phone that really suits his needs; if Benni spends more time on learning about how to be a good parent, he increases the likelihood of becoming a good parent to his daughter. The same direct relationship, however, does not hold for casting a ballot. If Benni spends more time on getting informed about politics, this will not significantly enhance his chances for obtaining a more desirable political outcome. Given that Benni does not enjoy getting informed about politics, and he has no chance to influence the result of political elections, there is little reason for him to spend much time to become well-acquainted with the political issues of the day.

Even though for the average citizen there is no instrumental value in getting informed, some people see intrinsic value in studying up on politics, economics and moral philosophy. Others see it as their civic duty to cast a well-informed ballot. Unfortunately, both studies on voter ignorance and the bestseller charts on Amazon show that the latter groups have always been a small minority of the electorate in modern democracies.

There are many reasons why people disagree about politics. In the previous sections I have mainly looked at epistemic explanations for political disagreements. In many cases, I have concluded that the reason why reasonable people disagree has to do with the evidential basis being inconclusive. However, another reason why there is disagreement in politics has to do with the fact that people are just not well-informed about politics. In this section, I want to point to two features of polycentric democracy that might help to ameliorate the problem of voter ignorance and thus lazy disagreements.

One of the central advantages of a polycentric democracy is that it allows for foot voting. A main difference between foot voting and ballot box voting is that foot voting is individually decisive. Thus, in polycentric democracies compared to centralized modus vivendi democracies, voters have additional reasons to get informed about political affairs. The legal scholar Ilya Somin explains:

> If a "foot voter" can acquire information about superior economic conditions, public policies, or other advantages in another state, he or she can move to that state and benefit from them even if all other citizens do nothing. This creates a much stronger incentive for foot voters to acquire

> relevant information about conditions in different jurisdictions than for ballot box voters to acquire information about public policy.[20]

A polycentric system thus rationalizes the public discourse by providing citizens with incentives to become more informed. Somin agrees:

> Unlike in the case of ballot box voters, information acquisition by foot voters is largely exempt from collective action problems.[21]

Note that Somin does not say that voters have a better incentive to get informed about politics per se in a political arrangement that allows for foot voting between different states. In a polycentric democracy, the citizens have a strong reason to get informed about the advantages of other political units, but not about politics per se. In a centralized modus vivendi arrangement there are not many reasons for the average citizen to get informed about different forms of democratic governments, different forms of organizing health care, different forms of organizing the welfare state and so forth. In a polycentric democracy, however, the individual has as much reason to get informed about mobile phones as she or he has to get informed about the available ways of organizing social life – simply because her choice for or against a particular way of organizing health care, primary education, a more just and thus more peaceful living environment, a more inclusive political environment, a more responsive way of governing the commons and so forth is individually decisive. If the individual identifies a more just, a more inclusive, a more peaceful polity, she or he has the option to move there. In a polycentric democracy the problem of voter ignorance is thus ameliorated through an invisible hand–type mechanism. Voter knowledge about the feasible set with regards to all domains of organizing social life should increase, simply because everyone has a personal interest in being better informed about existing, alternative ways of living together or organizing the production and distribution of collective goods.

Yardstick competition

Although the costs of moving have declined over recent years, moving between jurisdictions still comes with certain social costs. Leaving a jurisdiction often means leaving behind friends and family. For many people, thus, leaving their jurisdiction might be next to unthinkable. This seems to raise a problem for my argument. If Gabriel will not go on vacation, he will most likely not read through tourism prospects. However, if moving is no option for Gabriel, he will have no additional reason to be informed about the governing mechanisms of other communities. There are at least two things to say to this counterargument. First of all, moving is already a real option for many citizens today: According to Somin, "63 percent of Americans have moved at least once in their lives, and 43 percent have made at least one interstate move."[22] But the more important argument is that a polycentric system improves 'voice' through yardstick competition. Yardstick competition must be distinguished from mobility-based competition.[23] Mobility-based competition is mainly concerned with different jurisdictions competing over scarce resources such as individuals, capital goods and companies. In general, research on this kind of competition focuses on the effects of policy with regard to the interjurisdictional allocation of goods, firms and individuals. Yardstick competition, in contrast, is concerned with how political agents "are rewarded or sanctioned on the basis of comparative assessments of performance across jurisdictions."[24]

People have a hard time evaluating how the government performs if they lack a comparison. Imagine that the whole world had been organized according to the economic principles of the Soviet Union until this day.[25] In such a world, neither the politicians nor the public would have any idea what they are missing out on. Without a comparison, people might hope that there is a better alternative for X, but they would not know what it could be. Having an already established alternative to point to, however, makes it much easier to organize a critical mass that demands improvements. This, of course, also allows for better control over the government. If there is no comparison, the government can always purport that they are already doing the best job possible. If there is a comparison and people know with some certainty that there is actually a way to improve on X, this makes it easier for the public to adequately judge and influence public administration.[26] Yardstick competition, in summary, gives voters a better grasp of what they can reasonably expect from their political representatives.[27]

10.3.2 Defusing deep disagreement

In the last section, I outlined how a polycentric system could ameliorate 'shallow disagreement.' Unfortunately, it is highly likely that some of our normative disagreement is deep rather than shallow. Even if we could eradicate big parts of shallow disagreement, we should expect that we will be left with some deep disagreements. Historically, one of the central answers to deep disagreement is what Benjamin Constant calls the "liberty of the moderns"[28] and Gaus dubs "the rights of the moderns."[29] Gaus argues that modern political philosophy[30] tends to "conceive of the problem of moral legislation as finding a common way of regulating the moral decision space."[31] Such an approach, he tells us, can be understood as a "centralizing response."[32] The problem with such an approach is that "if we take as inputs a large body of diverse standards and seek to generate a single type of conduct that is required of all, we are unlikely to succeed."[33] Trying to come up with a single type of rule will theoretically lead – following Gaus – to an indeterminate set; in practice this will often lead to (violent) conflict. From an historical point of view, one of the most important devices to deal with deep disagreement is disaggregation or, in Gaus's words "partitioning the moral space."[34] He explains: "Rather than seeking a uniform way to regulate the moral space, we must partition it. We can devolve authority over different parts of it to different individuals."[35] Gaus refers here to the classical liberal solution to cope with deep disagreement. Since, so goes the classical liberal idea, we cannot reach unanimity on many moral questions – how to raise children, what to consume, which gods to praise and so on – leaving the decision about these things to the individuals, devolving jurisdictional rights, seems to be a reasonable solution that could help to keep the peace and to fulfill the preferences of everyone at least to some extent. Gaus, therefore, follows classical liberal thinkers in emphasizing jurisdictional rights (and especially private property rights as jurisdictional rights) as means to "economize on collective justification."[36]

This solution, however, seems to work only for private goods and for club goods in the technical sense. Granting individuals a relatively large sphere of moral authority gives people the chance to buy what they want, consume what they want and consume certain club goods – for example, practicing their religion with other believers in a certain location. What I am suggesting here is that we could also solve deep disagreement over 'common goods,' which includes questions of distribution and questions of collective decision-making, by devolving jurisdictional rights.

This is of course not an entirely new idea. Many political economists and philosophers have touched upon this.[37] Historically, thinkers viewed disaggregation – for instance through federalism – as a mechanism to diffuse tensions between different ethnicities and religions.[38] More recent contributions, however, view federalism as a viable mechanism for diffusing deep moral disagreement. Important contributions in this field are, as I pointed out earlier, Kukathas's *Liberal Archipelago* and Nozick's discussion of a meta-utopia in *Anarchy, State and Utopia*. Although many classical liberal thinkers have written about or commented on the idea of federalism, Buchanan's contribution to the theory of federalism sticks out for many reasons. In *Federalism and Individual Sovereignty*, Buchanan argues that a consistent classical liberal position must take "individual sovereignty" and not "individual liberty" as its central value. Buchanan argues that pressing to maximize individual liberty "would, to many of us, represent a leap backward into the Hobbesian jungle." Buchanan thinks that a more "meaningful maximand" would be "(equal) individual sovereignty."[39] The political economist explains:

> This objective allows for the establishment of political-collective institutions, but implies that these institutions be organized so as to minimize political coercion of the individual. Coercion is defined as being required to do things or to submit to things others do to you, that you do not, or would not, voluntarily agree to do yourself or to have done to you.[40]

Moving from 'individual liberty' to 'individual sovereignty' is consistent with Buchanan's (re)interpretation of classical liberalism as a second-order theory. Furthermore, it fits Buchanan's distinction between the "protective" and the "productive state."[41] In my framework, the protective state would be similar to the constitutional level, while the competing units are diverse kinds of productive states. Buchanan expects that

> small units, defined geographically or territorially, are likely to be more homogeneous in makeup than larger units, and the individual is more likely to share preferences for political action with his or her peers than would be the case where political interaction must include persons who are considered to be 'foreign,' whether the lines here be drawn racially, ethnically, religiously, economically, or otherwise.[42]

To summarize, the disaggregation approach might help to reduce the moral tensions produced by deep disagreement. Giving (deeply) diverse views the room for testing their ideas should considerably relax tensions and thus lead to more harmony within society.

10.3.3 The principal–agent problem

So far I have mainly discussed how a political polycentric system can disarm disagreements between citizens while focusing mostly on the horizontal dimension of modus vivendi. In this section, I will look at the vertical dimension of modus vivendi. One of the central political problems is how to restrain the government in such a way that it serves the people instead of abusing its power for its own profit. I am thus talking about the old question of *who will watch the watchmen*.

The relationship between the government and the citizens of a democratic state is marked by what political scientists and economists call a 'principal–agent problem'. A principal–agent problem exists if two conditions are fulfilled: First, there must be an information asymmetry between the principal and the agent. Second, the agent and the principal have different goals. The problem is that politicians can often use their positions of power for their own advantage if citizens – for epistemic reasons or lack of power – cannot hold them accountable. The solution to a principal–agent problem must (a) somehow reduce the information asymmetry and (b) present a mechanism that allows the principal to effectively enforce her or his goals and punish the agent for deviant behavior. In this section, I want to outline how a polycentric structure aids the democratic sovereign to overcome the principal–agent problem.

One of the most prominent examples of a principal–agent problem is the relationship between a doctor and his or her patient. Imagine that Anna is the only doctor in a little village, where there are few sick people. Under these conditions, Anna might maximize her profit not by treating her patients efficiently, but by deliberately keeping some of them ill. Anna's patients cannot compare her treatment with that of other doctors – and even if they could, Anna would still be the only viable medical expert in the vicinity. We thus have a divergence in goals: The patient wants to be healed and the doctor wants patients to be chronically ill. Of course, the fundamental problem is that the patient does not know whose goals the doctor is following. Huemer claims that a very similar relation at times holds between governmental agencies and the people:

> [When] some essential part of the government – say, the court system or law enforcement – fails chronically in ways that are complicated, difficult to understand, and not readily traceable to specific actions by a small number of individuals [then] that part of the government will more likely be rewarded than punished.[43]

The point here is this: Many agencies may face the same dilemma as the village doctor. If they solve the problem that they are supposed to solve, they become superfluous. There is no need to claim that the village doctor or the government agency will consciously try to make worse the disease that they are supposed to cure. This would surely be an unreasonable rational-choice claim. However, I must concede that such kinds of incentives will often lead agents to not give their very best to solve a given problem. This will often – via a positive feedback loop – lead to the result that especially "unsuccessful government programs [. . .] persist and grow."[44] The problem, as I pointed out, would not exist if voters had more complete information. The more information voters have, the easier it is for them to hold the government or particular agencies accountable. Unfortunately, in the political principal–agent problem the information asymmetry is amplified because voters have bad incentives to get informed. In addition, voters that overcome the incentive problem often face the problem that there is no yardstick with which to measure the performance of a certain agency.

A well-regulated polycentric system ameliorates the principal–agent problem by enhancing the alignment of public interest and administrative goals. The alignment of goals itself is an effect of competition. Let us go back to our village doctor for a second. Imagine that the village gets connected to the internet, and the patients now can access databases on medical issues that include the standard cost, treatment and treatment time for every particular illness. First of all, our village doctor certainly will have a rough time over the next few months. But what is more important is that the knowledge asymmetry between doctor and patients has been reduced. Unfortunately, this leveling of the playing field might not be enough to persuade Anna to enhance her services. She might find flimsy reasons why the web database is not reliable and defend her ways of treatment. In the end she might just dig in her heels and say that it is her way of treatment or no way. Faced with this alternative, the villagers might grudgingly continue to visit her office. Imagine now that the village gets connected to a nearby city through cheap and quick public transportation. Getting connected to the city has the effect that the villagers are now in a position to choose among a whole range of doctors. However, this dramatically changes the incentives of the village doctor. There is now the real threat that Anna will go out of business if she does not update her treatments according to educated preferences of her patients. Thus, if the doctor wants to turn a profit under the conditions of competition, she is now forced to respond to the preferences of her patients. Introducing competition thus aligned the preferences of the village doctor and her patients.

This little example illustrates the two important parts to the solution of the principal–agent problem: leveling the information asymmetry and creating a viable way of exit. Exit has two important functions: It motivates the principal to get informed and it puts her or him in an empowered position. Applying this insight to the political realm, it is now easy to see how a polycentric system (a) creates relevant information about public goods and (b) motivates voters to seek relevant information. As I have argued, the possibility of exit gives the individual an additional incentive to become educated about different institutional setups and alternative legislative problem-solutions. The existence of other polycentric units, however, makes comparison cognitively easier for the public. In addition, the exit option gives the principal an additional means to discipline an unruly agent. Furthermore, it is important to point out that the mechanisms that a polycentric system offers to ameliorate the principal–agent problem are not substitutes but supplements to the classical mechanisms that a democratic polity has to offer.

To summarize: In a highly centralized democratic system, the government has the option to advance its goals by advancing the goals of the voter, or to exploit the voter by abusing the knowledge asymmetry. In a polycentric system, competition severely limits the second option. I can conclude that there is good reason to believe that, in a polycentric system, the government and the state agencies have stronger incentives to efficiently produce public goods such as safety or justice.

10.3.4 Conclusion

A modus vivendi arrangement can be viewed as its total set of laws. From the viewpoint of Gabriel, the total set of laws can be divided into laws he would agree to and laws he would not agree to. Accordingly, Gabriel views the first set of laws as justified and the second set of laws as unjustified or subjugating. In this section, I argued that polycentric democracy reduces the set of unjustified laws from the perspective of every reasonable citizen. Polycentric democracy, I argued, has three principal ways of reducing the set of unjustified law: (a) reducing lazy and shallow disagreements, (b) ameliorating deep disagreements by disaggregation and (c) checking the power of government. The chart in Table 10.1 summarizes my results.

Table 10.1 Defusing Political Disagreement

Root Causes of Disagreement	*Polycentric Democracy*
The two epistemic problems of shallow disagreement	✓ Rationalizing the discourse by an institutional trial-and-error process.
• Shallow disagreement about means. • Shallow disagreement about goals.	✓ Ameliorating the problem of rational ignorance by exit and yardstick competition.
The problem of deep disagreement	
• Some disagreements in ethics will be stable – and are thus not based on facts.	✓ Disaggregation.
The principal–agent problem	✓ Solving the problem of rational ignorance by exit and yardstick competition.
• Sometimes government power is abused by private interests or particular ethical ideals.	✓ Institutional competition.

10.4 Unblocking Utopia Argument

Living under democratic modus vivendi arrangements means that each citizen will love, work, pray and play under rules that she or he deems only partly justified. However, living under such rules might be more acceptable if there was some real hope that the modus vivendi arrangement as a whole was steadily moving towards justice. One issue with democratic modus vivendi arrangements is then that the road to justice – to utopia, if you will – seems to be permanently blocked. The road to justice is blocked because reasonable people disagree about the principles of justice, and even the people who broadly agree about the principles of justice often disagree about what institutions best reflect the favored principles.

Some might think that if we only would debate a little bit longer, we might finally come to an agreement on the issues. However, it seems that there is not much evidence for that. More than two millennia ago, the Chinese philosopher Han Feizi pointed out that disagreements about morality are hardly ever resolved by philosophical debates. On the contrary, he thought that continuous philosophical inquiry has a tendency to produce further disagreements rather than to resolve them. In Chapter 50, titled *On the Prominent Schools of Thought*, he writes:

> The prominent schools of the age are Confucianism and Mohism. The greatest of the Confucians was Kong Qiu [i.e. Kongzi], and the greatest of the Mohists was Mo Di [i.e. Mozi]. Since the death of Kongzi, there has been the Zi Zhang school of Confucianism, the Zi Si school of Confucianism, the Yan family school of Confucianism, the Meng family school of Confucianism, the Qidiao family school of Confucianism, the Zhongliang family school of Confucianism, the Sun family school of Confucianism, and the Yuezheng family school of Confucianism. Since the death of Mozi, there has been the Xiangli family school of Mohism, the Xiangfu family school of Mohism, and the Dengling family school of Mohism. Thus, after Kongzi and Mozi, the Confucians split into eight factions and the Mohists split into three. The doctrines and practices that each of these factions accept and reject are divergent and conflicting, and yet each faction claims that they are the true representatives of the Way of Kongzi or Mozi.[45]

The ancient Chinese philosopher continues that Kongzi and Mozi themselves "claimed that they were the true transmitters of the Way of these sages" Yao and Shun and yet, he quips, "the doctrines and practices that each of them accepted and rejected are not the same."[46]

That the blade of reason is not as sharp in moral matters as we want it to be is an issue that philosophers – including myself – still grapple with. As

Rawls put in the introduction to *Political Liberalism,* pluralism indeed seems to be the "natural outcome of the activities of human reason under enduring free institutions."[47]

Even though there are some moral questions that we might never agree on, this does not mean that all moral and political disagreements might be unresolvable. In particular, I believe that many of our political disagreements are indeed shallow rather than deep: The desirability of political institutions for most of us depends heavily on the question of whether the advocated institution can deliver the desired effects. However, whether the political institution can deliver desired effects is an empirical question. The paradigmatic case on which my intuition rests here is the central politico-philosophical disagreement of the last century. For the greater part of the last century, there was huge disagreement about the moral advantages of socialism vis-à-vis capitalism. There were intense debates in not only moral philosophy and sociology but also in economics. Looking back to these debates, without being able to go into any detail here, it seems evident that reasonable experts during this time were not able to come to an agreement with regard to the central moral or economic issues that were at stake. Even after debating for decades, some philosophers remained convinced of the moral desirability of socialist institutions (even though the particular leaders of day were frowned upon) and economists of great standing remained convinced of the economic advantage of socialism. In my view, the reason why this debate continued for such a long time has to do with the fact that the evidence available during this debate was just inconclusive. Given the theoretical standards of the day and the evidence available, smart and well-meaning people came to different conclusions. Various experiments with varieties of socialism over time, however, generated enough evidence to settle the debate in both political philosophy and economics. For a decade, some seemed to think that that history had came to an end. This was foolish. Human creativity and ingenuity entail that we will always seek improvement. Thus, it cannot and should not surprise us that, in the last decades, theorists in both philosophy and economy have started to think up new and betters ways of living together (I mentioned some of these concepts in passing). As was the case with socialism 1.0, if you may, reasonable people now disagree about the desirability of these innovative ideas of organizing society. The reason why reasonable people disagree, in my view, is explained at least partly by the inconclusiveness of the available evidence. However, there is of course something to be learned from the history of social experimentation – one of the lessons being that if modern democratic societies should decide to experiment with alternative ways of organizing social life again, they should find smarter ways of doing so.[48]

There are then two distinct reasons the road between modern democracy and utopia is blocked. The first reason is that we currently have inconclusive evidence whether utopian institutions (or just much better ways of living together) are feasible, and we do not know what they look like. Because the evidence will remain inconclusive for at least some interesting utopian candidates, we should expect disagreements to remain relatively stable. Secondly, history has taught us that radical changes to the basic structure of society can derail easily and thus should be undertaken only if there is robust supporting evidence for it. These two factors together explain why the road to utopia in modern democracies appears to be blocked for good.

That the road to utopia is essentially blocked in modern democracies is a problem for different reasons. The most important reason might be that there is and always has been a desire for more just institutions. There is simply an interest in discovering better ways of living. Moreover, at least a subset of the RoCD would agree that there is a standing duty to discover the most just feasible institutional arrangement. Given that there is considerable interest in discovering just institutions – and maybe even a duty to do so – I want to advance a second argument in favor of a polycentric democracy. The second argument concludes that a polycentric democracy is far more likely to discover just institutions – or utopia, if you will – than our current modus vivendi democracies. A polycentric democracy thus keeps our hope of discovering utopia alive, and this is not a small feat.

10.4.1 Chasing utopia

Even though reasonable people disagree about the principles of a just society, and its economic and political systems, I believe that the RoCD nevertheless agree on some features of a just society. Reasonable people, I submit, should agree on the following sufficient condition: If the basic structure and the political process of a certain political unit are deemed just by the RoCD, it is most likely just. To put it in other terms, if any society was ever deemed to be just by its diverse, reasonable and well-educated citizens, we have good reason to believe that we have found a just institution.

However, this very thin definition of justice is not all that the RoCD should be able to agree about with relation to just institutions. I believe that the RoCD should also be able to agree at least on some desirable principles that should guide societies search for just institutions. I use the term 'principles' rather than 'constraints,' because the principles that I will enumerate should not be understand as necessary conditions, but rather as regulative principles. I want to call the first principle the 'voluntariness principle.' Nozick distinguishes between missionary and imperialist utopians. The essential difference between them is that although each is usually convinced that its own particular proposal for living together is essentially right, the missionary utopian "hopes to persuade or convince everyone to live in one particular kind of community but will not force them to do so."[49] The imperialist utopian on the contrary has no problem using force to introduce his or her utopian vision. The representatives of politico-philosophical approaches, I venture, are more drawn to the first camp of utopians. Every one of the RoCD – the Hayekian, the Rawlsian and the Marxian – is essentially convinced that he or she is right but is hesitant to force people to live according to his or her first-best option. Robert Audi writes that a "liberal democracy by its very nature resists using coercion, and prefers persuasion, as a means to achieve cooperation."[50] The issue of using force to reach morally desirable goals is a difficult one. However, we do not need to concern ourselves here with this question in any depth. The claim that I want to defend is simply that if we have two different mechanisms for discovery and reaching a just society, and both of these mechanisms are roughly similar with respect to all relevant normative dimensions, the RoCD would chose the one that scores higher in terms of the voluntariness principle.

The second principle is about reasonable caution. Every member of the RoCD agrees that in searching for better institution through policy experimentation, we have an overriding duty to prevent moral horrors. One of the problems associated with implementing new sets of institutions or an institutional reform (e.g. a change in our system of property rights as Rawls proposed it, or the curbing of state services as Nozick envisioned it) brings with it a lot of uncertainty. As Popper warned, "utopian social engineering" is prone – for various reasons that have to do with political sociology – to derail and result in catastrophic events.[51] Whereas the voluntariness condition should be viewed as a guiding principle, avoiding the risk of moral horrors should be understood as a hard constraint. This is particularly the case if our starting position is a relatively well-functioning democracy. Even though contemporary modus vivendi democracies are certainly not just (judged from the RoCD perspective), they are doubtless among the best politico-economical systems that have ever existed. Therefore, I doubt that any RoCD would propose to move from where we are to a new set of institutions, if this would entail a significant risk of ending up in a moral catastrophe.

The third principle that the search for a just society should follow is the defeasibility principle. In practical philosophy, as in the sciences in general, we are married to the idea of deliberation. The very practice of debate is founded on the belief that everyone is fallible and every proposal in principle subject to revision. What does the defeasibility principle imply for the societal search process for just institutions? The defeasibility principle and the voluntariness principle should be understood as regulative principles. Given that we have two methods for the collective search for the just society that are roughly equal across the relevant normative margins, we should choose the search mechanism that more closely confirms to the defeasibility principle. The principle itself advises us to design the institutionalized search process for justice in such a way that it is sensitive to feedback. A strong right to freedom of speech, academic freedom and democratic elections reflect the importance that modern societies attach to a principle of defeasibility.

The goal of this section is to argue that part of what makes polycentric democracy interesting from a normative point of view is that it unblocks the road towards a realistic utopia. The claim that I want to advance is comparative in nature. It states that a polycentric democracy is far more likely to discover just institutions monocentric than is a modus vivendi arrangement. Moreover, I want to argue that the search process in a polycentric democracy respects the principles guiding and constraining the societal search for a realistic utopia to a higher degree than its rival.

The argument advanced here can be put differently. The normative desirability of a polycentric democracy is peculiar in a specific sense. In political philosophy, since ancient times, theorists have put forward various proposals for the just society and various proposals for the best way of living together. The claim that I am putting forward is different. I am arguing that part of the normative desirability of a polycentric democracy stems from the fact that implementing a polycentric democracy is close to a necessary condition for finding the most just institutions. The claim I am advancing is simply that if a diverse society takes the pursuit of justice seriously, it should go for a polycentric institutional set-up to enhance its chances of discovering just institutions. I understand polycentric democracy thus as an intermediate step in our common search for justice, a launching pad towards a realistic utopia.

Some might wish to defend an even stronger claim for polycentric democracy. The argument might go something like this: Society has a normative duty to search for and implement just institutions. If a polycentric democracy gives society the best chance to discover just institutions, and if it is a prerequisite for finding just institutions, then the basic structure of a polycentric democracy itself has to be regarded as just or at least as mutually justified. I have great sympathies for this rather strong claim, but I have no space here to explore or even defend it. The normative goal of this essay, as stated in the introduction to this chapter, remains less ambitious. In the future, though, it might be a worthwhile pursuit to think through the stronger claim.

What reasons, then, are there to believe that it is far more likely that a polycentric democracy will discover genuinely just ways of living together than its competitor?

In his famous essay *A Letter Concerning Toleration*, Locke writes that "every church is orthodox to itself; to others," though, it is "erroneous or heretical."[52] This insight applies not apply to religions, but certainly also to comprehensive doctrines. Every member of the RoCD is convinced that his or her doctrine is right or at least most plausible, and that the full set of moral reasons speaks in favor of his or her theory. However, every one of the RoCD must also recognize that she or he evidently does not possess the argumentative resources to convince her or his reasonable peers, let alone the wider citizenship.

One way to understand the normative standoff between the RoCD is therefore that no party has enough argumentative resources to convince the other parties. A polycentric democracy has the advantage that enables it to shake up this standoff because it allows every party to generate new evidence for (and against) her or his position. A few centuries ago, Niccolo Machiavelli shared an interesting insight about any attempt to transform the institutions of society in a meaningful way. He wrote:

> It should be realized that [. . .] introducing a new form of government is [. . .] unlikely to succeed. The reason is that all those who profit from the old order will be opposed to the innovator, whereas all those who might benefit from the new order are, at best, tepid supporters of him. This lukewarmness arises partly from fear [. . .] partly from the sceptical temper of men, who do not really believe in new things unless they have been seen to work well.[53]

Machiavelli draws attention to a point that we have encountered on several occasions during this essay: Skillful innovators might be able to convince a small section of the potentially interested parties by argument alone. However, if an innovator is defending a hidden champion, he or she will simply lack the evidence necessary to convince the 'lukewarm,' let alone the indifferent and the doubters. To convince the lukewarm, the indifferent and the doubters of the value of a hidden champion, the innovator needs to produce additional evidence. From a social perspective, it is thus of paramount importance to give social innovators and their ideas the space to prove themselves.

Viewed from this perspective, the problem for the RoCD in our current democratic institutional environment is that they do not have the option to produce the evidences that they need to convince us of their proposals (or that allow us to disregard their proposals with confidence). Although it is at least imaginable that our disagreements are for the most part shallow, and a Rawlsian, a Hayekian, a Nozickian, or a Neo-Marxian world would be clearly superior to our current modus vivendi democracy, it is not likely that our current democratic searches will ever lead us to explore the Rawlsian or Nozickian landscapes. Innovation research teaches us two important lessons that seem to be broadly consistent with Machiavelli's observation: First, the adoption of any innovation is more likely if it "is perceived as being consistent with the existing values, past experiences, and needs of potential adopters."[54] Second, the adoption rate is negatively related to its complexity.[55] "In general, new ideas that are simpler to understand will be adopted more rapidly than innovations that require the adopter to develop new skills and understandings."[56] Unfortunately, most politico-philosophical proposals are both very complex and incompatible with current democratic institutions. Furthermore, it seems to be obvious that most people in democratic states could not come up with the names of even three political philosophers, let alone summarize their ideas. It thus seems very unlikely that politico-philosophical approaches that propose radical changes will ever see their ideas discussed deeply in the political arena, not to mention implemented. Of course, this is not only frustrating for intellectual elites but also most likely implies that society misses out on institutional reforms that would be clearly superior to the status quo.

In a polycentric democracy, the situation is different for three reasons: First, in a polycentric system, many institutional schemes or policy innovations can be tested simultaneously. This alone enhances the chances for every reasonable political approach to be considered for implementation. Second, at the very outset, reasonable politico-philosophical approaches need to convince far fewer people in order to be implemented. In a centralized democratic polity, every politico-philosophical approach needs to convince the majority of the people before it can be implemented. In a polycentric system, on the contrary, a certain approach just needs to convince a small, entrepreneurially spirited fraction of the public. The third and most important argument, though, is this: In a centralized democratic polity, politico-philosophical approaches can rely on arguments and on rhetorical means to convince the majority. As we have seen in Chapter 7, it is very difficult to convince a majority of any cognitively peripheral idea for psychological and epistemic reasons. In a polycentric democracy, on the contrary, every approach can rely on 'sequential persuasion' to communicate its advantages in a manner that is psychologically adequate (see Chapter 8, Section 8.3.1). 'Psychologically adequate' means that the advantages and disadvantages of a certain implemented approach are tangible and thus relevant for the early majority. As I pointed out earlier, it makes no sense for a great part of the society to deeply engage with political theory. In the event that a new institutional set gets implemented, and moving to this new unit becomes an option, however, there are additional reasons for the early majority to get acquainted with the results of the new unit. Moreover, the first people who live in a new unit will speak the same language as the people around them and thus confer information about the new unit that is more accessible to peers. To quote Rogers again:

> The results of various diffusion investigations show that most individuals do not evaluate an innovation on the basis of scientific studies of its consequences, although such objective evaluations are not entirely irrelevant, especially to the very first individuals who adopt. Instead, most people depend mainly upon a subjective evaluation of an innovation that is conveyed to them from other individuals like themselves who have previously adopted the innovation. This dependence on the communicated experience of near-peers suggests that the heart of the diffusion process is the modeling and imitation by potential adopters of their network partners who have adopted previously.[57]

As I argued earlier, many innovative ideas for reforming systems of solidarity that ex post would find approval might be neither discussed seriously nor implemented because they are cognitively peripheral. In a polycentric system, however, many of these ideas would get implemented locally and then diffuse via sequential persuasion. To give an example, the idea of an unconditional basic income is certainly a cognitively peripheral idea in politics. Presumably, this idea would have a hard time prevailing under our current institutions. In a polycentric democracy, however, it is quite possible that a city with a particularly progressive population (a high population of innovators) would implement a basic income. If this city develops very positively, early adopters among the other cities would be encouraged to follow the example. If the concept proves successful ex post, it can be expected that cities with more conservative populations will seriously start to consider reform.

Let me summarize: In a centralized democratic polity, even reasonable politico-philosophical approaches have very slim chances of being considered for implementation. In a polycentric system, on the contrary, every reasonable politico-philosophical approach has comparatively better chances to be implemented. Furthermore, a polycentric system allows reasonable approaches to convince the majority in a way that is psychologically adequate. A polycentric democracy thus gives every reasonable politico-philosophical approach a fair chance to persuade the majority in a way that is psychologically adequate. As a result, society as a whole increases its chance to find the most just feasible institutions, or at least better modus vivendi arrangements.

At any given time, new institutional experiments might take place and others might be terminated. Citizens, by ballot and by foot voting, select which institutional schemes they deem most choice-worthy and in doing so put pressure on the existing cities and the main body of the national state to adapt. In a slow process of institutional learning, cities that lose ground may therefore see themselves forced to change their institutional structure. At the same time, the main body of the nation state – while being under a certain pressure to adapt – needs to choose which institutional innovations to adopt or to reject. By *using and defusing* instrumental and evaluative diversity, polycentric democracy should then be able to continuously discover new and better institutional arrangements and policies. To put it differently, polycentric democracy takes diverging normative views and contending socio-economic theories as fuel to discover new heights in the institutional search space. Although, at this point, I cannot be sure whether the RoCD actually view polycentric democracy as a Pareto improvement, I have at least prevailed – it seems – in my attempt to formulate a second-order theory that is based on utilizing rather than taming diversity.

Let me add a final comment. In recent history, say the last four centuries, there have been huge developments in social morality and institutions. Thus, there is of course a possibility for huge changes even in relatively centralized democratic units. The claim that I am defending here is thus decidedly comparative.

However, it does not suffice to show that polycentric democracy is more likely to find just institutions than its alternative. I also need to show that a polycentric democracy has a significantly better chance of finding better institutions without violating any of the principles meant to guide the societal search for better institutions. Let me then proceed to compare how a polycentric democracy fares vis-à-vis its alternative with regard to the guiding principles.

10.4.2 Does polycentric democracy respect the constraints of searching for utopia?

An interesting distinction in innovation studies is the distinction between optional innovation decisions and collective innovation decisions. When deciding for or against a certain innovation, a group can always choose between two modes of adoption. The first mode is a collective innovation decision. In this mode, a group employees a particular decision rule to decide for all of its members whether to adopt an innovation. However, the group could also decide to let any member individually decide whether to adopt an innovation. In the latter case, the group allows for optional innovation decisions. Innovation studies show that optional innovation decisions have two advantages over collective decisions. The first point relates to the speed of innovation diffusion. "Optional decisions," Rogers tells us, "can usually be made more rapidly than collective decisions."[58] Thus, social learning processes that allow for optional individual decisions are often faster than collective decisions. The second point is normative: Leaving room for optional innovation decisions not only allows for faster adoption rates, but also respects that different individuals need different sets of reasons to become convinced. Polycentric democracy, as is evident, entails optional innovation decisions for both political units and individual citizens. In a polycentric democracy, political units can decide whether they collectively adopt an innovative policy, and individuals can decide whether they want to be part of a more innovative or a more conservative political unit. Our current democratic modus vivendi arrangements, on the contrary, put heavy emphasis on collective innovation decisions with all their familiar normative and epistemic problems. While it is certain that there are advantages and disadvantages to both systems, it seems evident that the principle of voluntariness – which I am concerned with in this section – is more thoroughly respected by the institutional arrangements of a polycentric democracy.

The principle of reasonable caution says that every societal process of searching for better political institutions needs to proceed with caution to prevent moral horrors. Of course, the same is not true – or at least not to the same degree – for purely intellectual inquiries into justice. I have already pointed out that when it comes to dealing with the risks and uncertainties that are involved in implementing institutional reforms, a polycentric system has obvious advantages. In a polycentric system there will always exist various modes of living together at the same time. This makes it easier for citizens to evaluate their own polity in economic, moral and social terms (see Section 10.3). A second, more unfamiliar, argument in favor of polycentric democracy is this: According to innovation researchers, early adopters are usually not only open to innovations, but also comparatively more affluent. This suggests that the people who incur the costs of failed innovations across domains are usually in a relatively good position to absorb the damage. Of course, it is an empirical question whether this regularity will also hold for political experiments.

However, the robustness argument remains the most important one in favor of a polycentric democracy. To outline a simple case, imagine that one polity in a polycentric democracy chooses to experiment with a radical policy reform that ex post turns out to be very bad. If one political unit fails in a polycentric unit, there will be – as a rule – plenty of resources in the remaining units to help. Moreover, a well-regulated polycentric democracy will know how to respond to such a case. The agency associated with the regulative framework will be responsible for responding to such scenarios with an appropriate fail-safe procedure.

Now, imagine what happens if an experiment with the very same dangerous policy in a more centralized democracy fails. The effects of the policy would not only be felt in parts of the country, but also throughout the whole nation. More people would be harmed, and the whole country would have considerably less means to mitigate the damage.

However, the case for polycentric democracy in terms of precaution might not be quite so univocal. Even though polycentric democracy will prove to be more robust against failures of experimentation, we should keep in mind that polycentric democracies on average will also have a higher rate of experimentation. A higher rate of local experimentation, though, will most likely lead to a higher absolute rate of unsuccessful or failed experiments. Now, a failed experiment does not necessarily mean that some moral bad was incurred. At the same time, since the goal of polycentric democracy is to incentives more policy experiments in general and more radical experiments in particular, it would be surprising if – despite all efforts of democratic supervision – morally problematic experiments would not occur over time. In conclusion, it seems safe to say, that modus vivendi democracies – especially if they experiment with radical changes in their basic structures – face a higher risk of moral catastrophe. However, polycentric democracies might more frequently experience morally problematic situations on the local level because there is simply more experimentation going on. The task of the regulatory framework for institutional competition is therefore important. It needs to define the rules for local experimentation in a way that prevents moral horrors and closely supervises the development of local experiments.

The defeasibility principle is meant to reflect the burdens of judgment. Each of the RoCD believes that that her or his own political position best concurs with the moral reasons as she or he understands them and the evidence available. At the same time, each of the RoCD also recognizes that every other party to the deliberation conceives of himself or herself and his or her position in the same fashion; moreover, the RoCD are also aware of the various psychological biases, some of which we talked about in earlier chapters. What we should keep in mind, however, is that the RoCD are primarily interested in seeing justice itself (whatever it may be) prevail. Their main objective is thus to move from where we are over time to the most just feasible world. Naturally, on one hand the RoCD have certain beliefs about what moral and political rules justice entails. On the other hand, they know that they might be wrong about these matters. For these reasons the RoCD value open inquiry. In particular, I believe, given two institutional search processes, they should choose the one that, ceteris paribus, prevents societies from getting stuck on suboptimal institutional arrangements.

Now, one of the great advantages of a well-regulated polycentric democracy is that is comparatively much less prone to get stuck on local optima. The reason for this is that a polycentric democracy offers all of the modes of contestation of modus vivendi democracies, but on top of that, *offers an additional means of contestation: realizing alternative modes of living together.*

In a polycentric democracy, various alternatives to the dominant way of organizing society will be present and thus salient not only for intellectuals, academics, journalists, politicians but also for citizenry as a whole. For human beings, it is in general very hard to assess how well their own set of institutions works in absolute terms. Just because a certain institution – be it the criminal justice system, the health care system, the mode of production – seems to be deficient across a whole range of evaluative criteria, it does not mean that we can actually do better. This is the point of option regret. Sometimes every single option in a choice set is deeply undesirable compared to what we would hope for. As Machiavelli wrote, because of the "sceptical temper of men, who do not really believe in new things unless they have been seen to work well,"[59] it is hard for many to believe that the democratic world with its familiar institutions is not already the best of all possible worlds. The principle of defeasibility suggests that we should organize society in a way that better institutional arrangements will be recognized as such and thus be adopted in time. The better an institutional arrangement is in terms of discovering hidden champions, the better it scores in terms of the principle of defeasibility. If Machiavelli is right, as innovation diffusion theory suggests, and people believe in new things only if they have seen them to work well, then a polycentric democracy should score higher in terms of the defeasibility principle than modus vivendi democracy.

Conclusion

The case for polycentric democracy is built on two arguments. In this section I have focused on the *Unblocking Argument*. On an abstract level, the claim tries to capture the following idea: In reality, as well as in our model, the RoCD are stuck, (almost) every argument has been voiced and every card has been played. The result is a stalemate, a political deadlock that effectively blocks the 'road to utopia.' One of the great advantages of a polycentric democracy, then, is that it holds the promise of unblocking the road to utopia. To put this in other words, polycentric democracy holds the promise of discovering institutional hidden champions by giving every reasonable political doctrine a chance to generate additional and maybe decisive evidence for its own doctrine. New ideas in general, as I argued in Chapter 8, need space to prove themselves. Concurrently, innovators across domains need space to demonstrate the value of their ideas to generate the evidence that is necessary to convince the 'lukewarm supporters' and eventually the doubters. If utopia (or just a better modus vivendi arrangement) is possible, it should be found through a polycentric democracy. Polycentric democracy, as an institution, thus might not be just itself, but it may very well be our best bet for discovering just institutions.

10.5 The feasibility and stability of polycentric democracy

Just because some political order would be desirable, this does not necessarily mean that there is a path from our current state of affairs to the desired state. Any political philosophy should tell a plausible story of how actual people can climb a ladder from where they are to where they are supposed to go. A philosophical conception – to be relevant to this question – needs to tell something about how our world that is marked by deep disagreement can be transformed into a more desirable world. In the following sections, I want to argue that polycentric democracy is reasonably feasible. Later, I will discuss the stability of polycentric democracy.

As I have discussed in previous sections, polycentrism is not a binary concept, since a system can be more or less polycentric. In fact, important nations like the United States of America, Germany and Japan, to name just a few, are already polycentric to a certain degree. The same is true for the European Union. Furthermore, Europe has a long tradition of federalism, free cities, municipal autonomy and subsidiarity.

Moreover, if the Domination Claim is right, there is a good chance that pushing towards a more consciously framed polycentric system will be supported by an overlapping consensus between political theorists. Such an overlapping consensus between theorists would surely, over time, influence public opinion and thus eventually trigger political action.

Up to this point, I have painted a very positive picture of a well-regulated polycentric system – so positive, indeed, that we might wonder why we are not yet living in this 'wonderland,' if the case for it is so unambiguous. There are several answers to this question; I want to confine myself to two replies here. Later, I will review some of the more specific objections to my proposal. Let me start off with a historical explanation of why we are not living in a more polycentric system. I can make the case that centralized political units have historically proved to be *militarily* more efficient than decentralized political units. In Europe, the result of evolutionary competition between nation states over the last six hundred years apparently resulted in a push towards more centralized political systems. This explains, at least in part, why Europe lost so much diversity over the last centuries. A certain degree of peace and respect for human autonomy are thus necessary conditions for a polycentric system. Fortunately, the world in its entirety is becoming more peaceful and increasingly respects human autonomy[60] – and thus, the conditions under which polycentric systems seem feasible are probably within our reach.

There is another set of reasons that might help explain why we aren't yet living in a more polycentric world. The set of reasons I am hinting at are academic in nature. First, most discussions, in elite as well as public forums, are still dealing with the question of *who is right*. The very idea of employing cognitive diversity, in contrast, is still relatively foreign. Second, the idea of an institutional system employing diversity is even more foreign. This might be due to the fact that "despite the prevalence of federalism in the practice of liberal constitutional democracies," federalism still "remains understudied and poorly understood."[61]

In summary, I think there are good reasons to believe that a more polycentric system is feasible, because in large parts of the Western world, we already have a tradition of decentralization. What is needed to enable us to move towards an even more polycentric system is, foremost, a better understanding of its advantages and disadvantages. The other necessary conditions that seem critical for the success of polycentrism – peace and respect for the individual – are conditions that seem to be increasingly realized.

10.5.1 Stability

The question that we have to tackle next is whether a polycentric polity can be stable. Stability can be conceptualized in many different forms. Two notions seem to be especially important here: stability in the sense of robustness and stability understood as a Nash equilibrium. Let me comment on both concepts. If an institutional system is robust, it will be resilient against transgressions within the system and adaptable with regard to changing tasks or a changing environment. In Bednar's words: "Compliance maintenance makes the robust federation effective; adaptability keeps it relevant."[62] Furthermore, if the system is in the general interest, making the rules of the game robust is primarily a technical problem and thus does not need to concern us here.[63] However, in this chapter I attempted to show that a polycentric polity is in the general interest. This leaves us with the notion of stability in the sense of the Nash equilibrium. The Nash equilibrium basically obtains in a non-cooperative game if none of the players can gain anything by unilaterally changing their strategy. If we apply this concept, we may ask whether any faction within a polycentric polity can achieve an institutional arrangement that better fulfills its goals by unilateral action. This brings us back to the *Domination Claim,* which states $RoCD_i: Pol_i > PD \geq D_{MV}$. With reference to the Domination Claim, there is a clear answer to the question. As long as there is no faction with the power to enforce its favorite system Pol_i unilaterally, the polycentric system is in Nash equilibrium.[64] Being able to enforce a favored system, however, seems to presuppose that there is not much diversity in society to begin with. Thus, a polycentric system is especially unstable under conditions of relative homogeneity.[65]

Since the standard social science concepts of stability have not led us to any especially interesting results, we should switch to a more philosophical analysis. Now, we can ask about the necessary conditions for a polycentric system to be stable. I want to propose that a polycentric polity is a reasonably stable modus vivendi arrangement if at least three conditions are met.

1 The Amelioration Argument is based on a correct descriptive account of the political processes within a polycentric polity.

2 It is public knowledge that the institutions of a polycentric democracy ameliorate political conflict in the ways described.
3 The instrumental and evaluative diversity found in current democracies does not decrease dramatically due to the process described in the Amelioration Argument.

It seems that all three conditions are necessary for the stability of a polycentric polity. Let me discuss briefly why these conditions are necessary. First, if the first claim is not a reasonably good approximation of the political process, and the desired benefits will not obtain, then the citizens might rightly judge that the costs of such a system will outweigh the benefits. The costs of such a system consist, for instance, of an additional layer of bureaucracy that administers the framework for competition and supervises the experiments.

Second, the polycentric polity will not be stable if a majority of the public wrongly rejects the Amelioration Argument even though it is mostly true.[66] Human beings are fallible and often confuse the salience of an event with its relative importance. For example, it might be the case that a random shooting takes places in one of the experimental zones and a group of schoolchildren are killed. Although such shootings happen regularly throughout the country, public opinion might wrongly attribute the shootings to the institutional framework of that specific experimental zone. This in turn might lead the public to wrongly lose faith in the system.

Third, it is at least conceivable that the evolutionary discovery process of a polycentric polity is so successful that it will find one or a very small number of institutional systems that Pareto dominates its rivals with respect to all important values. Furthermore, when it comes to establishing new institutional arrangements, human creativity might be not as potent as we imagine, so that at some point the existing institutional system will no longer be challenged. If that is the case, the institutional framework that allows for experimentation will essentially die off, because it is no longer of any use. This should not surprise us, since the very idea of a polycentric polity is tailored to a society that struggles with deep and shallow disagreement. If there is no longer such diversity in society, then there is also no need for a polycentric system.[67]

10.6 Objections and rejoinders

The goal of the third part of this essay was mainly to make the argument that from the perspective of the RoCD a polycentric polity arrangement is a better arrangement than the modus vivendi arrangements we currently live in. In this essay, I have addressed many particular normative concerns with respect to polycentrism. Although I have tried to address many legitimate concerns and objections, there are surely a lot of questions unanswered. One of those issues might be: What counts as a reasonable political stance, and what kinds of institutional experiments are permissible? However, as I said earlier, to expect a definite answer to this question is to misunderstand the project of this essay. This essay asks: Can't we live in a better world, despite our shallow and deep disagreements? Since we are facing normative disagreement, the answer to these questions can be settled only in a bargaining process between relevant factions in a polycentric society. How a polycentric polity solves these questions is thus contingent on the relative bargaining power of the different factions.

This is a crucial difference to two approaches that might – at face value – seem somewhat similar to my own approach. I have in mind Kukathas's *Liberal Archipelago* and Nozick's discussion of a libertarian meta-utopia, both of which I have already mentioned a few times throughout this essay. I want to point here to some crucial differences. The first one concerns the genesis and goals of the three approaches.

1 Kukathas and Nozick are both defending first-order theories. Kukathas's conception is founded on the idea of the sanctity of the private conscience. The liberal archipelago is then presented as a deduction from the sanctity of conscience and the related principle of freedom of association. Nozick's political philosophy, in contrast, is founded on a strong conception of natural rights. The libertarian meta-utopia is then presented as a deduction from natural rights and a certain conception of libertarian property rights. The polycentric institutional grid that emerges from their normative premises, by itself, though, does not do any justificatory work.

In contrast, the conception that I am defending is a second-order theory. The polycentric system that I defend is not a deductive outcome of certain principles, but is itself the centerpiece of polycentric democracy.

2 The difference between these approaches and the one presented can be further elaborated with regard to their respective stance on the tasks of government, noninterference and freedom of association. In Kukathas's approach the task of government is to secure peace. That implies that in Kukathas's polycentric system, there are no restraints with regard to freedom of association, nor does the government have any right to interfere with the internal affairs even of strongly illiberal communities. Even in the case that people are "held within the community against their will"[68] or cases in which the community holds people in "ignorance of any possibility of leaving,"[69] the state should not interfere or prevent these communities from existing in the first place. Nozick, on the contrary, favors a minimal state that protects the negative rights of its people. Consequently, in Nozick's meta-utopia the state has the obligation to protect the rights of all persons regardless of the association they choose to live in. Although the reference to rights seems like a clear criterion that would allow the government to judge which practices an association is allowed to carry out, these questions become much more intricate when it comes to concrete cases. Nozick acknowledges this and states explicitly that there are a lot of open questions when it comes to the tasks of government in a Nozickian polycentrism.[70]

In polycentric democracy, of course, things look quite differently. First, my proposal supposes that existing national states simply add charter cities and grant another set of cities greater municipal authority. This means that my approach is silent about the tasks of the state. My approach starts from the 'here and now' and asks how we could achieve a better modus vivendi. In my concrete proposal, this means that the state does not change the rules of the game for its main territory. Second, any plausible framework for institutional competition will surely define the search scope so as to outlaw a huge part of possible associations. Furthermore, such a regulatory framework will surely leave room for interference in emergency cases and for adapting the regulations for polities as it sees fit. As I said in the beginning of this essay, modus vivendi arrangements produce modus vivendi bargains. These modus vivendi bargains shift over time as new governments introduce new laws and the judiciary changes its interpretation of the law. Since modus vivendi bargains are always shifting, we also expect that at least the details of the framework for institutional competition will change. Renegotiating parts of the framework also has two important connected functions. First, the option of renegotiation makes the framework adaptable to new knowledge and thus ensures that institutional experiments can be undertaken in safe and moral way. Second, democratic renegotiations of the framework can help to ensure that the framework is at all times in the interest of all.

In the last sections of this chapter I want to address two more pressing and somewhat connected questions: The first asks whether institutional competition tends to dissolve the cohesion of democracy, while the second asks whether institutional competition leads to a race to the bottom.

10.6.1 Does the option of exit dissolve the social cohesion of democratic societies?

The ideal of democracy is a very fuzzy one. It entails such ideas as collective deliberation and ideals of social cohesion, non-domination and solidarity. In a sense, democracy is about *us*. It is about inclusion and about finding solutions together that are in the interest of all that are affected: It is about *voice*.[71] On the contrary, at least at first glance the polycentric polity seems to be about *exit*. Commonly, we think that voice belongs to the realm of politics, while exit belongs to the realm of the market. Reviewing the literature about exit and voice in political philosophy and political theory, Mark Warren writes:

> Tellingly, "exit" is not to be found in the indexes of works of contemporary democratic theory. When the concept does make an appearance, it is often viewed as an undesirable alternative to democracy understood as common choice, one that atomizes collectivities and damages collective loyalties, erodes collective choice and undermines provision of common goods, encourages excessive individualism, drains collectivities of their best and brightest, and substitutes silence for voice.[72]

The worry is thus that the very option of exit discourages citizens to take part in practices of collective deliberation. Or, to put it in the words of Albert Hirschman: "The presence of the exit alternative can [. . .] tend to *atrophy the development of the art of voice*."[73] He might be right: Where exit is cheap relative to voice, as in regular market interactions, the option of exit alone tends to discourage participants from utilizing voice. However, leaving one city for another, or one country for another, is not cheap, but very expensive.[74] Nevertheless, there is also a strong case for the reverse claim that – under the right conditions – exit enhances voice. I have already talked about how well-regulated competition between polities might enhance the quality of expert and popular discourse (see Section 10.3.1). Thus, I have already based much of my argument for the polycentric polity on the claim that exit enhances voice. Furthermore, I want to point to two other features of institutional competition that should improve voice drastically. First, in my discussion about deliberative democracy, I emphasized that there are very diverse views on how to best moderate deliberation (see Chapter 3, Section 3.2). Goodin writes:

> Some [deliberative democrats] place their hopes in conventional institutions of government such as legislatures or courts, some in civil society, others in e-networks or mass-mediated deliberation, yet others in empathetic imaginings. Still other deliberative democrats place their hope in 'mini-publics'.[75]

Secondly, there are many ideas on how to best implement such mini-publics, as, for instance, citizen summits, deliberative polls, community policing programs, citizen juries and planning cells.[76] Thus, within deliberative democracy itself there is a large degree of instrumental diversity. A polycentric polity should be in the best interest of deliberative democrats, because it gives them a better chance to experiment with new modes of organizing voice. Thus, a polycentric polity should be seen as a playground for deliberative democrats to experiment with deliberation-devices to further citizen empowerment and more meaningful public debates. More generally, of course, I should emphasize that a polycentric polity is an important device for generating new mechanisms of accommodating divergent interests. In a sense, a polycentric system is a mechanism that explores the search space of second-order search mechanisms.[77]

Let me now turn to the second argument against the charge that institutional competition necessarily undermines democratic values. The argument basically states that exit should be seen in a more favorable light by democrats, because it empowers those groups in society that often lack representation and voice. One of the central problems of democratic legislation is its sheer complexity. It is often not possible for well-intentioned experts – and even less so for the general public – to get the full picture. This means that it is often really hard to fully understand the intended and unintended consequences of a certain body of legislation. It seems evident that unintended consequences are especially difficult to notice when they hit only those small fractions of society that are also particularly bad in articulating their interests – or, to put it differently, it is exactly in those cases where highly vulnerable people are affected that these effects might be especially hard to discover.[78] In those situations, exit becomes an important tool for empowering the especially vulnerable parts of society that might have a hard time finding recognition through the usual communication channels of democracy. This claim can be substantiated by historical evidence.[79] The importance of exit for minorities under authoritarian regimes, I would venture, is undisputed:

> The asylum which (the American people) opens to the oppressed of all nations must console the earth. The ease with which it will now be possible to take advantage of this situation, and thus to escape from the consequences of a bad government, will oblige the European governments to be just and enlightened.[80]

I should also mention that especially vulnerable people might not even know what kind of laws might have caused their precarious situation. It is not inconceivable that long-term unemployed people might vote for parties that advocate a high minimum wage, even though it might very well be the case that these laws lessen their chances for entering the workforce. Another (maybe less controversial) example would be violence. People in poor and violent neighborhoods might not be aware of the exact socio-economic reasons that caused the poverty and violence, and they might have no idea how to fix these problems. This lack of knowledge, though, will certainly not prevent them from recognizing better living conditions in other polycentric units. The reason behind this is that comparing the outcome of two different situations is a much simpler task than understanding the causal factors that brought them into being. Similarly, nobody needs to understand the technology that makes smartphones work in order to judge which one is faster, cheaper and more beautiful.

To summarize, voice and exit should not be understood as rival or mutually exclusive concepts. The insight that voice can actually be amplified when exit options exist, is, of course, not new. Hirschman, the inventor of these very notions, writes:

> That even the most loyal member can exit is often an important part of his bargaining power vis-a-vis the organisation. The chances for voice to function effectively as a recuperation mechanism are appreciably strengthened if voice is backed up by the threat of exit.[81]

I can conclude that neither exit and voice nor polycentric and deliberative democracy are necessarily rival conceptions.[82]

10.6.2 Institutional competition: a race to the bottom?

In the final part of this essay, I want to confront a worry that is especially prevalent in debates about globalization. The worry is that competition between nation states might lead to an erosion of the welfare state; or, to put it differently, the worry that institutional competition might necessarily lead to a race to the bottom. Let me start with two comments on this debate and how it relates to the polycentric account that I developed in this essay. First, it is evident, as one study laconically puts it, that "the dire predictions of early doom theories have not materialized; welfare states are still welfare states and are likely to persist in the future."[83] So, even under current conditions – where an overarching system that regulates competition between nation states is missing – welfare regimes persist. This brings me to the second point. As I pointed out in Chapter 9, the international order does not qualify as a polycentric polity because it lacks an international framework for polycentric competition.[84] Even if competition between welfare states under the current conditions were to lead to a race to the bottom and to the erosion of welfare states, this would not tell us much about the effects of institutional competition within a regulated polycentric system. As should be clear from the preceding chapters, if people prefer to live in welfare states, it is of course of the utmost importance to regulate the competition between polities in such a way as to counteract tendencies towards the erosion of welfare states. Furthermore, some critics not only worry about unregulated competition between nation states but also fear that all kinds of institutional competition will necessarily turn every nation state into some kind of minimal or small state. Since the whole argument for a polycentric polity hinges on the very idea that it will *increase* institutional diversity, it is important for us to understand under which conditions competition between polities could lead to institutional homogenization. Let me then turn to the arguments on which the 'race to the bottom' worry rests.

Since it is not possible to review the literature about institutional competition comprehensively, I will focus on Hans-Werner Sinn's "influential criticism of institutional competition."[85] Sinn starts out by distinguishing what he calls "new systems competition" and "old systems competition."[86] The old systems competition is a competition between states with closed-off borders. What he has in mind here is the competition between communism and capitalism. The new systems competition, in contrast, is a competition between nation states with open borders for goods and people, like that within the European Union.[1] I discuss the relationship between institutional competition and social security in the context of the European Union in Müller and Lütge (2014b). While Sinn approvingly notes that the old systems competition "forced communism to its knees,"[87] he is highly skeptical with regard to the effects of "migration-induced competition."[88]

Sinn's criticism of an unregulated mobility-based competition between nations is based on a simple economic model that will help us to get a better understanding of the tasks of a framework for competition in a polycentric polity. This economic model is founded on a rational-choice model of human agency and a set of strong assumptions about government activity. The first assumption Sinn calls the "selection principle."[89] The selection principle says that governments have "taken over all those activities which the private market has proved to be unable to carry out."[90] Furthermore, the model assumes that each government aims at "maximizing national welfare, given the behavior of other countries."[91] What is important to note is that Sinn's selection principle thus assumes away three important problems:

1 The principal–agent problem.
2 The problem of deep disagreement.
3 The problem of shallow disagreement.

In fact, Sinn's model assumes away the majority of the problems that motivated the project of my project in the first place. Of course, this should not discourage us from trying to get a better understanding of the model, since it might nevertheless identify important causal mechanisms within institutional competition that are not easily discernible without the model. Let us then look at how Sinn's basic model works. Sinn sees the modern welfare state as an insurance agency. The insurance activity of the state in this model is not limited to providing social security, but instead encompasses "the whole system of redistributive taxation" and the provision of "public goods."[92] Here again, Sinn interprets the notion of public goods rather liberally. The insurance consists of net-payers and net-recipients. From a rational-choice perspective, the only reason why a net-payer, such as Benni, contributes to the insurance is that he cannot know ex ante whether he will be a net-recipient or a net-payer. If Benni, as an economic agent, knows with certainty that he will never be in need, he will have no reason to pay for insurance. Now Sinn's interesting idea is this: When a citizen enters adulthood, he or she can already, with some certainty, ascertain whether he or she will be a net-recipient or a net-payer during his or her life span. Becoming an adult is thus, in some sense, akin to lifting the veil of uncertainty. As long as there are no open borders, though, the individual cannot profit from this new information. However, if there is mobility-based competition between nation states, the situation will change considerably. In a state of institutional competition, two effects become instantly relevant. Assuming that the nation states are more or less homogeneous, Benni now has strong incentives to migrate to the state that has the lowest tax rate (and thus the smallest welfare state) since he knows that he will be a net-payer. In contrast, Benni's sickly and lazy brother Philipp will have strong incentives to migrate to a state that has a particularly comprehensive welfare state. The national governments, at the same time, will start to compete for particularly wealthy and healthy individuals by lowering their tax rates. The competition between states for wealthy individuals by lowering taxes will then necessarily drive down the tax rates and thus in the end starve the welfare state.

How should we evaluate this model and its predictions? Let me first highlight two further premises of this model. The model is based on the premises that agents are money maximizers and that exit is very cheap. Both premises are very strong. Real-world agents maximize over a very heterogeneous bundle of goods. Furthermore, since real-world agents often highly value the very goods that are not easily substitutable – old friends, the familiarity, cuisine and dialect of their hometown – exit for most is not a particularly cheap option. Nevertheless, I think that Sinn points to a problem that we need to take seriously when thinking about the polycentric polity. The goal of a polycentric polity is, among other things, to discover better, more humane and more efficient social welfare systems. Let us imagine a polity that has introduced a basic income policy and everything works out fine. Now, imagine that, after a while, even lazy Phillip has become aware that there is a city that would provide him with a basic income. It seems not unlikely that, in that case, Phillip might migrate to the basic income polity. Unfortunately, if many lazy people followed the same incentives, providing a basic income might not be feasible anymore. How should we cope with such problems in a polycentric polity? Interestingly, Sinn, the alleged "arch-critic of institutional competition,"[93] not only describes the problem but also provides an interesting solution. Instead of proposing a homogenization of welfare states, Sinn suggests *the principle of delayed integration*, a rather pragmatic solution:

> According to the principle of delayed integration, immigrants would immediately be included in the tax and contribution system of the host country and they would have free access to all public facilities and contribution financed social benefits. However, certain tax-financed benefits such as social aid and subsidized government housing would be available only after a transition period of, say, seven years so as to secure a rough fiscal balance during this period of time.[94]

Although this solution might not find the approval of libertarian economists – who indeed sometimes seem to propose institutional competition as a means to curb the welfare state (and thus use institutional competition as a Trojan horse) – Sinn's solution is fully in line with the idea of political polycentrism as developed in this essay. As I have emphasized throughout the essay, the concept of polycentrism consists of three parts: a framework for competition, multiple decision centers and the competition between these decision centers. The function of the framework for competition is to diagnose potential problems like a tendency for a race to the bottom, and then to find pragmatic solutions in light of the goals of polycentric democracy.

Notes

1 Yamamoto (2014).

2 This is of course an oversimplification. There could also be other reasons why she views income inequality as a problem.

3 I use 'ϕing is unjustified from the perspective of X' and 'ϕing is subjugating from the perspective of X' as synonyms.
4 Horton (2007, p. 52).
5 Horton (2007, p. 52).
6 This should be read as morally mandated according to Benni's evaluative standards.
7 If Benni had thought a bit more about Y, he would have recognized that Y cannot be morally mandated, since Y violates moral standard A, which he ranks very highly.
8 The same line of reasoning of course applies in exactly the same way also to lazy agreements and disagreements.
9 Compare Wendt's discussion of a 'second-best' (Wendt 2015).
10 Wall (2013).
11 Compare this case: Imagine you are the slave of a very brutal slaveholder. On one beautiful autumn day, a very rich slaveholder offers to buy you as a teacher for his son. The rich slaveholder seems to be a very nice and gentle person, so you urge him to buy you. He agrees and you become a teacher for his son. He treats you very well, so well indeed, that you have more money to spend in a month than most of the free people in your city. The point is this: Even though your situation now is a lot better than under the brutish slaveholder, you might still reasonably hold that you are treated unfairly, because you are still prevented from exercising some of the rights you think every person ought to have.
12 Aiming for a 'simple' Pareto improvement as well the idea of 'utilizing rather than taming diversity' reflects the intellectual roots of polycentric democracy in 'order ethics,' see Homann (1988), Homann and Blome-Drees (1992), Homann (2002), Homann and Lütge (2005), Lütge (2005), Lütge (2012), Lütge (2015), Müller and Lütge (2014a), Pies (1993). Order ethics, as I mentioned before, is an approach in political philosophy that is based on constitutional economics and the German tradition of 'ordoliberalism.'
13 Landemore (2013, p. 216).
14 We will never be able to do controlled experiments as in biology or physics. There are two main reasons for this. First, we cannot sufficiently control for all important variables. Second, we cannot conduct a large enough number of experiments to achieve the same quality of results.
15 Kofman (2012, p. 249).
16 Mises (1985, pp. 7–8).
17 Cohen (2003, pp. 244–245).
18 Schumpeter (2008, p. 262).
19 For an overview, see Caplan (2007), Somin (2011), and Achen and Bartels (2016).
20 Somin (2011, p. 210).
21 Somin (2011. pp. 210–211).
22 Somin (2011, p. 214).
23 Vaubel (2008, p. 55).
24 Salmon (2015, p. 85). Italics in original.
25 The example is from Wegner (2014).
26 See also Rincke (2009).
27 Padovano and Petrarca (2014).
28 Constant (1988).
29 Gaus (2011c, p. 334).
30 Gaus singles out Kant and Rousseau, but I am sure he would also include Rawls and many others.
31 Gaus (2011c, p. 373).
32 Gaus (2011c, p. 373).
33 Gaus (2011c, p. 373).
34 Gaus (2009, p. 119).
35 Gaus (2011c, p. 373).
36 Gaus (2011c, p. 374).

37 Economists discuss this topic for instance under the rubric of 'Tiebout sorting.' See Tiebout (1956).
38 Mises (1983).
39 For a project that seems to have interesting parallels, see Lu *et al.* (2011).
40 Buchanan (1996, p. 267).
41 Buchanan (2000, p. 88).
42 Buchanan (1996, p. 263). As Feld (2014) points out, Buchanan's thinking about federalism went through at least three stages. In his later work, Buchanan began to think about federalism as an ideal political order. In this period, his concept of ideal federalism overlaps considerably with ideas of polycentrism as outlined by Aligica, Boettke and the Ostroms. In Chapter 9 (Section 9.3), I briefly discussed the differences between their understanding of polycentrism and my own approach.
43 Huemer (2013, p. 220).
44 Huemer (2013, p. 220).
45 Han Feizi (2005, pp. 335–336).
46 Han Feizi (2005, p. 336).
47 Rawls (2005b, p. xxiv).
48 Even contemporary left-leaning theorists agree that we lack a good understanding of how to put the socialist ideal into practice in a way that is morally permissible and economically feasible. These theorists agree that we do need careful experimentation to find out (Unger 2007; Honneth 2017).
49 Nozick (1999, p. 319).
50 Audi (1997, p. 16).
51 Popper (2002b).
52 Locke (2010, p. 21). Capitalization altered.
53 Machiavelli (2003, p. 20–21).
54 Rogers (1983, p. 15).
55 Rogers (1983, p. 231).
56 Rogers (1983, p. 15).
57 Rogers (1983, p. 18).
58 Rogers (1983, p. 30).
59 Machiavelli (2003, p. 21).
60 Huemer (2013, section 13.1).
61 Levy (2007, p. 459). Furthermore, the existing literature focuses for the most part on a very different set of questions than this essay. For an in-depth overview about the literature in political science, see Bednar (2009). For an in-depth overview about the economic literature, see Sinn (2003).
62 Bednar (2009, p. 3).
63 The principles of robust federation design as lined out by Bednar (2009) are certainly also relevant for questions of robust polycentric design in general.
64 Of course, even if a faction had the power to enforce its favorite institutional system, it might not be willing to do so, because of the moral costs of enforcement.
65 This is not too surprising. The question that I attempt to answer in this essay is based on the premise that there *is* diversity and that nobody is able to achieve their first-best option. At the moment when one faction is able to achieve its first-best option, the very problem that I set out to answer vanishes.
66 The whole discussion of stability is based on the premise that a polycentric polity is already established. This means that at least a big part of society must have been convinced of the benefits of such a system, in order for it to be implemented.
67 Of course, a perfectionist can argue that it is the responsibility of the government to incentivize new experiments, since becoming complacent is a bad in itself. But this would be a defense of a polycentric system founded on a particular normative view, and not one built on an overlapping consensus.

68 Kukathas (2009, p. 3).
69 Kukathas (2009, p. 3).
70 Nozick (1999, p. 329).
71 Hirschman (1970).
72 Warren (2011, pp. 683–684).
73 Hirschman (1970, p. 42). Italics in original.
74 Compare my argument in Section 10.3.
75 Goodin (2008, p. 11).
76 For an overview, see Grönlund *et al.* (2013) and Fung (2011).
77 This opens the question whether our approach is actually a second-order or a third-order theory.
78 Warren (2011, p. 688).
79 Somin (2011, p. 214, section 4).
80 Turgot 1810, quoted after Vaubel (2008, p. 35).
81 Hirschman (1970, p. 82).
82 Compare Müller (2018) for a more in-depth discussion of how to think about the relation of polycentric and epistemic democracy.
83 Troeger (2013, p. 10).
84 For example, the World Trade Organization is just a framework for international trade. A framework for a polycentric polity, though, encompasses much more than trade.
85 Bergh and Höijer (2008b, p. x).
86 Sinn (2003, pp. 1–2).
87 Sinn (2003, p. 1).
88 Sinn (2003, p. 7).
89 Sinn (2003, p. 6).
90 Sinn (2003, p. 6).
91 Sinn (2003, p. 9).
92 Sinn (2003, p. 66).
93 Vaubel (2008, p. 55).
94 Sinn (2003, p. 81).

11 Concluding remarks

Persistent disagreement is perhaps one of the defining features of modern liberal democracy. As I have emphasized throughout this essay, disagreement is not merely a philosophical nuisance, but also a source of friction and conflict. Modern societies, I argued, rely on a complex social machinery – modus vivendi arrangements – to secure peaceful cooperation in the face of pervasive instrumental and evaluative diversity. In a continuous stream of political bargains, modus vivendi arrangements attempt to provisionally settle and resolve conflicts. Although this process, at least in some Western countries, has undoubtedly led to a general rise in prosperity and has been able to eradicate some of the gravest injustices, modus vivendi arrangements nevertheless come with an undeniable cost. There is tremendous dissatisfaction with some of the institutional aspects of such arrangements, and a considerable number of the resulting bargains may be seen as unjustified by some or even found to be outright oppressive. Our current modus vivendi arrangements thus entail both mutual benefit and overlapping dissatisfaction.

Based on this initial observation, this essay set out to raise a simple question: Can modern societies – despite their pervasive disagreements – do better than to settle for our current modus vivendi arrangement?

The aim of this essay was to inquire, to put it a bit more precisely, whether we can conceive of a political order that might be judged as superior to our current modus vivendi arrangement from a very diverse set of normative standards or perspectives. In this essay, I was therefore not concerned with first-order, but with second-order theory. While first-order theories are mainly concerned with establishing who is right, second-order theories inquire how we can live together despite our prevailing disagreements.

11.1 Part I: escaping modus vivendi

The first part of the essay had two main objectives. First, I set out to get more traction on the guiding question. In particular, I had to define the term 'modus vivendi arrangement,' explain why there is a common interest to 'escape' modus vivendi arrangements, and determine what counts as a 'successful escape.' In order to judge whether a proposal qualifies as desirable, I constructed the

RoCD Test. This test essentially models a discussion between the representatives of a wide range of comprehensive doctrines. A given proposal will pass the test if the RoCD Test determines that it is (a) inter-subjectively justified or (b) constitutes at least a Pareto improvement over our current modus vivendi arrangements. Furthermore, a proposal counts as inter-subjectively justified if all parties – from their own perspective – think of it as justified, while a proposal counts as a Pareto improvement if no one prefers the current arrangement over the proposal, and at least some prefer the proposal over the current situation.

Building on the RoCD Test, the second objective of the first part was to review three of the most well-known second-order theories and test their institutional recommendations. Let me highlight two important results of my analysis. First, none of the proposals that I reviewed – Rawls' justice as fairness, Gutmann and Thompson's deliberative democracy and Buchanan's constitutional economics – passed the RoCD Test. Looking back on the institutional proposals reviewed, it is not particularly surprising that none of the approaches could come up with convincing answers to the problem of modus vivendi. The intuitive and persuasive idea behind constructing second-order theories is that we need some kind of a fair arbitration between the parties in disagreement. Although these theories start out by acknowledging our pervasive disagreements, their normative discussions, nevertheless, conclude with proposals that are highly controversial: Rawls, as well as Gutmann and Thompson, essentially propose something akin to 'egalitarian utopias' while Buchanan defends a political arrangement that comes close to a 'libertarian utopia.'

Second, although these theories differ in many respects, they nevertheless share one distinct feature: They view existing evaluative and instrumental diversity primarily as a nuisance that needs to be properly hedged and tamed, if society wants to have the chance of escaping modus vivendi. To put it differently: All three approaches agree that, unless we can attain a considerable normalization of our normative and socio-economic beliefs, we are actually stuck with modus vivendi. Both Rawls's and Gutmann and Thompson's approach for escaping modus vivendi require that a subset of the RoCD revise at least parts of their normative views and socio-economic beliefs. Buchanan's proposal is a little more modest in the sense that it requires only a substantial change in socio-economic beliefs by a large subset of the RoCD.

11.2 Part II: how to make use of diversity?

My analysis in Part I suggests that any politico-philosophical solution for the problem of modus vivendi that requires a substantial normalization of existing evaluative and instrumental diversity is bound to fail. This result led me to reconsider diversity. I argued that in a world of bounded rationality, diversity is not only – and may not even be primarily – a nuisance, but also a potential resource. Building on these first few insights, I decided to take a philosophical U-turn and construct a second-order approach that is based on utilizing rather than on taming existing instrumental and evaluative diversity.

The goal of the second part, then, was mainly to get a deeper understanding of diversity and of the mechanisms that enable us to profit from diversity. In particular, I looked at two approaches for utilizing diversity: 'deliberative' and 'polycentric.' The deliberative approach views collective deliberation as a universal tool for unlocking and communicating the benefits of diversity. This approach reflects our everyday experience rather well, since whenever we are confronted with difficult and important problems, we will consult with friends or experts before we make up our minds. The polycentric approach, however, emphasizes that (especially when it comes to hard problems) the best way to collectively gain from diversity is to provide a multitude of diverse agents, or decision centers, sufficient space to put their ideas into practice and – to simplify a bit – let the results speak for themselves.

I compared both approaches with regard to their capacity to make use of diversity in order to solve hard problems. My conclusion was that the polycentric approach outperforms the deliberative approach, because the latter suffers from a host of shortcomings that prevent deliberation from making adequate use of diverse perspectives. Here I will highlight only three: the epistemic problems associated with bounded rationality, psychological biases, and problems of transaction costs. The first problem with collective deliberation is that, for epistemic reasons, it is often not possible to determine who knows best. Second, people abhor being the sole dissenter – as Andersen's "The Emperor's New Clothes" teaches and laboratory experiments confirm – and thus often refuse to share important information. Third, meaningful deliberation is only feasible in relatively small groups, because of the transaction costs it involves. Therefore deliberative groups are usually not able to take into account all relevant perspectives. My analysis suggests that polycentric systems can to some degree ameliorate the inhibitors of collective deliberation and thus are better suited to reap the benefits from diversity. Polycentric systems, in short, mitigate the outlined inhibitors by allowing innovations to demonstrate their utility in a process of sequential persuasion; moreover, they incentivize dissent and are able to facilitate an unlimited number of diverse cognitive models.

11.1 Part III: polycentric democracy

In the third part, building on the previous results, I tried to outline the concept of polycentric democracy – a philosophical second-order approach that is based on *utilizing* rather than on *hedging* evaluative and instrumental diversity. Building on Aligica's work, I defined 'polycentric democracy' as an institutional arrangement involving a multiplicity of polities acting independently, but under the constraints of a democratically supervised framework for institutional competition.[1] As I discussed in Chapter 9, there are several options for implementing *ideal* polycentric democracy. I decided for an implementation strategy that seems most feasible given the existing disagreements. A polycentric democracy, in my scheme, differs institutionally from our current modus vivendi democracies in two respects. First, a polycentric democracy features a multitude of 'free cities' (i.e. cities with a rather large degree of municipal autonomy). In addition, a polycentric democracy allows – and incentivizes – the founding of new free cities, so-called charter cities. Creating free cities from scratch essentially allows for a more homogeneous constituency and thus for (more) radical experiments. Second, a polycentric democracy features a regulatory framework that defines boundaries for institutional experiments and supervises the institutional competition within a polycentric democracy. Let me now comment on just two of the advantages of this implementation strategy with regard to the conundrum that this essay attempts to solve. First, in contrast to other second-order theories, polycentric democracy does not propose a sweeping institutional change. Second, polycentric democracy – in contrast to the systems outlined in Chapter 1 – prima facie seems not to be biased towards any first-order theory.

From a normative point of view, polycentric democracy is rather modest. My goal in sketching polycentric democracy was simply to create a *better modus vivendi arrangement*. The core normative claim of this essay, the *Domination Claim*, reflects the modest normative ambitions. Its short version can be stated like this: $RoCD_i$: $PD \geq D_{MV}$. The claim essentially states that a move towards polycentric democracy would be, from the viewpoint of all RoCD, either neutral or an improvement. To support this claim, I conceptualized two arguments.

1 **The Amelioration Argument**: Polycentric democracy ameliorates the problem of subjugation by improving public discourse, by defusing deep disagreement and by mitigating the political principal–agent problem.
2 **The Unblocking Utopia Argument:** Social innovators need space to demonstrate the value of their ideas, to generate the evidence that is necessary to convince the 'lukewarm supporters' and eventually the skeptics. By giving every reasonable political doctrine space to generate additional and maybe decisive evidence for its own principles, a polycentric democracy will discover better institutional solutions and perhaps even 'utopia' if it exists.

Let me comment further on these two claims. Under the rubric of 'ameliorating the hazards of disagreement,' I discussed how the institutional setup of polycentric democracy tends to resolve conflict by reducing *lazy* and *shallow disagreement*, by defusing *deep disagreement* and by ameliorating the *principal–agent problem* through exit and yardstick competition. Under the second rubric, I addressed the RoCD more directly as 'political entrepreneurs.' In a polycentric democracy, I argued, every reasonable political faction has not only a better chance to live according to its own principles, but also to *demonstrate* the advantages of their own ideal to the rest of society in a safe, morally responsible and psychologically adequate manner. By *diffusing* disagreement (i.e. by giving reasonable parties space to generate more evidence for their proposal) polycentric democracy should be uniquely capable of *using* the creative potential of diversity while at the same time *defusing* the lingering hazards of disagreement.

On an abstract level, the Unblocking Utopia Argument tries to capture the following idea: In the current political discourse almost every argument has been voiced, and every card has been played. The result is a stalemate, a political deadlock that effectively blocks the 'road to utopia.' One of the advantages of a polycentric democracy is that it holds the promise of unblocking the road to utopia by giving every reasonable political doctrine a chance to generate additional and maybe decisive evidence for its own doctrine. New ideas in general need space to prove themselves. Concurrently, innovators defending hidden champions across domains need space to demonstrate the value of their proposals – to generate the evidence that is necessary to convince their 'lukewarm supporters' and eventually their doubters. To put it even more emphatically, the second argument suggests that if we want justice, polycentric democracy is our best shot. This is not because it is just, but because it is our best shot at discovering feasible, just institutions.

Furthermore, I want to draw attention to a final point. As I said earlier, Rawls's, as well as Buchanan's and Gutmann and Thompson's approach for escaping modus vivendi, require that a subset of the RoCD revise at least parts of their normative views or socio-economic beliefs. The same is not true for my proposal. Realizing my proposal does not require a subset of RoCD to change either their normative views or their socio-economic beliefs.

Although, in the end it remains an open question whether polycentric democracy is indeed a Pareto improvement over our current modus vivendi arrangement, I nevertheless succeeded in my second endeavor: creating a second-order approach that – in contrast to traditional approaches – is based on *utilizing* rather than on *taming* existing instrumental and evaluative diversity.

Note

1 Aligica and Tarko (2013, p. 727)

References

Achen, C.H. and Bartels, L.M. (2016), *Democracy for Realists: Why Elections Do Not Produce Responsive Government*, Princeton University Press, Princeton, NJ.

Aligica, P.D. (2014), *Institutional Diversity and Political Economy: The Ostroms and Beyond*, Oxford University Press, New York, NY.

Aligica, P.D. and Boettke, P.J. (2009), *Challenging Institutional Analysis and Development: The Bloomington School*, Routledge, London.

Aligica, P.D. and Boettke, P.J. (2011a), "Institutional Design and Ideas-Driven Social Change: Notes from an Ostromian Perspective", *The Good Society*, Vol. 20 No. 1, pp. 50–66.

Aligica, P.D. and Boettke, P.J. (2011b), "The Two Social Philosophies of Ostroms' Institutionalism", *Policy Studies Journal*, Vol. 39 No. 1, pp. 29–49.

Aligica, P.D. and Tarko, V. (2012), "Polycentricity: From Polanyi to Ostrom, and Beyond", *Governance*, Vol. 25 No. 2, pp. 237–262.

Aligica, P.D. and Tarko, V. (2013), "Co-Production, Polycentricity, and Value Heterogeneity: The Ostroms' Public Choice Institutionalism Revisited", *American Political Science Review*, Vol. 107 No. 04, pp. 726–741.

Anderson, E. (2006), "The Epistemology of Democracy", *Episteme*, Vol. 3 No. 1–2, pp. 8–22.

Aristotle (1998), *Politics, Oxford World's classics*, trans. E. Barker, R.F. Stalley (Ed.), Oxford University Press, Oxford, New York, NY.

Asch, S.E. (1951), "Effects of Group Pressure upon the Modification and Distortion of Judgments", in Guetzkow, H. (Ed.), *Groups, Leadership and Men*, Carnegie Press, Pittsburgh, PA, pp. 177–190.

Asch, S.E. (1952), *Social Psychology*, Prentice Hall, Englewood Cliffs, NJ.

Audi, R. (1997), "Liberal Democracy and the Place of Religion in Politics", in Audi, R. and Wolterstorff, N. (Eds.), *Religion in the Public Square: The Place of Religious Convictions in Political Debate, Point/counterpoint*, Rowman & Littlefield Publishers, Lanham, MD, pp. 1–66.

Backer, T.E. (2005), "Introduction", *Journal of Health Communication*, Vol. 10 No. 4, pp. 285–288.

Bednar, J. (2009), *The Robust Federation: Principles of Design, Political Economy of Institutions and Decisions*, Cambridge University Press, Cambridge, New York, NY.

Bell, D. and De-Shalit, A. (2011), *The Spirit of Cities: Why the Identity of a City Matters in a Global Age*, Princeton University Press, Princeton, NJ.

Bergh, A. and Höijer, R. (Eds.) (2008a), *Institutional Competition, New Thinking in Political Economy*, Edward Elgar, Cheltenham, UK, Northampton, MA.

Bergh, A. and Höijer, R. (2008b), "Preface", in Bergh, A. and Höijer, R. (Eds.), *Institutional Competition, New Thinking in Political Economy*, Edward Elgar, Cheltenham, UK, Northampton, MA.

Binmore, K.G. (2009), *Rational Decisions, the Gorman Lectures in Economics*, Princeton University Press, Princeton, NJ.

Bladel, J.P. (2005), "Against Polanyi-centrism: Hayek and the Re-emergence of "Spontaneous Order", *The Quarterly Journal of Austrian Economics*, Vol. 8 No. 4, pp. 15–30.

Bohman, J. (1997), "Deliberative Democracy and Effective Social Freedom: Capabilities, Resources, and Opportunities", in Bohman, J. and Rehg, W. (Eds.), *Deliberative Democracy: Essays on Reason and Politics*, MIT Press, Cambridge, MA, pp. 321–348.

Brennan, G. (2012a), "Politics-as-exchange and the Calculus of Consent", *Public Choice*, Vol. 152 No. 3–4, pp. 351–358.

Brennan, G. and Buchanan, J.M. (2000), *The Reason of Rules: Constitutional Political Economy*, Liberty Fund, Indianapolis, IN.

Brennan, J. (2012b), *The Ethics of Voting*, Princeton University Press, Princeton, NJ.

Brennan, J. and Jaworski, P. (2016), *Markets Without Limits: Moral Virtues and Commercial Interests*, Routledge Press, New York, NY.

Brown, R. (2001), *Group Processes: Dynamics Within and Between Groups*, 2nd ed., Blackwell Publishers, Oxford, UK, Malden, MA.

Buchanan, J.M. (1986), *Liberty, Market and State. Political Economy in the 1980s*, Oxford University Press, Oxford, UK.

Buchanan, J.M. (1987), "The Constitution of Economic Policy", *American Economic Review*, Vol. 3 No. 77, pp. 243–250.

Buchanan, J.M. (1990), "The Domain of Constitutional Economics", *Constitutional Political Economy*, Vol. 1 No. 1, pp. 1–18.

Buchanan, J.M. (1996), "Federalism and Individual Sovereignty", *Cato Journal*, Vol. 15 No. 2–3, pp. 259–268.

Buchanan, J.M. (2000), *The Limits of Liberty: Between Anarchy and Leviathan*, Liberty Fund, Indianapolis, IN.

Buchanan, J.M. and Congleton, R.D. (1998), *Politics by Principles, Not Interest: Toward Nondiscriminatory Democracy*, Cambridge University Press, Cambridge.

Buchanan, J.M. and Tullock, G. (1999), *The Calculus of Consent: Logical Foundations of Constitutional Democracy*, Liberty Fund, Indianapolis, IN.

Buchthal, B. (2013), *Komplexitätsprobleme und die Gestaltung sozialer Ordnungen*, Wissenschaftliche Hausarbeit zur Erlangung des 1. Staatsexamens, Philosophie, Universität Hamburg, Hamburg, 2013.

Caplan, B.D. (2007), *The Myth of the Rational Voter: Why Democracies Choose Bad Policies*, Princeton University Press, Princeton, NJ.

Cohen, G.A. (2003), "Facts and Principles", *Philosophy & Public Affairs*, Vol. 31 No. 3, pp. 211–245.

Cohen, G.A. (2008), *Rescuing Justice and Equality*, Harvard University Press, Cambridge, MA.

Cohen, J. (1998), "Democracy and Liberty", in Elster, J. (Ed.), *Deliberative Democracy, Cambridge Studies in the Theory of Democracy*, Cambridge University Press, Cambridge. [u.a.], pp. 185–231.

Collins, B.E. and Guetzkow, H. (1964), *A Social Psychology of Group Processes for Decision-making*, Wiley, New York, NY.

Constant, B. (1988), "The Liberty of Ancients Compared with that of Moderns", in Constant, B. and Fontana, B. (Eds.), *Political Writings, Cambridge Texts in the History of Political Thought*, Cambridge University Press, Cambridge [Cambridgeshire], New York, NY, pp. 307–328.

D'Agostino, F. (2004), "The Legacies of John Rawls", *Journal of Moral Philosophy*, Vol. 1 No. 3, pp. 349–365.

D'Agostino, F. (2010), *Naturalizing epistemology: Thomas Kuhn and the 'Essential Tension'*, Palgrave Macmillan, Houndmills, Basingstoke, Hampshire, UK, New York, NY.

Darwin, C. (2010), *The Variation of Animals and Plants Under Domestication, Cambridge Library Collection – Darwin, Evolution and Genetics*, Cambridge University Press, Cambridge.

DePaul, M.R. (1993), *Balance and Refinement*, Routledge, London, New York, NY.

Eckermann, J.P. (2001), *Conversations of Goethe with Eckermann and Soret*, Adamant Media Corporation, London.

Eichenberger, R. and Funk, M. (2011), "Stadtstaaten: Der Schlüssel zu einer besseren Welt", in Hummler, K. and Jäger, F. (Eds.), *Stadtstaat – Utopie oder Realistische Modell? Theoretiker und Praktiker in der Debatte*, Verlag NZZ, Zürich, pp. 115–131.

European Commission (2015), "Directives and Regulations – Motor Vehicles", available at: http://ec.europa.eu/enterprise/sectors/automotive/documents/directives/motor-vehicles/index_en.htm (accessed 25 April 2015).

Farrelly, C. (2007), "Justice in Ideal Theory: A Refutation", *Political Studies*, Vol. 55 No. 4, pp. 844–864.

Feld, L.P. (2014), "James Buchanan's Theory of Federalism: From Fiscal Equity to the Ideal Political Order", *Constitutional Political Economy*, Vol. 25 No. 3, pp. 231–252.

Festinger, L. (1954), "A Theory of Social Comparison Processes", *Human Relations*, Vol. 7 No. 2, pp. 117–140.

Frankena, W.K. (1973), *Ethics, Prentice-Hall Foundations of Philosophy Series*, 2nd ed., Prentice-Hall, Englewood Cliffs, NJ.

Freeman, S.R. (2007a), "Consequentialism, Publicity, Stability, and Property-Owning Democracy", in Freeman, S.R. (Ed.), *Justice and the Social Contract: Essays on Rawlsian Political Philosophy*, Oxford University Press, Oxford, New York, NY, pp. 75–110.

Freeman, S.R. (Ed.) (2007b), *Justice and the Social Contract: Essays on Rawlsian Political Philosophy*, Oxford University Press, Oxford, New York, NY.

Freiman, C. (2013), "Cosmopolitanism Within Borders: On Behalf of Charter Cities", *Journal of Applied Philosophy*, Vol. 30 No. 1, pp. 40–52.

Frey, B.S. (2005), "Functional, Overlapping, Competing, Jurisdictions. Redrawing the Geographic Borders of Administration", *European Journal of Law and Reform*, Vol. 5 No. 3/4, pp. 543–555.

Friedman, J. (2005), "Popper, Weber, and Hayek: The Epistemology and Politics of Ignorance", *Critical Review*, Vol. 17 No. 1–2, pp. 1–58.

Fukuyama, F. (2012), *Origins of Political Order: From Prehuman Times to the French Revolution*, Farrar, Straus and Giroux, New York, NY.

Fuller, L. (1995), "The Forms and Limits of Adjudication", in Freeman, Michael D.A. (Ed.), *Alternative Dispute Resolution, International Library of Essays in Law and Legal Theory. Areas*, New York University Press, New York, NY, pp. 3–60.

Fung, A. (2005), "Deliberation Before the Revolution: Toward an Ethics of Deliberative Democracy in an Unjust World", *Political Theory*, Vol. 33 No. 3, pp. 397–419.

Fung, A. (2011), "Minipublics: Designing Institutions for Effective Deliberation and Accountability", in Odugbemi, S. and Lee, T. (Eds.), *Accountability Through Public Opinion*, The World Bank, Washington, DC, pp. 183–202.

Gaus, G. (2007), "On Justifying the Moral Rights of the Moderns: A Case of old Wine in new Bottles", *Social Philosophy and Policy*, Vol. 24 No. 01, pp. 84–119.

Gaus, G. (2009), "Recognized Rights as Devices of Public Reason", in Hawthorne, J. (Ed.), *Ethics, Philosophical Perspectives*, Wiley Periodicals, Malden, MA, pp. 111–136.

Gaus, G. (2010), "Coercion, Ownership, and the Redistributive State: Justificatory Liberalism's Classical Tilt", *Social Philosophy and Policy*, Vol. 27 No. 01, pp. 233–275.

Gaus, G. (2011a), "A Tale of Two Sets: Public Reason in Equilibrium", *Public Affairs Quarterly*, Vol. 25 No. 4, pp. 305–325.

Gaus, G. (2011b), "Between Discovery and Choice: The General Will in a Diverse Society", *Contemporary Readings in Law and Social Justice*, No. 2, pp. 75–90.

Gaus, G. (2011c), *The Order of Public Reason: A Theory of Freedom and Morality in a Diverse and Bounded World*, Cambridge University Press, New York, NY.

Gaus, G. (2013), "The Turn to a Political Liberalism", in Mandle, J. and Reidy, D.A. (Eds.), *A Companion to Rawls*, John Wiley & Sons, Inc, Hoboken, NJ, pp. 233–250.

Gauthier, D. (1986), *Morals by Agreement*, Oxford University Press, New York.

Gigerenzer, G. and Selten, R. (2001), *Bounded Rationality: The Adaptive Toolbox*, MIT Press, Cambridge, MA.

Gigone, D. and Hastie, R. (1993), "The Common Knowledge Effect: Information Sharing and Group Judgment", *Journal of Personality and Social Psychology*, Vol. 65 No. 5, pp. 959–974.

Gigone, D. and Hastie, R. (1997), "Proper Analysis of the Accuracy of Group Judgments", *Psychological Bulletin*, Vol. 121 No. 1, pp. 149–167.

Goldschmidt, N. and Zweynert, J. (2013), *Neue Ordnungsökonomik, Untersuchungen zur Ordnungstheorie und Ordnungspolitik*, 1., neue Ausg, Mohr Siebeck, Tübingen.

Goodin, R.E. (2008), *Innovating Democracy: Democratic Theory and Practice After the Deliberative Turn*, Oxford University Press, Oxford, New York, NY.

Google (2014), "Google – Our History in Depth", available at: www.google.com/about/company/history/ (accessed 22 September 2014).

Gray, J. (2000), *Two Faces of Liberalism*, New Press, Distributed by W.W. Norton, New York, NY.

Grönlund, K., Bächtiger, A. and Setälä, M. (Eds.) (2013), *Deliberative Mini-publics: Involving Citizens in the Democratic Process*, ECPR – Studies in European Political Science, Colchester.

Grüne-Yanoff, T. (2007), "Bounded Rationality", *Philosophy Compass*, Vol. 2 No. 3, pp. 534–563.

Gürerk, Ö. (2013), "Social learning increases the acceptance and the efficiency of punishment institutions in social dilemmas", *Journal of Economic Psychology*, Vol. 34, pp. 229–239.

Gürerk, O., Irlenbusch, B. and Rockenbach, B. (2006), "The Competitive Advantage of sanctioning Institutions", *Science (New York, N.Y.)*, Vol. 312 No. 5770, pp. 108–111.

Gutmann, A. and Thompson, D. (1995), "Moral Disagreement in a Democracy", *Social Philosophy and Policy*, Vol. 12 No. 01, pp. 87–110.

Gutmann, A. and Thompson, D. (1996), *Democracy and Disagreement*, Belknap Press of Harvard University Press, Cambridge, MA.

Gutmann, A. and Thompson, D. (2000), "Why Deliberative Democracy is Different", *Social Philosophy and Policy*, Vol. 17 No. 01, p. 161.

Gutmann, A. and Thompson, D. (2004), *Why Deliberative Democracy?*, Princeton University Press, Princeton, NJ. [u.a.].

Habermas, J. (1990), *Moral Consciousness and Communicative Action, Studies in Contemporary German Social Thought*, MIT Press, Cambridge, MA.

Habermas, J. (1995), "Reconciliation Through the Public Use of Reason: Remarks on John Rawls's Political Liberalism Jürgen Habermas", *The Journal of Philosophy*, Vol. 3 No. 92, pp. 109–131.

Habermas, J. (1996), *Between Facts and Norms: Contributions to a Discourse Theory of Law and Democracy, Studies in Contemporary German Social Thought*, MIT Press, Cambridge, MA.

Han Feizi (2005), "Han Feizi", trans. Joal Sahleen in Ivanhoe, P.J. and Van Norden, B.W. (Eds.), *Readings in Classical Chinese Philosophy*, Seven Bridges, London, pp. 311–362.

Harsanyi, J. (1975), "Can the Maximin Principle Serve as a Basis for Morality? A Critique of John Rawls' Theory", *American Political Science Review*, Vol. 69 No. 2, pp. 594–606.

Hausman, D.M. and McPherson, M.S. (1996), *Economic Analysis and Moral Philosophy, Cambridge Surveys of Economic Literature*, Cambridge University Press, Cambridge, UK, New York, NY.

Hayek, F.A. von (1945), "The Use of Knowledge in Society", *The American Economic Review*, Vol. 35 No. 4, pp. 519–530.

Hayek, F.A. von (Ed.) (1980), *Individualism and Economic Order*, Midway Reprint, University of Chicago Press, Chicago, IL.

Hayek, F.A. von (2002), "Competition as a Discovery Procedure", trans. Marcellus S. Snow, *The Quarterly Journal of Austrian Economics*, Vol. 5 No. 3, pp. 9–23.

Hayek, F.A. von (2007), *The Road to Serfdom: Text and Documents: The Definitive Edition*, The Collected Works of Friedrich August Hayek, W.W. Bartley and Caldwell, B. (Eds.), Vol. 2, University of Chicago Press, Chicago, IL. [u.a.].

Hayek, F.A. von (2012), *Constitution of Liberty, Routledge classics*, Routledge, London.

Hayek, F.A. von (2013), *Law, Legislation, and Liberty: A new Statement of the Liberal Principles of Justice and Political Economy, Routledge classics*. Routledge, London.

Hill, G.W. (1982), "Group versus Individual Performance: Are N+1 Heads Better Than One?" *Psychological Bulletin*, Vol. 91 No. 3, pp. 517–539.

Hirschman, A.O. (1970), *Exit, Voice, and Loyalty: Responses to Decline in Firms, Organizations, and States*, Harvard University Press, Cambridge, MA.

Homann, K. (1988), *Rationalität und Demokratie*, Die Einheit der Gesellschaftswissenschaften, Vol. 57, J.C.B. Mohr, Tübingen.

Homann, K. (2002), *Vorteile und Anreize: Zur Grundlegung einer Ethik der Zukunft*, C. Lütge (Ed.), Mohr Siebeck, Tübingen.

Homann, K. and Blome-Drees, F. (1992), *Wirtschafts- und Unternehmensethik*, Uni-Taschenbücher, Vol. 1721, Vandenhoeck & Ruprecht, Göttingen.

Homann, K. and Lütge, C. (2005), *Einführung in die Wirtschaftsethik*, 2nd ed., LIT-Verl., Münster.

Honneth, A. (2017), *The Idea of Socialism*, Polity Press, Cambridge, UK.

Horton, J. (2007), "John Gray and the Political Theory of Modus Vivendi", in Horton, J. and Newey, G. (Eds.), *The Political Theory of John Gray*, Routledge, London, New York, NY, pp. 43–58.

Horton, J. (2010), "Realism, Liberal Moralism and a Political Theory of Modus Vivendi", *European Journal of Political Theory*, Vol. 9 No. 4, pp. 431–448.

Huemer, M. (2012), "In Praise of Passivity", *Studia Humana*, Vol. 1 No. 2, pp. 12–28.

Huemer, M. (2013), *The Problem of Political Authority: An Examination of the Right to Coerce and the Duty to Obey*, Palgrave Macmillan, Basingstoke.

Hume, D. (2006), *Essays, Moral, Political, and Literary, Cosimo Classics Philosophy*, Cosimo Classics, New York, NY.

IXDA (2005), "Automotive Design Standards/Guidelines", available at: www.ixda.org/node/19948 (accessed 25 April 2015).

Jacobs, S. (2000), "Spontaneous Order: Michael Polanyi and Friedrich Hayek", *Critical Review of International Social and Political Philosophy*, Vol. 3 No. 4, pp. 49–67.

Janis, I.L. (1982), *Groupthink: Psychological Studies of Policy Decisions and Fiascoes*, 2nd ed., Houghton Mifflin, Boston, MA.

Johnson, J. (1998), "Arguing for Deliberation: Some Skeptical Considerations", in Elster, J. (Ed.), *Deliberative Democracy, Cambridge Studies in the Theory of Democracy*, Cambridge University Press, Cambridge. [u.a.], pp. 161–184.

Kahneman, D. and Thaler, R. (1991), "Economic Analysis and the Psychology of Utility: Applications to Compensation Policy", *American Economic Review*, Vol. 81 No. 2, pp. 341–346.

Kahneman, D. and Tversky Amos (1979), "Prospect Theory: An Analysis of Decision under Risk", *Econometrica*, Vol. 47 No. 2, pp. 263–292.

Kameda, T., Yohsuke, O. and Masanori, T. (1997), "Centrality in Sociocognitive NetWorks and Social Influence. An Illustration in a Group Decision-Making Context", *Journal of Personality and Social Psychology*, Vol. 73 No. 2, pp. 296–309.

Kant, I. (1991), "Idea for a Universal History with a Cosmopolititan Purpose", in Reiss, H.S. (Ed.), *Kant: Political Writings, Cambridge Texts in the History of Political Thought*, 2nd ed., Cambridge University Press, Cambridge, UK, New York, NY, pp. 41–53.

Kauffman, S. (1996), *At Home in the Universe: The Search for the Laws of Self-Organization and Complexity*, Oxford University Press, New York, p. 252.

King, J. (2012), *Judging Social Rights*, Cambridge Studies in Constitutional Law, Cambridge University Press, Cambridge, New York, NY.

Kitcher, P. (2001), *Science, Truth, and Democracy, Oxford Studies in Philosophy of Science*, Oxford University Press, Oxford, New York, NY.

Knight, J. and Johnson, J. (1997), "What Sort of Political Equality Does Deliberative Democracy Require?", in Bohman, J. and Rehg, W. (Eds.), *Deliberative Democracy: Essays on Reason and Politics*, MIT Press, Cambridge, MA, pp. 279–320.

Kofman, D. (2012), "How Insensitive: Principles, Facts and Normative Grounds in Cohen's Critique of Rawls", *Socialist Studies/Études Socialistes*, Vol. 8 No. 1, pp. 246–266.

Kordig, C.R. (1978), "Discovery and Justification", *Philosophy of Science*, Vol. 45, pp. 110–117.

Kuhn, T.S. (2012), *The Structure of Scientific Revolutions*, I. Hacking (Ed.), 4th ed., The University of Chicago Press, Chicago, IL, London.

Kukathas, C. (2007), *The Liberal Archipelago: A Theory of Diversity and Freedom, Oxford Political Theory*, Oxford University Press, Oxford.

Kukathas, C. (2009), "Two Constructions of Libertarianism", *Libertarian Papers*, Vol. 1.

Lafont, C. (2015), "Deliberation, Participation, and Democratic Legitimacy: Should Deliberative Mini-publics Shape Public Policy?" *Journal of Political Philosophy*, Vol. 23 No. 1, pp. 40–63.

Lakatos, I. (1980), *Philosophical Papers*, 1st ed., Cambridge University Press, Cambridge, New York, NY.

Landemore, H. (2013), *Democratic Reason: Politics, Collective Intelligence, and the Rule of the Many*, Princeton University Press, Princeton, Oxford.

Landemore, H. and Page, S.E. (2015), "Deliberation and Disagreement: Problem Solving, Prediction, and Positive Dissensus", *Politics, Philosophy & Economics*, Vol. 14 No. 3, pp. 229–254.

Larmore, C. (1996), "Pluralism and Reasonable Disagreement", in Larmore, C. (Ed.), *The Morals of Modernity*, Cambridge University Press, Cambridge, pp. 152–174.

Larson, J.R. (2010), *In Search of Synergy in Small Group Performance*, Psychology Press, New York, NY.

Laudan, L. (1980), "Why Was the Logic of Discovery Abandoned?" in Nickles, T. (Ed.), *Scientific Discovery, Logic, and Rationality, Boston Studies in the Philosophy of Science*, D. Reidel Pub. Co, Sold and distributed in the USA and Canada by Kluwer Boston, Dordrecht, Holland, Boston, Hingham, MA, pp. 173–183.

Laughlin, P.R. and Adamopoulos, J. (1980), "Social Combination Processes and Individual Learning for Six-person Cooperative Groups on an Intellective Task", *Journal of Personality and Social Psychology*, Vol. 38 No. 6, pp. 941–947.

Laughlin, P.R. and Ellis, A.L. (1986), "Demonstrability and Social Combination Processes on Mathematical Intellective Tasks", *Journal of Experimental Social Psychology*, Vol. 22 No. 3, pp. 177–189.

Levy, J.T. (2007), "Federalism, Liberalism, and the Separation of Loyalties", *American Political Science Review*, Vol. 101 No. 03, p. 459.

Lewis, D. (2004), "What Experience Teaches", in Ludlow, P., Nagasawa, Y. and Stoljar, D. (Eds.), *There's Something About Mary: Essays on Frank Jackson's Knowledge Argument*, MIT Press, Cambridge, MA, pp. 77.–104.

Licuanan, B.F., Dailey, L.R. and Mumford, M. (2007), "Idea Evaluation: Error in Evaluating Highly Original Ideas", *The Journal of Creative Behavior*, Vol. 41 No. 1, pp. 1–27.

Lippmann, W. (1982), *The Essential Lippmann: A Political Philosophy for Liberal Democracy*, C. Rossiter and Lare, J. (Eds.), Harvard University Press, Cambridge, MA.

List, C. and Goodin, R.E. (2001), "Epistemic Democracy: Generalizing the Condorcet Jury Theorem", *Journal of Political Philosophy*, Vol. 9 No. 3, pp. 277–306.

Lister, A. (2010), "Public Justification and the Limits of State Action", *Politics, Philosophy & Economics*, Vol. 9 No. 2, pp. 151–175.

Locke, J. (2010), *A Letter Concerning Toleration and Other Writing*, M. Goldie (Ed.), The Thomas Hollis Library, Liberty Fund, Indianapolis, IN.

Lu, L., Yuan, Y.C. and McLeod, P.L. (2011), "Twenty-Five Years of Hidden Profiles in Group Decision Making: A Meta-Analysis", *Personality and Social Psychology Review*, Vol. 16 No. 1, pp. 54–75.

Lütge, C. (2001), *Ökonomische Wissenschaftstheorie*, Königshausen & Neumann, Würzburg.

Lütge, C. (2003), "Saving Science from Science Studies: Aa Constitutional Economics Approach", *Energeia*, Vol. 2 No. 1–2, pp. 187–204.

Lütge, C. (2004), "Economics in Philosophy of Science: A Dismal Contribution?" *Synthese*, Vol. 140 No. 3, pp. 279–305.

Lütge, C. (2005), "Economic Ethics, Business Ethics and the Idea of Mutual Advantages", *Business Ethics: A European Review*, Vol. 2 No. 14, pp. 108–118.

Lütge, C. (2012), *Wirtschaftsethik ohne Illusionen: Ordnungstheoretische Reflexionen*, Mohr Siebeck, Tübingen.

Lütge, C. (2015), *Order Ethics or Moral Surplus: What Holds a Society Together?* Lexington Books, Lanham, MD.

Machiavelli, N. (2003), *The Prince, Cambridge Texts in the History of Political Thought*, Skinner, Quentin and Price, Russel (Eds.), Cambridge University Press, Cambridge, UK, New York, NY.

Mantzavinos, C. (2001), *Individuals, Institutions, and Markets, Political Economy of Institutions and Decisions*, Cambridge University Press, Cambridge, UK, New York, NY.

Mantzavinos, C. (2013), "Explanatory Games", *The Journal of Philosophy*, Vol. 110 No. 11, pp. 606–632.

Marengo, L. (2000), "The Structure of Problem-solving Knowledge and the Structure of Organizations", *Industrial and Corporate Change*, Vol. 9 No. 4, pp. 757–788.

McGinnis, M.D. (1999), *Polycentricity and Local Public Economies: Readings from the Workshop in Political Theory and Policy Analysis, Institutional Analysis*, University of Michigan press, Ann Arbor.

McMahon, C. (2009), *Reasonable Disagreement: A Theory of Political Morality*, Cambridge University Press, Cambridge, UK, New York, NY.

Meadowcroft, J. (2013), *James M. Buchanan, Major Conservative and Libertarian Thinkers*, Vol. 17, Bloomsbury Academic, London.

Mill, J.S. (1989), *On Liberty: With the Subjection of Women: And Chapters on Socialism, Cambridge Texts in the History of Political Thought*, S. Collini (Ed.), Cambridge University Press, Cambridge, UK, New York, NY.

Mises, L. von (1944), *Bureaucracy*, Yale University Press, New Haven.

Mises, L. von (1983), *Nation, State, and Economy: Contributions to the Politics and History of Our Time, The Institute for Humane Studies Series in Economic Theory*, New York University Press, New York, NY.

Mises, L. von (1985), *Liberalism, The Classical Tradition*, B.B. Greaves (Ed.), Foundation for Economic Education, Cobden Press, New York, NY, San Francisco, CA.

Mitchell, M.T. (2006), *Michael Polanyi: The Art of Knowing, Library of Modern Thinkers*, ISI Books, Wilmington, DE.

Moberg, L. (2014), "The Political Economy of Special Economic Zones", *Journal of Institutional Economics*, pp. 1–24.

Moehler, M. (2014), "The Scope of Instrumental Morality", *Philosophical Studies*, Vol. 167 No. 2, pp. 431–451.

Mueller, D.C. (2003), *Public Choice III*, Cambridge University Press, Cambridge, New York, NY.

Muldoon, R. (2016), *Social Contract Theory for a Diverse World: Beyond Tolerance*, Routledge, New York, NY.

Mullen, B., Johnson, C. and Salas, E. (1991), "Productivity Loss in Brainstorming Groups: A Meta-analytic Integration", *Basic and Applied Social Psychology*, Vol. 12 No. 1, pp. 3–23.

Müller, J.F. (2013), "Die Sozialphilosophie Ludwig von Mises' im Lichte klassischer Liberalismus-Konzeptionen", in Conze, E., Scholtyseck, J., Weede, E., Frölich, J. and Grothe, E. (Eds.), *Jahrbuch zur Liberalismus-Forschung*, 1. Aufl, Nomos, Baden-Baden, pp. 353–363.

Müller, J.F. (2014), "Large-scale Social Experiments in Experimental Ethics", in Lütge, C., Rusch, H. and Uhl, M. (Eds.), *Experimental Ethics: Towards an Empirical Moral Philosophy. Toward an Empirical Moral Philosophy*, Palgrave Macmillan, New York, NY, pp. 247–263.

Müller, J.F. (2016), "Advancing Justice by Appealing to Self-Interest: The Case for Charter Cities", *Moral Philosophy and Politics*, Vol. 3 No. 2, pp. 223–245.

Müller, J.F. (2018), "Epistemic Democracy: Beyond Knowledge Exploitation", *Philosophical Studies*, Vol. 75 No. 5, pp. 1267–1288.

Müller, J.F. and Lütge, C. (2014a), "Ordnungsethik als übergreifender methodischer Ansatz zur Analyse von bereichsethischen Fragestellungen", in Maring, M. (Ed.), *Bereichsethiken im interdisziplinären Dialog, Schriftenreihe des Zentrums für Technik- und Wirtschaftsethik am Karlsruher Institut für Technologie*. Hrsg. von Matthias Maring, KIT Scientific Publishing, Karlsruhe, Baden, pp. 79–94.

Müller, J.F. and Lütge, C. (2014b), "Wettbewerb der Solidarsysteme", in Hruschka, J. and Joerden, J.C. (Eds.), *Jahrbuch für Recht und Ethik/Annual Review of Law and Ethics*, 1. Aufl, Duncker et Humblot, Berlin, pp. 329–348.

Mumford, M.D., Blair, C., Dailey Lesley, Leritz, L.E. and Osburn, H.K. (2006), "Errors in Creative Thought? Cognitive Biases in a Complex Processing Activity", *The Journal of Creative Behavior*, Vol. 40 No. 2, pp. 75–109.

Nietzsche, F.W. (2006), *Thus Spoke Zarathustra: A Book for All and None*, trans. A. Del Caro, R.B. Pippin (Ed.), Cambridge Texts in the History of Philosophy, Cambrige University Press, Cambridge, New York, NY.

Nozick, R. (1994), "Invisible-Hand Explanations", *The American Economic Review, Papers and Proceedings of the One Hundred Fifteenth Annual Meeting of the American Economic Association*, Vol. 84 No. 2, pp. 314–318.

Nozick, R. (1999), *Anarchy, State and Utopia*, Blackwell, Oxford, Cambridge.

Ostrom, E. (2005), *Understanding Institutional Diversity*, Princeton University Press, Princeton, NJ.

Ostrom, V. (1991), *The Meaning of American Federalism: Constituting a Self-governing Society*, ICS Press, San Francisco, CA.

Ostrom, V. (1997), *The Meaning of Democracy and the Vulnerability of Democracies: A Response to Tocqueville's Challenge*, University of Michigan press, Ann Arbor.

Ostrom, V., Tiebout, C.M. and Warren, W. (1961), "The Organization of Government in Metropolitan Areas: A Theoretical Inquiry", *American Political Science Review*, Vol. 55 No. 4, pp. 831–842.

Padovano, F. and Petrarca, I. (2014), "Are the Responsibility and Yardstick Competition Hypotheses Mutually Consistent?" *European Journal of Political Economy*, Vol. 34, pp. 459–477.

Page, S.E. (2007b), *The Difference: How the Power of Diversity Creates Better Groups, Firms, Schools, and Societies*, Princeton University Press, Princeton, NJ.

Parijs, P.P. (1991), "Why Surfers Should be Fed: The Liberal Case for an Unconditional Basic Income", *Philosophy & Public Affairs*, Vol. 20 No. 2, pp. 101–131.

Paul, L.A. (2014), *Transformative Experience*, 1st ed., Oxford University Press, Oxford.

Pennington, M. (2008), "Classical Liberalism and Ecological Rationality: The Case for Polycentric Environmental Law", *Environmental Politics*, Vol. 17 No. 3, pp. 431–448.

Pennington, M. (2010), "Democracy and the Deliberative Conceit", *Critical Review*, Vol. 22 No. 2–3, pp. 159–184.

Pennington, M. (2011), *Robust Political Economy: Classical Liberalism and the Future of Public Policy, New Thinking in Political Economy*, Edward Elgar, Cheltenham, UK, Northampton, MA.

Pies, I. (1993), *Normative Institutionenökonomik: Zur Rationalisierung des Politischen Liberalismus*, Die Einheit der Gesellschaftswissenschaften, Bd. 78, J.C.B. Mohr (Paul Siebeck), Tübingen.

Polanyi, M. (1997), *Society, Economics & Philosophy: Selected Papers*, R.T. Allen (Ed.), Transaction Publishers, New Brunswick, NJ.

Polanyi, M. (1998), *The Logic of Liberty: Reflections and Rejoinders*, Liberty Fund, Indianapolis, IN.

Popper, K.R. (2002a), *The Open Society and its Enemies*, 5th ed., Routledge, London.

Popper, K.R. (2002b), *The Poverty of Historicism, Routledge Classics*, Routledge, London.

Popper, K.R. (2005), *The Logic of Discovery, Routledge Classics*, Routledge, London, p. 7.

Rawls, J. (1999a), "Preface for the French Edition of a Theory of Justice", in Rawls, J. and Freeman, S.R. (Eds.), *Collected papers*, Harvard University Press, Cambridge, MA, pp. 415–420.

Rawls, J. (1999b), "The Idea of an Overlapping Consensus", in Rawls, J. and Freeman, S.R. (Eds.), *Collected Papers*, Harvard University Press, Cambridge, MA, pp. 421–448.

Rawls, J. (1999c), "The Law of Peoples", in Rawls, J. and Freeman, S.R. (Eds.), *Collected Papers*, Harvard University Press, Cambridge, MA, pp. 529–565.

Rawls, J. (2001), *Justice as Fairness: A Restatement*, E. Kelly (Ed.), Belknap Press of Harvard University Press, Cambridge, MA. [u.a.].

Rawls, J. (2005a), *A Theory of Justice*, Original ed., Belknap Press, Cambridge, MA.

Rawls, J. (2005b), *Political Liberalism, Columbia Classics in Philosophy*, Expanded ed., Columbia University Press, New York, NY.

Rawls, J. (2007), "Themes in Kant's Moral Philosophy", in Rawls, J. (Ed.), *Lectures on the History of Political Philosophy*, Belknap Press of Harvard University Press, Cambridge, MA, pp. 497–529.

Read, L.E. (1999), "I, Pencil: My Family Tree as Told to Leonard E. Read", available at: www.econlib.org/library/Essays/rdPncl1.html (accessed 16 September 2014).

Reisman, D.A. (1990), *The Political Economy of James Buchanan*, Palgrave Macmillan, Basingstoke.

Rescher, N. (1993), *Pluralism: Against the Demand for Consensus, Clarendon Library of Logic and Philosophy*, Clarendon Press, Oxford University Press, Oxford, New York, NY.

Rescher, N. (1998), *Complexity: A Philosophical Overview, Science and Technology Studies*, Transaction Publishers, New Brunswick, NJ.

Rincke, J. (2009), "Yardstick Competition and Public Sector Innovation", *International Tax and Public Finance*, Vol. 16 No. 3, pp. 337–361.

Rogers, E.M. (1983), *Diffusion of Innovations*, 3rd ed., Free Press, Collier Macmillan, New York, NY, London.

Rogers, E.M. (2003), *Diffusion of Innovations*, 5th ed., Free Press, New York, NY.

Rousseau, J.J. (2008), *Discourse on Political Economy and the Social Contract, Oxford World's Classics*, Oxford University Press, Oxford, New York, NY.

Rousseau, J.J. (2009), "The Social Contract", in Rousseau, J.J. (Ed.), *Discourse on Political Economy and the Social Contract, Oxford World's classics*, Oxford University Press, Oxford, New York, NY, pp. 43–168.

Salmon, P. (2015), "Horizontal Competition in Multilevel Governmental Settings", in Ahmad, E. and Brosio, G. (Eds.), *Handbook of Multilevel Finance*, Edward Elgar, pp. 85–106.

Schumpeter, J.A. (2008), *Capitalism, Socialism, and Democracy*, 1st ed., Harper Perennial Modern Thought, New York, NY.

Sen, A. (2009), *The Idea of Justice*, Belknap Press of Harvard University Press, Cambridge, MA.

Shearmur, J. (1996), *Hayek and After: Hayekian Liberalism as a Research Program, Routledge Studies in Social and Political Thought*, Vol. 1, Routledge, London, New York, NY.

Simmons, A.J. (2010), "Ideal and Nonideal Theory", *Philosophy & Public Affairs*, Vol. 38 No. 1, pp. 5–36.

Simmons, R.T. and Mitchell, W.C. (2011), *Beyond Politics: The Roots of Government Failure*, Rev. and updated ed., Independent Institute, Oakland, CA.

Sinn, H.W. (2003), *The new Systems Competition, Yrjö Jahnsson Lectures*, Blackwell Publishing, Malden, MA.

Somin, I. (2011), "Foot Voting, Political Ignorance, and Constitutional Design", *Social Philosophy and Policy*, Vol. 28 No. 01, pp. 202–227.

Somin, I. (2014), "Why Political Ignorance Undermines the Wisdom of the Many", *Critical Review: A Journal of Politics and Society*, Vol. 26 No. 1–2, pp. 151–169.

Sophocles (2007), "Trachiniae", in Sophocles (Ed.), *Dramas of Sophocles*, Rockville, MD: Wildside Press, pp. 174–210.

Stasser, G. (1999), "The Uncertain Role of Unshared Information in Collective Choice", in Levine, J.M., Thompson, L.L. and Messick, D.M. (Eds.), *Shared Cognition in Organizations: The Management of Knowledge, Series in Organization and Management*, Taylor and Francis, Hoboken, pp. 49–70.

Stasser, G., Abele, S. and Parsons, S.V. (2012), "Information Flow and Influence in Collective Choice", *Group Processes & Intergroup Relations*, Vol. 15 No. 5, pp. 619–635.

Stasser, G. and Dietz-Uhler, B. (2001), "Collective Choice, Judgment, and Problem Solving", in Hogg, M.A. and Tindale, R.S. (Eds.), *Group Processes, Blackwell Handbook of Social Psychology*, Blackwell, Malden, MA. [u.a.], pp. 31–55.

Stasser, G. and Titus, W. (1985), "Pooling of Unshared Information in Group Decision Pooling of Unshared Information in Group Decision Making: Biased Information Sampling During Discussion", *Journal of Personality and Social Psychology*, Vol. 48 No. 6, pp. 1467–1478.

Stasser, G. and Titus, W. (1997), "Effects of Information Load and Percentage of Shared Information on the Dissemination of Unshared Information During Group Discussion", *Journal of Personality and Social Psychology*, Vol. 53 No. 1, pp. 81–93.

Stasser, G. and Titus, W. (2003), "Hidden Profiles: A Brief History", *Psychological Inquiry*, Vol. 14 No. 3–4, pp. 304–313.

Stasson, M.F. and Bradshaw, S.D. (1995), "Explanations of Individual-Group Performance Differences: What Sort of "Bonus" Can Be Gained Through Group Interaction?" *Small Group Research*, Vol. 26 No. 2, pp. 296–308.

Streit, M.E. (1992), "Welfare Economics, Economic Order, and Competition", in Giersch, H. (Ed.), *Money, Trade, and Competition: Essays in Memory of Egon Sohmen*, Springer, Heidelberg, pp. 255–278.

Sunstein, C.R. (2006), "Deliberating Groups versus Prediction Markets (or Hayek's Challenge to Habermas)" *Episteme*, Vol. 3 No. 03, pp. 192–213.

Tetlock, P.E. (2005), *Expert Political Judgment: How Good Is It? How Can We Know?* Princeton University Press, Princeton, NJ.

Thaler, R.H. and Sunstein, C.R. (2003), "Libertarian Paternalism", *The American Economic Review, Papers and Proceedings of the One Hundred Fifteenth Annual Meeting of the American Economic Association*, Vol. 93 No. 2, pp. 175–179.

Thaler, R.H. and Sunstein, C.R. (2010), *Nudge: Improving Decisions About Health, Wealth, and Happiness, Concentrated Knowledge for the Busy Executive*, Soundview Executive Book Summaries, Distributed by Books24x7.com, Concordville, PA, Norwood, MA.

Thornton, M. and Thommesen, S. (1987), "An Interview with Nobel Laureate James Buchanan", *Austrian Economics Newsletter*, pp. 3–4, 10, available at: https://mises.org/sites/default/files/aen9_1_1_1.pdf (accessed 26 January 2015).

Tiebout, C. (1956), "A Pure Theory of Local Expenditures", *The Journal of Political Economy*, Vol. 64 No. 5, pp. 416–424.

Tindale, R.S., Meisenhelder, H.M., Dykema-Engblade, A.A. and Hogg, Michael A. (2001), "Shared Cognition in Small Groups", in Hogg, M.A. and Tindale, R.S. (Eds.), *Group Processes, Blackwell Handbook of Social Psychology*, Blackwell, Malden, MA. [u.a.], pp. 1–30.

Tocqueville, A. de (2002), *Democracy in America*, trans. H.C. Mansfield and D. Winthrop, University of Chicago Press, Chicago, IL, London.

Tomasi, J. (2012a), "Democratic Legitimacy and Economic Liberty", *Social Philosophy and Policy*, Vol. 29 No. 01, pp. 50–80.

Tomasi, J. (2012b), *Free Market Fairness*, Princeton University Press, Princeton, NJ.

Troeger, V. (2013), "Tax Competition and the Myth of the 'Race to the Bottom'. Why Governments Still Tax Capital", *The CAGE-Chatham House Series*, No. 4.

Tullock, G. (1964), *Politics of Bureaucracy*, Washington, DC: Public Affairs.

Tversky, A. and Kahneman, D. (1981), "The Framing of Decisions and the Psychology of Choice", *Science*, Vol. 211 No. 4481, pp. 453–458.

Unger, R.M. (2007). *The Self Awakened: Pragmatism Unbound*, Harvard University Press, Cambridge, MA.

Vallier, K. and D'Agostino, F. (2014), "Public Justification", in Zalta, E.N. (Ed.), *The Stanford Encyclopedia of Philosophy*, available at https://plato.stanford.edu/entries/justification-public/ (accessed 11 March 2019).

Vanberg, V. (2008), "Can Competition Between Governments Enhance Democracy", in Bergh, A. and Höijer, R. (Eds.), *Institutional Competition, New Thinking in Political Economy*, Edward Elgar, Cheltenham, UK, Northamption, MA, pp. 113–128.

Vanberg, V. and Kerber, W. (1994), "Institutional Competition among Jurisdictions: An Evolutionary Approach", *Constitutional Political Economy*, Vol. 5 No. 2, pp. 193–219.

Vaubel, R. (2008), "A History of Thought on Institutional Competition", in Bergh, A. and Höijer, R. (Eds.), *Institutional Competition, New Thinking in Political Economy*, Edward Elgar, Cheltenham, UK, Northamption, MA, pp. 29–66.

Wall, S. (2013), "Political Morality and Constitutional Settlements", *Critical Review of International Social and Political Philosophy*, Vol. 16 No. 4, pp. 481–499.

Warren, M.E. (2011), "Voting with Your Feet: Exit-based Empowerment in Democratic Theory", *American Political Science Review*, Vol. 105 No. 04, pp. 683–701.

Wegner, G. (2008), *Political Failure by Agreement: Learning Liberalism and the Welfare State, New Thinking in Political Economy*, Edward Elgar, Cheltenham, UK, Northampton, MA.

Wegner, G. (2014), "Hayek und die Konstruktivismusfalle", available at: http://wirtschaftlichefreiheit.de/wordpress/?p=14656 (accessed 25 April 2015).

Weithman, P.J. (2010), *Why Political Liberalism? On John Rawls's Political Turn, Oxford Political Philosophy*, Oxford University Press, Oxford, New York, NY.

Wendt, F. (2015), *Political Morality Beyond Justice. An Essay on Compromise, Peace and Public Justifiability*, Habilitationsschrift, Universität Hamburg, Hamburg, 2015.

Wiens, D. (2012), "Prescribing Institutions Without Ideal Theory", *Journal of Political Philosophy*, Vol. 20 No. 1, pp. 45–70.

Wiens, D. (2015), "Against Ideal Guidance", *The Journal of Politics*, Vol. 77 No. 2, pp. 433–446.

Williams, B. (2008), "Realism and Moralism in Political Theory", in Williams, B. and Hawthorn, G. (Eds.), *In the Beginning was the Deed: Realism and Moralism in Political Argument*, Princeton University Press, Princeton, NJ, pp. 1–18.

Wohlgemuth, M. (2008), "Learning Through Institutional Competition", in Bergh, A. and Höijer, R. (Eds.), *Institutional Competition, New Thinking in Political Economy*, Edward Elgar, Cheltenham, UK, Northamption, MA, pp. 67–89.

Wolterstorff, N. (2007), "The Paradoxical Role of Coercion in the Theory of Political Liberalism", *Journal of Law, Philosophy and Culture*, Vol. 1 No. 1, pp. 135–158.

Yamamoto, T. (2014), *Hagakure. the Secret Wisdom of the Samurai*, trans. A. Bennett, Tuttle Publishing, Tokyo.

Index

Note: Figures and tables are denoted with *italicized* and **bold** page numbers, respectively.